THE · ART · OF
Eating In

Fast,
Easy and
Fabulous

Jane Horn
Writer/Editor

CALIFORNIA CULINARY ACADEMY

Jane Horn is the author and editor of *Cooking A to Z*, the award-winning culinary encyclopedia and cookbook. In the California Culinary Academy series of cookbooks, she has contributed to *Chicken and Other Poultry, Microwave and More,* and other titles. She also is the co-author of *The New Harvest* (published by The Cole Group/101 Productions), a guide to exotic and specialty produce. Her column on culinary equipment, "Cook's Tools," appears regularly in *Bay Food* magazine. Although eating out is a favorite activity, Jane Horn enjoys even more the pleasures of eating in with family and friends at her home in Piedmont, California, or at her vacation home in the Sierra Nevada mountains near Lake Tahoe.

The California Culinary Academy In the forefront of American institutions leading the culinary renaissance in this country, the California Culinary Academy in San Francisco has gained a reputation as one of the most outstanding professional chef training schools in the world. With a teaching staff recruited from the best restaurants of Western Europe, the Academy educates students from around the world in the preparation of classical cuisine. The recipes in this book were created in consultation with the chefs of the Academy. For information about the Academy, write the Office of the Dean, California Culinary Academy, 625 Polk Street, San Francisco, CA 94102.

Front Cover: Saffron, orange peel, and fennel contribute to the exquisite flavor and aroma of Mary's Bourride, an updated version of a classic French fish soup (see page 49).

Title Page: Fresh tomatoes and spinach highlight this version of everybody's favorite pasta dish: Lasagne With Three Cheeses (see page 99).

Contributors

Contributing Writers
Bruce Aidells, Mary Harrison Carroll, Ron Clark, Olivia Erschen, Janet Fletcher, Lonnie Gandara, Jay Harlow, Hallie Donnelly Harron, Janet Jue, Carole Latimer, Faye Levy, Susan E. Mitchell, Julie Renaud, Vicki Barrios Schley, Cynthia Scheer, Angelo Villa, Susan Walter, Naomi Wise

Photographers
Patricia Brabrant, Victor Budnik, Alan Copeland, David Fischer, Ernie Friedlander, Joel Glenn, Marshall Gordon, Dennis Gray, Michael Lamotte, Fred Lyon, Patrick Lyons, Bob Montesclaros, Kit Morris, Keith Ovregaard, Kevin Sanchez, Chris Shorten, Richard Tauber

Food Stylists
Sandra Cook, Susan Devaty, Joanne Dexter, Stephanie Greenleigh, Karen Hazarian, Robert Lambert, Amy Nathan, Susan Massey-Weil, Cherie Miller, Cynthia Scheer, Doug Warne, Clay Wollard

Illustrator
Edith Allgood

Project Editor
Annette Gooch

Copyeditor
Anna Morgan Pendergrass

Indexer
Carolyn Chandler

Editorial Assistants
Nicole Aronescu and Alexis McDowell

Cover Design
Glenn Martinez & Associates

Series Format Interior Design
Octavo and Steve Lux

Production
Octavo

Separations, Film, and Printing
Regent Publishing Services Limited

The California Culinary Academy Series is published by the staff of The Cole Group.

Publisher
Brete C. Harrison

Associate Publisher
James Connolly

Director of Operations
Linda Hauck

Senior Editor
Annette Gooch

Director of Production
Steve Lux

Copyright © 1992 The Cole Group
All rights reserved under international and Pan-American copyright conventions.

A B C D E F
2 3 4 5 6 7 8 9

ISBN 1-56426-000-3

Address all inquiries to
The Cole Group
4415 Sonoma Highway PO Box 4089
Santa Rosa, CA 95402-4089

C O N T E N T S

THE · ART · OF
Eating In

Having a good selection of eggs, pasta, tortillas, and other versatile, easy-to-store foods on hand in your pantry provides limitless possibilities for delicious, easily prepared dishes.

EATING IN WITH FAMILY AND FRIENDS

Good news! The dining room is off the endangered list. We've rediscovered that most delightful form of social interaction—eating in with family and friends. This book is a tested collection of almost 200 exciting, easy-to-follow, and easy-to-prepare recipes that will make it fun again to cook at home. It's all there—appealing ideas for simple weeknight meals or dress-up weekend dinners—organized to make menu planning a simple matter of mix-and-match. The recipes reflect the exciting cultural diversity that typifies today's cuisine: hints of Asia, Latin America, and the more familiar European and American classics. Technique is straightforward, "keep it simple" the guiding principle. Throughout are special features and tips culled from cooking professionals who know the best tricks of the trade, to make it all work even better.

GET READY, GET SET, RELAX

The best meals are a blend of good food and good company. And that good company should include you—the cook—who, after all, provides the reason to gather together in the first place. But sometimes the cook is too busy in the kitchen to be part of the party.

Appetizing food and pleasant surroundings are important to the success of any get-together, but a relaxed and self-assured host is even more important. Can you be a guest at your own table? Yes, if the menu is one that you can pull off easily.

What appears effortless of course never is. The most successful endeavors are usually the result of a little planning and a familiarity with procedure so that there are no unwelcome surprises to rattle composure.

Realistically, even the simplest, most impromptu meal requires some orchestration. What can I make in under an hour? In 30 minutes? On the spot? Do I have enough food in my pantry or do I have to make a quick trip to the market? Are the napkins ironed? Can I set the table with what's in the closet? Even more behind-the-scenes preparation might be necessary if the menu is complicated and the presentation dressy.

It helps to become a dedicated listmaker if you're not one already. Make up a shopping list. Jot down what has to be done and in what order, and estimate about how much time it will take to complete each task. If it's a high-pressure situation—dinner party for your boss, or for guests that you don't know very well—fall back on recipes that are guaranteed to go smoothly because you've made them before. Save your experiments for a casual gathering of family and good friends. They'll be more inclined to give you points for effort, even if the finished dish doesn't look quite like a magazine cover.

At cooking time, organize each dish using the traditional French method of *mise en place*—gathering measured amounts of ingredients together on a tray or baking sheet, ready to sauté, mix, or bake. When all the ingredients are right there, you can prepare the recipe rapidly and efficiently without interruptions caused by the need for additional preparation or by lack of an ingredient.

Break recipe procedures into small, manageable steps such as washing, slicing, dicing, or puréeing. For example, the preparation of a simple green salad includes making the dressing; washing the salad greens; cutting the accents such as tomatoes, cucumbers, or bell peppers; and tossing all ingredients together just before serving. Combining comparable tasks from several recipes will save time and effort. Wash all produce before proceeding, chop onions for two or three recipes at once, or toast nuts while the oven is being used for another baking job.

THE PANTRY: SOCIAL SECURITY

A carefully planned and stocked pantry is a form of social security. It will enable you to put together a satisfying meal for just about any entertaining situation without stepping outside the kitchen door, or with the purchase of just a few perishables.

The word *pantry* evokes images of old-fashioned home-canned foods, cured meats, and out-of-season produce stocked in storage bins and cellars—but today the reality is different. Modern pantries tend to be smaller than those of two generations ago. The advent of supermarkets, with their long shopping hours, has made extensive stocking unnecessary. However, the pantry, now defined to include the refrigerator and the freezer as well as a dry goods cupboard, is still one of a cook's most important assets.

A pantry (from the French *paneterie,* a wooden wall-hung storage cupboard with lattice doors, used to store bread) can be as small as two shelves, a tiny freezer, and a section of the refrigerator. It can also be the traditional storage room separate from the kitchen. The size of a pantry is less important than what it should contain—a carefully chosen selection of purchased and homemade staples. Your pantry should be designed to allow you the flexibility to entertain whenever you want and as easily as possible. The key to pantry management is to choose staples that will be used regularly and to replenish them when necessary.

STOCKING THE PANTRY

The usual pantry items—flour, sugar, and butter—can be expanded to include favorite foods stashed in the cupboard, freezer, and refrigerator, ready to turn into last-minute meals.

Stocking a pantry doesn't mean overpurchasing items to cover every appetite or to anticipate every crisis. It does mean taking into consideration your palate, the recipes you make most often, and your cooking style. When you buy foods you enjoy eating, the pantry will work for you.

Start with the basics and then personalize the food choices. Take time to sample the high-quality prepared foods that can be purchased from delicatessens and specialty stores. Also look for brands of canned, packaged, and frozen foods that meet your standards.

A well-planned pantry can also include fresh foods. Ripe, red tomatoes or fresh asparagus can be tossed with pasta for a quick first course. Some ingredients, such as onions, cabbage, potatoes, pumpkins and other winter squash, although perishable, will keep for several weeks if properly stored. Dry goods can be enhanced by fresh tomatoes, herbs, green onions, peaches, raspberries, and other seasonal perishables that appear in the marketplace.

With a carefully selected pantry and a working knowledge of favorite, successful recipes, you will be able to handle drop-in guests and to extend spur-of-the-moment invitations. As further reward, cooking will become creative as well as fun.

THE BASIC PANTRY

Pantry upkeep revolves around shopping bimonthly to restock basic ingredients and maintain a selection of prepared sauces, condiments, and other staples. Once or twice a week, you will need to add fresh meat, poultry, seafood, dairy products, fruit, and vegetables in moderate amounts to supplement the frozen and dry goods. Leftovers, a starting point for creative cooking, can be incorporated into pantry menus. Planned leftovers can reduce cooking time and allow you to prepare impromptu meals.

Tableware is also an important component of the basic pantry. A supply of serving pieces and attractive tableware is essential. For versatility, choose tableware that has simple lines. Buy a large quantity of one size of glasses and dinner plates rather than the same number of dishes in an assortment of sizes. For example, several dozen all-purpose glasses, holding 8 to 10 ounces, can be used for white wine, red wine, and non-alcoholic drinks as well as for fruit compotes and dessert mousses. A dozen white dinner plates can be dressed up with elegant accents or made festive with bright colors. On the other hand, if you have a set of dishes that you really love to look at and to use, and that is easy to store and to care for, by all means make that pattern your entertaining signature. Stock an abundant supply of cocktail napkins, serving trays, toothpicks, bamboo skewers, paper doilies, vases for cut flowers, and casserole dishes and platters in a variety of sizes and style to complement your dinnerware.

The following foods are recommended as staples for a basic pantry. The lists are based on the recipes that appear in this book and are probably quite different from ones that might have been written even five years ago. They draw from many cuisines, including traditional European such as Italian and French, plus Latin American, Asian, and Middle Eastern cooking. These cross-cultural groceries reflect how international our cuisine has become, even the foods we cook every day. Most of the foods are available at well-stocked supermarkets. Sometimes a trip to a gourmet foods store or Latin American

or Asian market (if one is available to you) may be in order to track down something special.

Adapt these lists to suit your needs and style:

Basic fruits and vegetables
Apples, carrots, celery, lemons, lettuce, onions, oranges, garlic, shallots, fresh ginger, cabbage, potatoes, sweet potatoes, selection of seasonal vegetables and fruits

Cupboard staples
Bread, dried beans and grains (long-grain rice, basmati rice, Arborio rice, lentils, wheat berries, and other favorite grains), dried Italian pasta and Asian noodles, couscous, granulated sugar, confec-

tioners' sugar, brown sugar, honey, flour, cornmeal, rolled oats, vanilla extract, almond extract, unsweetened and semisweet chocolate, semisweet chocolate chips, unsweetened cocoa, baking powder, baking soda, cornstarch, apricot and raspberry jams, preserves, maple syrup, salt, pepper, dried herbs and spices, canned plum tomatoes, tomato paste, tomato sauce, hot-pepper sauce, Worcestershire sauce, canned chicken and beef broth, Dijon-style mustard, olive oil, vegetable oil, peanut oil, varietal-wine vinegars (Cabernet, Chardonnay, sherry) and fruit vinegars, dried apricots, and raisins

Fancy and specialty foods
Dried mushrooms (*porcini, shiitake*), red and white wines, rum, brandy, vermouth, orange-flavored liqueur, jars of roasted red peppers and marinated artichoke hearts, soy sauce, tamari, Asian sesame oil, rice wine vinegar, rice wine (sake or Shaoxing), assorted canned beans (black, cannellini, kidney), canned oysters, chutneys, *cornichons* or dill pickles, olives (black, Niçoise, Greek, oil-cured, green), capers, and crackers

Freezer staples
Corn, cherries, peas, peaches, blueberries, blackberries, strawberries, raspberries, good-quality tortellini, ice cream, puff pastry, Parmesan cheese, bread crumbs, spinach, stock (chicken, beef, and fish), butter, nuts (almonds, hazelnuts, pecans, pine nuts, walnuts), sausages, bacon, chicken breasts, Cornish game hens, turkey breasts and fillets, ground beef and pork, chops (veal, pork, and lamb), flank steak, pesto sauce, and orange juice

Refrigerator staples
Blue cheese, goat cheese, Cheddar cheese, Swiss cheese, cream cheese, Monterey jack cheese, butter, cream, milk, sour cream, plain nonfat yogurt, eggs, parsley and other fresh herbs, bacon, fresh meat (or poultry or seafood), and corn or flour tortillas

EQUIPPING THE BASIC KITCHEN

Although it is always fun to buy culinary paraphernalia, most cooks function extremely well with a collection of well-chosen, high-quality equipment that suits their needs. It's better to have a few items that last than many poor-quality pieces that must be replaced often. As you work in the kitchen, decide which cookware and appliances to add in order to save time and give the best results. The following items will make certain jobs easier:

Bakeware

Baking pans and sheets are kitchen workhorses. They give shape to batters; hold cookie doughs, rolls, free-form yeast breads, biscuits, and meringues; and help organize setup by serving as a catchall for ingredients and equipment. Also useful: round 8- or 9-inch cake pans and pie plates, muffin pans, loaf pans, tube pans, quiche pans, and wire cooling racks.

Casseroles and baking dishes

Many of these are multipurpose. Primarily intended for slow cooking such as making stews and braises, which require extended cooking to tenderize tough cuts of meat, they are also suitable for roasting and for baking such combination dishes as layered entrées, vegetable accompaniments, and fruit desserts. Casseroles have lids. Baking dishes are fairly shallow in comparison with casseroles, don't have covers, and usually don't have handles either. The more attractive casseroles and baking dishes can be presented at the table. Capacity ranges from as little as 2 cups to sizes for a crowd. Useful sizes include 1, 2, and 3 quarts.

Food processor

Many cooks consider this multifunctional machine their most valuable kitchen appliance. It makes quick work of many tedious and time-consuming culinary chores. With one machine, a cook can chop, slice, shred, mix, and purée almost instantaneously. Food processors vary in capacity and power, from the very compact for households of one or two persons to machines intended for cooks who prepare food on a large scale. Which processor you buy depends on how often you will use the machine and the amount of food you will need to prepare at any one time.

Grater

A four-sided, standing hand grater should have both coarse and fine sides. The coarse holes are used for grating cheeses such as Swiss or Gruyère, the fine holes for grating citrus peel and hard cheeses, such as Parmesan.

Heavy-duty electric mixer

There is no better way to whip cream, beat egg whites, and mix up light, airy cake batters than with an electric mixer. If you do a lot of baking, you need a mixer with a strong motor to handle dense cookie doughs, plus a paddle beater for general mixing, a balloon whisk for whipping, and a dough hook for kneading.

Knives

A basic set of well-constructed knives will make kitchen work much easier. A chef's knife with an 8-inch blade, a boning knife, a serrated knife for slicing bread, and a 3- or 4-inch paring knife are most useful. A good knife has a blade that extends the length of the handle and should feel balanced in your hand. Knives made of high-carbon stainless steel will take a good edge and won't rust.

Measuring cups and spoons

Measuring tools are kitchen necessities. It makes sense to have several sets of cups and spoons—at least one set for liquids and another for dry ingredients. The most useful sizes of cups for liquids are 1-, 2-, and 4-cup capacities.

Meat thermometer

The most accurate way to check meat for doneness is with a meat thermometer. For a true reading, the thermometer should be inserted in the thickest part of the meat and should not touch bone. An instant-read thermometer, which rises quickly to the proper reading and is then removed from the meat, is an excellent investment.

Mixing bowls

Every kitchen needs a generous assortment of these very versatile, multipurpose bowls, matched in capacity, shape, and material to the tasks performed most often. Tall, narrow shapes are best for creaming and beating; the high sides prevent liquids or solids from flying out of the bowl onto counter or face. Wide, shallow bowls keep all ingredients in view and within reach; nothing gets lost on the bottom. In general, use bowls larger than seems necessary for the job; the extra capacity will help control messes and reduce cleanup. Look for containers that sit flat on the work surface and that are easy to pick up and not too heavy to move or store. Overall, stainless steel is the preferred material. It is highly durable, nonreactive (it won't discolor batters, doughs, or high-acid foods), and resistant to thermal shock (it can withstand sudden changes of temperature—setting a dish of hot custard in a bowl of ice water, for example).

Pepper mill

For grinding whole peppercorns easily, a pepper mill is a necessity.

Roasting pan and rack

Buy a low, open roasting pan that will fit in your oven with several inches of space all around for air circulation. It should be sturdy enough to support a large roast or turkey, but not so heavy that lifting is a struggle. A rack provides open space beneath a roast so the heat can reach its underside and drippings can fall into the pan. Without a rack, the bottom of the roast will stew in the pan juices instead of staying dry and crisp. The most practical racks collapse for easy storage and are adjustable. Rigid racks are sturdy, but require more storage space when not in use.

Salad spinner

Nothing dilutes a good vinaigrette and ruins a good salad more quickly than wet lettuce. The plastic salad spinner, a relatively new kitchen device available at houseware shops, makes drying lettuce and other greens quick and easy.

Saucepans

The versatile saucepan is ideal for making sauces, cooking vegetables and rice, and reheating and warming. Have an assortment of sizes—ranging from 1 to 8 quarts—and shapes—wide and shallow, narrow and deep—all with tight-fitting lids. A saucepan should heat quickly and evenly, sit firmly on the burner, pour without dripping, and be well balanced, easy to clean, not too heavy, and nonreactive to acid foods. Because a saucepan is moved around a great deal, the handle should be in proportion to the pan's size and weight for easy lifting.

Saucepots (Dutch ovens and casseroles)

These large, useful pans are invaluable for cooking in large quantities: pasta, vegetables, soups, and stews. Because they are used for slow cooking, which requires holding a simmer for long periods of time, they should be made of a material that conducts and holds heat well, such as aluminum, copper, or clad metals. A 5- to 6-quart pot will meet the needs of most households.

Skillets

The flare-sided skillet and the straight-sided French sauté pan evolved as slightly different approaches to the same process—rapid stove-top cooking in fat of some sort. The skillet is shallower than the sauté pan, with less bottom surface, but still tall enough to contain liquid for a sauce or stir-fry. Buy several skillets: large (12 or 14 inches in diameter), medium (10 inches in diameter), and small (6, 7, or 8 inches).

A well-chosen selection of high-quality cookware is one of the most important investments you can make in your kitchen.

Small tools and gadgets

Gadgets range from the familiar, such as citrus zesters and vegetable peelers, to the unidentifiable. If they are well made and perform their job well, they are invaluable. Be sure the edges of cutting tools are sharp. The following hand tools should be in your kitchen drawer: citrus zester, garlic press, metal and rubber spatulas, slotted spoon, tongs, vegetable peeler, whisk, wooden spoons.

Stove-top grill

A hybrid, this pan functions as a combination griddle, skillet, and grill. It is available in several types. One is a flat, ridged pan with raised sides like a skillet. Another is a round pan that looks like a hubcap. The grill's greatest appeal is that food doesn't cook in its own fat—a boon to those on restricted diets or anyone trying to limit fat intake.

Wok

It is hard to imagine a more versatile or better-designed piece of cookware than this most famous symbol of Chinese cooking. Its rounded bottom allows food to be stir-fried or deep-fried with a minimum of oil. With a cover and a steaming rack or basket, the wok becomes a steamer for everything from whole birds and fish to bite-sized pastries. You can simmer, braise, and even smoke foods in a wok. A 14-inch pan is good for quantity cooking of any type of food, not just Chinese.

BASICS

VERSATILE STAPLES: EGGS, PASTA, AND TORTILLAS

A practical pantry should include eggs, dried pasta, and corn and flour tortillas. Eggs, the critical ingredient in soufflés, omelets, crêpes, and many baked goods, give every pantry limitless possibilities. They fit well into any menu, are easily stored, and can be prepared at the last minute. Pasta, one of the most versatile pantry foods, is delicious simply tossed with butter and cheese or as part of a do-ahead lasagne. Dried pasta stores well in the pantry for up to one year. Fresh pasta, available in many supermarkets or from specialty stores, can be held in the freezer, ready to use as part of a speedy and savory supper. In most recipes, use 50 percent more fresh pasta when substituting fresh for dried (12 ounces fresh pasta for 8 ounces dried, for example). Tortillas, both flour and corn, are a great foundation for snack, lunch, and supper casseroles.

ROASTED PEPPER AND BACON OMELET

A perfect omelet is a slightly scrambled egg that cooks in about 1 minute. Omelets are best made in one- or two-portion servings. Using a pan of the proper size is critical to the speed of cooking: The egg should coat the bottom of the pan to a depth of about ¼ to ½ inch. Too much egg in the pan and the omelet will start to overcook in some spots and undercook in others. The method for this Roasted Pepper and Bacon Omelet can be used for a variety of fillings, such as cheese, mushroom, ham, or spinach.

> 12 eggs
> ½ teaspoon salt
> ¼ teaspoon freshly ground pepper
> 4 tablespoons unsalted butter

Roasted Pepper and Bacon Filling

> 6 slices bacon (about 8 oz)
> 1 medium onion, sliced
> 3 cloves garlic, minced
> 1 jar (7 oz) roasted red peppers, diced
> 1 teaspoon dried oregano
> ¼ teaspoon freshly ground pepper

1. Prepare filling. Beat eggs with salt and pepper in a medium bowl. In a large skillet over high heat, melt 2 tablespoons butter and swirl to coat bottom and sides of pan.

2. Pour one half of the egg mixture into pan. Grasp handle of pan with one hand and gently shake pan to keep omelet from sticking. With other hand, lightly scramble top of eggs with a fork, taking care to let bottom set slightly so bottom surface is cooked and top stays moist. Cook about 1 minute (omelet should still be moist).

3. Place one half of filling in a thin line down center of omelet at a right angle to pan handle. Using a spatula or fork, fold third of omelet nearest handle over filling. Lifting handle of omelet pan, place edge of pan on a serving plate. Push omelet over onto itself and gently roll it onto serving plate (underside of omelet will be on top). Cut omelet in half and serve immediately. Repeat with remaining egg mixture.

Serves 4.

Roasted Pepper and Bacon Filling

Slice bacon into ½-inch-long pieces. Set a small skillet over medium heat, add bacon pieces, and cook until bacon starts to brown (about 3 minutes). Stir in onion and garlic; sauté about 2 minutes. Add red peppers, oregano, and pepper; stir to mix; cook over low heat for about 2 minutes. Keep warm over low heat while omelet cooks.

Makes about 2 cups.

Cheese and Bacon Omelet Grate 6 ounces Monterey jack cheese. Place 3 ounces of cheese in center of each omelet on top of bacon mixture before folding.

Dessert Omelet Omit ground pepper in egg mixture. Stir 4 tablespoons sugar and 2 tablespoons dark rum into beaten eggs. Omit filling. Proceed as directed. Dust finished omelet with confectioners' sugar.

PASTA PUTTANESCA

Onions, canned tomatoes, olives, and dried herbs—all from the pantry—combine to make this simple pasta sauce. Vary it with additions of salami, cooked chicken breast, or kidney beans, or add fresh seasonal produce such as asparagus, broccoli, sugar snap peas, or bell peppers.

> 2 onions, diced
> 4 tablespoons olive oil
> 4 cloves garlic, minced
> 1 can (28 oz) whole plum
>   tomatoes, drained and
>   diced
> 24 black olives, pitted and halved
> 1 teaspoon hot-pepper flakes
> 1 teaspoon dried oregano
> 1 teaspoon dried basil
> 1 teaspoon salt
> ¼ teaspoon freshly ground pepper
> 12 ounces dried fusilli or other
>   dried pasta
> ½ cup (2½ oz) grated Asiago or
>   Parmesan cheese (optional),
>   for garnish

1. In a medium saucepan or large skillet over medium heat, sauté onions in oil until translucent (about 4 minutes). Add garlic and cook 3 minutes. Stir in tomatoes, olives, hot-pepper flakes, oregano, basil, salt, and pepper; reduce heat to medium-low and simmer 15 minutes.

2. In a large saucepan, bring 4 quarts water to a boil. Cook pasta until tender, but slightly resistant to the bite (*al dente;* about 12 minutes or according to package instructions). Drain thoroughly and toss with sauce. Serve immediately, sprinkled with Asiago or Parmesan cheese (if desired).

Serves 6 as a main course.

QUESADILLAS

A quesadilla is a south-of-the-border grilled cheese sandwich. When prepared with Cheddar, Monterey jack, goat cheese, or Brie, layered between two flour tortillas, quesadillas make an appealing hors d'oeuvre or accompaniment to soup or salad.

> 1 cup (5 oz) grated Cheddar
>   cheese
> 1 cup (5 oz) grated Monterey jack
>   cheese
> 12 medium-sized flour tortillas
> 6 green onions, diced
> 24 sprigs cilantro (optional)
> 3 tablespoons vegetable oil
>   Fresh Pineapple Salsa (see
>   page 114) or purchased
>   hot salsa

1. In a small bowl combine cheeses. Sprinkle one sixth of the cheese mixture on 1 flour tortilla. Dot with diced green onions and 2 sprigs cilantro (if used). Cover with a second tortilla. Repeat with remaining tortillas.

2. In a 10-inch skillet over medium-high heat, heat 1 teaspoon oil. Cook stuffed tortillas, one at a time, until very lightly browned and crispy (about 3 minutes). Turn and cook second side until tortilla is lightly browned and cheese is melted (about 2 minutes).

3. Remove from pan and reserve in a warm oven until all quesadillas are done. Cut each in 6 pieces at serving time and serve with salsa.

Serves 12 as an hors d'oeuvre, 6 as a sandwich, or 6 as an accompaniment.

The variety of colors and shapes in this assortment of Crudités—raw fresh vegetables—complements any dip.

STARTERS

APPETIZERS AND HORS D'OEUVRES

Sometimes an hors d'oeuvre is as simple as a bowl of nuts set down on the kitchen counter to stave off hunger pangs until a quickly organized, casual meal is ready. On other occasions it's something more—the overture to a well-orchestrated menu. In either situation—spur-of-the-moment or planned-in-advance—the hors d'oeuvre is not the main event, but a tempting bite or two that precedes it. "Keep it light" should be the cardinal rule pre-dinner. This chapter offers dozens of quick-to-prepare nibbles that will get your next gathering off to a good start.

PARTY STARTERS

Coordinating hors d'oeuvres with one another and with the rest of the meal is just common sense, but many hosts overlook this step. Serve like with like, both in terms of cuisine—Italian starters with Italian meals—and in terms of style—elegant starters with elegant meals.

If you're serving several hors d'oeuvres with no meal to follow, the hors d'oeuvres should complement one another. Balance textures and flavors, hot and cold, cooked and raw, simple and hearty. And it's best to avoid mixing metaphors: an assortment of Latin-inspired hors d'oeuvres makes a far more pleasing spread than a couple of Latin dishes paired with sushi and Chinese egg rolls.

How Much is Enough?

Knowing how many hors d'oeuvres to make, and how much of each one, takes common sense coupled with some educated guesswork. If your hors d'oeuvres will be followed by a full-course dinner, keep them few and simple. For dinner parties of eight or fewer, serve a single hors d'oeuvre. As the guest list grows, add another selection or two, but that's all; two or three pre-dinner hors d'oeuvres are enough, no matter how large the party. Count five to six "bites" per person during the standard cocktail hour.

Of course, heartier hors d'oeuvres go farther than nuts or olives. If you're concerned about having enough, make 10 to 20 percent extra of any items you can use as leftovers: sauces or pickles that will keep for a while or meats that can be frozen.

Keep it Simple and Stylish

Most foods look their best and are more inviting in casual settings and simple presentations. A low-key, less-fuss approach keeps the mood relaxed and the logistics manageable. Don't feel compelled to compose still lifes on every tray. Your guests may hestitate to disturb such picture-perfect arrangements and

the food might sit there uneaten. That's not what it's all about.

And, unless you're a caterer, you don't need a closetful of serving platters, bowls, and baskets. A few containers and trays that you particularly enjoy using, in several sizes that match your entertaining style, will get you through almost any situation. More than that isn't really necessary.

About Wine and Spirits

What you choose to pour with hors d'oeuvres is certainly a matter of personal taste: wine, cocktails, soft drinks or mineral water, or all of these.

Wine is almost always a good choice, and is becoming increasingly popular. In general, the best appetizer wines are light-bodied, crisp, and fruity. Among whites, the dry Alsatian Rieslings and Gewürztraminers stand up to slightly spicy foods particularly well. Fruity California Chenin Blancs and French Chenin Blanc from the Loire Valley are lovely with fish, shellfish, and pork. The crisp California Sauvignon Blancs are excellent fish and hors d'oeuvre wines, as are many of the simple whites from Italy.

Among reds, the fruity Beaujolais wines are delightful with pâtés and grilled foods. Beaujolais is a versatile, likeable red that marries well with many dishes; if you're pouring only one wine, it's a good choice.

California Zinfandels made in a light style, simple French Côtes-du-Rhône, Spanish reds from Rioja, and light-bodied Italian Chiantis can also make good appetizer wines, and most are modestly priced.

Pickled or spicy hors d'oeuvres present problems for wine and may be better with cocktails or beer.

Champagne is an appetizer par excellence. Its high acid content stimulates the gastric juices; its fresh, clean flavors awake the palate, and its bubbles lighten the spirit. With pâtés, fish, and shellfish, it is truly at its best. There are dozens of excellent values in sparkling wine made by the Champagne method,

from California, Italy, Spain, and France. Ask your wine merchant for recommendations.

NUTS AND OLIVES: CLASSIC AND EASY

Light, slightly salty, and, in the most basic sense of the word, appetizing, nuts and olives are the epitome of cocktail fare. You can prepare any of the following hors d'oeuvres in very short order. The marinated olives require a half-day's lead time, but they can be made far ahead and put aside for the proper moment.

CREOLE PECANS

Louisiana flavors spice up these deep-fried nuts—a hard-to-resist companion to tequila-based drinks and beer. Choose only the best-looking pecan halves and, if possible, taste before you buy to make sure they're fresh and moist.

> 2 tablespoons melted butter
> 1 teaspoon each ground cumin, celery seed, and minced garlic
> ½ to 1 teaspoon cayenne pepper
> 1 teaspoon hot curry powder (optional)
> 1 pound shelled pecans
> Corn oil, for deep frying
> Salt, to taste

1. In a bowl stir together butter, cumin, celery seed, garlic, cayenne, and curry powder (if used). Add nuts and stir to coat well. Let rest at room temperature at least 1 hour or up to 12 hours.

2. In a medium skillet, heat at least 2 inches of oil to 375° F. Fry nuts in hot oil until golden and fragrant. Drain on paper towels, salt lightly, and let cool 10 minutes before serving.

Makes 1 pound.

FEATURE

EFFORTLESS APPETIZERS

Each cook needs a few hors d'oeuvres that will be a snap to prepare. However, other than a wedge of cheese and a box of crackers, there are very few work-free appetizers. Simplicity and good planning will help lessen the burden of coming up with that perfect little something before dinner.

Bacon-Wrapped Dried Fruit
Wrap dried pears, apples, or apricots in a 3-inch length of bacon, spear with a toothpick, and broil until bacon is crisp (2 to 3 minutes).

Baked Brie
Place a 1-pound wedge of Brie on an ovenproof serving platter with a 1-inch-deep rim. Bake in a preheated 350° F oven until softened and slightly runny (20 minutes). Serve with crackers.

Crostini of Salami and Parmesan Cheese
Cut a baguette into ¼-inch-thick slices. Top with a slice of salami and grated Parmesan cheese. Bake in a preheated 350° F oven until warmed (2 to 3 minutes).

Cucumber Rounds With Sour Cream and Chutney
Slice English cucumbers crosswise about ¼ inch thick. Top each slice with 1 teaspoon sour cream and ½ teaspoon purchased chutney.

Endive Spears With Guacamole, Bay Shrimp, and Salsa
Trim root end from a head of Belgian endive; separate endive into spears. Place ½ teaspoon prepared guacamole near cut end, 2 or 3 bay shrimp next to guacamole, and ¼ teaspoon tomato salsa next to shrimp.

Endive Spears With Gorgonzola and Toasted Walnuts
Wash and pat dry 24 endive spears. Place ½ teaspoon Gorgonzola cheese on each spear and garnish with 1 large toasted walnut half.

Grilled Sausage With Spicy Mustard
Grill or broil mild Italian sausage; cut into pieces and serve on skewers, accompanied with favorite spicy mustard.

Herring in Cherry Tomatoes
Remove stems from 1 basket of cherry tomatoes. Slice top off stem end and hollow out interior by gently squeezing out seeds. Dice prepared herring in sour cream sauce and spoon into tomatoes.

Jane's Pesto–Crème Fraîche
Stir together 1 cup crème fraîche and 1 cup Pesto Sauce (see page 115; or use prepared sauce). Serve as a dip for skewered tortellini and crudités.

Parmesan Pita Triangles
Cut 8-inch pita circles in 6 wedges; split each wedge, brush with garlic oil (see page 36), sprinkle with 1 teaspoon grated Parmesan cheese, and bake in a 375° F oven until crispy and lightly browned (about 5 minutes).

Prosciutto-Wrapped Bread Sticks
Wrap a paper-thin piece of prosciutto diagonally along the length of a good-quality bread stick. Leave a small amount of bread stick showing for a handle.

Skewered Chicken Breast With Italian Salsa Verde
Cut boned chicken breast halves into 8 to 10 cubes (about ½ inch) and thread on a bamboo skewer. Broil 3 inches from heat for 2 minutes; turn and cook for 1 minute more. Serve with a vinaigrette flavored with red wine vinegar, anchovy paste, capers, garlic, and chopped parsley for dipping.

Smoked Salmon Mousse
In a blender or food processor, purée 4 ounces smoked salmon, 4 ounces softened cream cheese, and juice of ½ lemon. Place in a small serving dish and serve with baguette slices or crackers.

Steamed Potatoes With Aioli
Steam 2 pounds (about 16) tiny red-skinned potatoes until tender when pierced with a knife (30 to 35 minutes). Cool slightly. Slice and arrange around a bowl of garlicky Aioli (mince 3 cloves garlic and stir into 1 cup mayonnaise).

Steamed Potatoes With Sour Cream and Caviar
Steam 2 pounds red-skinned potatoes as directed above. Using a melon ball cutter, scoop a small ball of flesh from the top of each potato. Fill with 1 teaspoon sour cream and dot with tiny caviar.

CRISP SUGARED WALNUTS

This traditional Asian dish—perfect snack food for cocktail parties—can be made in a skillet or wok, or baked in a preheated 325° F oven for 10 minutes.

- *2 cups boiling water*
- *2 cups walnut or pecan halves*
- *6 tablespoons sugar*
- *Pinch of salt*
- *2 cups peanut oil*

1. In a medium bowl combine boiling water and walnuts; soak 3 minutes. Drain nuts and pat dry. While nuts are hot, toss with sugar and salt to coat. Spread on waxed paper or parchment paper and let stand until dry (at least 1 hour).

2. In a medium skillet or wok, heat at least 2 inches of oil to 325° F. Add nuts and deep-fry until they glisten and begin to caramelize (about 5 minutes). Remove, drain, and let cool on waxed paper or parchment paper, separating nuts so that they harden.

Makes 2 cups.

GARLIC AND HOT-PEPPER ALMONDS

Pepper-toasted almonds make a quick nibble to accompany cocktails or wine. Take a batch to the ballgame; they're excellent with beer! Almonds can be made up to two weeks ahead if stored in an airtight container.

- *2 tablespoons olive oil*
- *2 tablespoons butter*
- *1 tablespoon minced garlic*
- *½ teaspoon hot-pepper flakes*
- *3 cups whole blanched almonds*
- *Salt, to taste*

In a large skillet over moderate heat, heat olive oil and butter. When butter foams, add garlic and stir until fragrant. Add pepper flakes and stir an additional 15 seconds. Add almonds and stir continuously until nuts are well coated and lightly toasted. Season with salt. Drain nuts on paper towels and let cool. Serve cool, but not cold.

Makes 3 cups.

PARTY MIX

This concoction is addictive, whether you call it trail mix, party mix, or bridge mix, and is best when you make your own. This recipe yields a large batch; store any extra in an airtight container.

- *1 pound Brazil nuts, unskinned*
- *1 pound almonds, unskinned*
- *1 pound blanched cashews*
- *½ pound pine nuts*
- *¼ pound muscat raisins or seedless dark raisins*
- *⅓ pound golden raisins*
- *⅓ cup Marsala or sweet vermouth*
- *½ pound shelled pistachio nuts*
- *¼ cup shredded unsweetened coconut*
- *¼ cup lightly salted sunflower seeds*
- *¼ cup finely minced dried apricots*
- *Salt, to taste*
- *Worcestershire sauce, to taste (optional)*

1. Preheat oven to 350° F. Toast Brazil nuts, almonds, cashews, and pine nuts on cookie sheets until lightly browned and fragrant. Set aside to cool.

2. In a medium saucepan, combine dark and golden raisins with Marsala. Bring to a boil, reduce heat, and simmer gently until liquid has evaporated (20 to 30 minutes). Set aside to cool.

3. Combine cooled toasted nuts with raisins, pistachios, coconut, sunflower seeds, and apricots. Season with salt and Worcestershire sauce (if used).

Makes about 10 cups.

ORANGE AND FENNEL OLIVES

Overnight marinating infuses these olives with the flavors of tangy citrus peel, garlic, and fennel. Use only best-quality unpitted olives here: Greek Kalamata or French Niçoise olives are good choices if available.

- *2 pounds black olives, rinsed of any brine*
- *Peel of 2 oranges (discard bitter white pith), cut into long strips*
- *Peel of 2 lemons (discard bitter white pith), cut into long strips*
- *Juice of 4 lemons*
- *3 to 4 tablespoons fennel seeds*
- *4 large cloves garlic, peeled*

Combine olives, orange peel, lemon peel, lemon juice, fennel seeds, and garlic. Pack into clean glass jars, cover, and marinate overnight at room temperature. Olives can be stored up to 6 months in the refrigerator.

Makes 2 pounds.

HERBED OLIVES AND ONIONS

Buy unpitted olives, either green or black, rinse off any brine under cold running water, and then marinate them. Use a good-quality oil and vinegar for the best flavor. The mixture must marinate at least 12 hours before serving.

- *1 pound olives, rinsed of any brine*
- *2 tablespoons white wine vinegar*
- *2 tablespoons tarragon vinegar*
- *½ cup olive oil*
- *1 jar (3 to 4 oz) cocktail onions*
- *2 tarragon sprigs*
- *2 parsley sprigs*
- *Salt, to taste*

In a large clean glass jar with lid, combine olives, vinegars, olive oil, cocktail onions, tarragon sprigs, parsley sprigs, and salt. Shake well. Marinate at room temperature, shaking jar occasionally, for at least 12 hours. Serve immediately with a little of the marinade and the onions, and the parsley sprigs for garnish, or store in marinade up to 6 months in the refrigerator.

Makes 1 pound.

FEATURE

PREPARING HORS D'OEUVRES FOR ENTERTAINING

When planning your selection of appetizers for a party, consider the following:

Serving temperature Try to offer variety—a few hot hors d'oeuvres, a few at room temperature, and one or two chilled.

Shape Vary the shapes, arranging both round shapes and long, thin shapes on the same platter. For example, offer a scooped-out red bell pepper, filled with a dip, accompanied by round melba toasts and raw vegetable sticks.

Color Serve an assortment of warm colors—red, orange, yellow (tomatoes, oranges, and squash)—and cool colors—green, purple, blue (lettuce, eggplant, blueberries)—for alluring hors d'oeuvre combinations. The contrasts are especially effective when combined on the same platter.

Texture Choose crunchy- and smooth-textured foods. For example, serve a creamy dip with a crisp spear of Belgian endive or a crunchy slice of bell pepper. Strive for good texture throughout the setting as well. Use woven baskets, polished brass or copper trays, rattan mats, or bright cotton cloths as backgrounds for the food.

Preparing Vegetables for A Crudités Platter

Many vegetables can be transformed into wonderful dip containers or stuffed for appetizers. Small pumpkins, eggplants, bell peppers, or large, ripe tomatoes can be hollowed out to hold dips for a crudités platter. Smaller vegetables can be scooped out with a melon baller, stuffed with a cheese mixture or a vegetable pâté, and served as finger food.

To prepare a crudités platter, you can line the serving dish with lettuce that has been washed and checked for brown spots. Good vegetables for crudités platters include cherry tomatoes, celery and carrot sticks, broccoli and cauliflower florets, red or green bell pepper strips, whole banana peppers or small sweet chiles, green onions, whole snow peas or pea pods, diagonal slices of yellow summer squash, whole button mushrooms, endive spears, and asparagus tips. You may want to heat a small pot of water to boiling and blanch the hard vegetables—broccoli, squash, peppers, carrots, and cauliflower.

When arranging the prepared vegetables on the platter, try to create interest by placing different colors and shapes together. For example, a long, green asparagus stalk might be placed next to a round, red cherry tomato for a colorful effect.

SPREADS AND DIPS

A little something smooth and creamy on a round of crunchy toast or cracker or slice of chewy country loaf is one of the most popular kinds of hors d'oeuvres. It's also one of the easiest because most can be made in advance; the flavor of some actually improves if they are left to sit for a day or so. Crudités—raw fresh vegetables—are always welcome as a partner for dips. Choose the best vegetables the season has to offer, prepare them in bite-sized pieces, and arrange them in an eye-catching still life, with a dip or two.

CHIVE TOASTS

These crunchy toasts make a great snack food. They also marry well with a first-course soup. A regular baguette is fine if you can't find whole-wheat.

    3 ounces French goat cheese
    4 tablespoons butter
    ¼ cup minced chives
    1 tablespoon dried rosemary
    1 whole-wheat baguette, cut in
      24 to 28 slices

Preheat oven to 350° F. In a small bowl, mix together cheese and butter. Add chives and rosemary. Mix well. Spread 1 teaspoon on each baguette slice. Bake toasts until cheese is melted (10 minutes). Serve warm.

Makes 24 to 28 toasts.

LITTLE CRUSTS

Crostini are crisp slices of French or Italian bread topped with just about anything. Here, the topping is a fennel-laced mixture of sausage and cheese that is broiled until bubbly—a sort of quickly-made mini pizza.

    1½ pounds ricotta cheese
    ½ cup grated Parmesan cheese
    ¼ cup grated Romano cheese
    3 tablespoons olive oil
    3 cloves garlic, minced
    3 to 4 hot Italian sausages, about
      4 inches long
    1½ tablespoons fennel seed
      Salt and freshly ground pepper,
      to taste
    36 two-and-a-half-inch baguette
      slices

1. Preheat broiler. In a large bowl, combine ricotta, Parmesan, and Romano cheeses. In a medium skillet over moderate heat, heat olive oil. Add garlic and cook 45 seconds. Add sausages and cook slowly until they are well browned and cooked through (15 to 20 minutes). Remove from pan and cool completely, then remove casings.

2. Crumble sausage and add to cheeses, along with any oil and garlic in the skillet. Add fennel seed and season with salt and pepper; mix well.

3. Spread cheese mixture on bread slices and broil until bubbly and lightly browned. Serve immediately.

Makes 3 dozen crostini.

BLUE CHEESE CROSTINI

Whirl cheeses, brandy, and pecans in a food processor or mixer for a smoother spread. Bringing the cheese to room temperature will allow it to blend more easily with the other ingredients.

    4 ounces Roquefort cheese,
      softened
    4 ounces cream cheese, softened
    ½ tablespoon brandy
    ¼ cup pecans, coarsely chopped
    12 slices baguette

Preheat oven to 425° F. Thoroughly mix cheeses. Stir in brandy and pecans. Arrange bread slices on a baking sheet. Spread cheese mixture over bread slices. Bake until cheese is lightly browned (about 10 minutes). Serve immediately.

Makes 1 dozen crostini.

SICILIAN TOMATO SPREAD

This is a disarmingly simple topping—tomato paste spruced up with garlic and fresh herbs—but remarkably tasty when slathered on bread sticks, toasted or grilled bread rounds, or a crusty Italian loaf.

    ½ cup tomato paste
    1 teaspoon red wine vinegar
    1 tablespoon olive oil
    ½ teaspoon chopped fresh thyme
    1 large clove garlic, minced

Combine all ingredients thoroughly. Pack into a small crock. Serve immediately or cover with a thin film of olive oil and refrigerate for up to a week.

Makes ½ cup.

COUNTRY FRENCH CAVIAR

A creamy eggplant purée to spread on warm and chewy Italian *(foccacia)* or French *(fougasse)* flatbread will get your dinner off to a delectable start. For an intriguingly smoky flavor, cook eggplant over charcoal, turning often, until flesh is soft and skin is blackened. Specialty bakeries and delicatessens are two sources for flatbread, or serve the spread with baguette slices or pita-bread triangles.

    2 pounds (about 2 large) egg-
      plant
      Half large onion, peeled
    1 clove garlic, peeled
    2 tablespoons olive oil
    1 tablespoon red wine vinegar
    2 tablespoons lemon juice
      Salt and freshly ground pepper,
      to taste
    ½ cup tomato sauce
    3 tablespoons minced fresh basil

1. Preheat oven to 350° F. With a small, sharp knife, cut a half-dozen slits in skin of each eggplant to allow steam to escape. Place eggplants on a baking sheet. Bake until very soft (about 1 hour).

2. When cool enough to handle, peel eggplants and place pulp in a food processor or blender with onion and garlic. Blend until smooth. Add oil, vinegar, and lemon juice, and pulse to blend. Transfer mixture to a bowl. Season with salt and pepper. Stir in tomato sauce and basil. The spread can be made up to 2 days ahead without the basil. Refrigerate, but serve at room temperature; just before serving, mince basil and stir in; taste and adjust seasonings, if necessary.

Makes about 4 cups, 8 servings.

WATERCRESS DIP WITH BASIL AND PECANS

This dip is a showstopper—a nutty, coarse-textured creation fragrant with basil and brilliantly green. Arrange a basket of crudités beside it: cherry tomatoes, cauliflower and broccoli florets, snow peas, endive leaves, zucchini and carrot spears, artichoke hearts, radishes, or fennel.

> *3 cups watercress, stems trimmed*
> *¾ cup fresh small basil leaves*
> *¼ cup minced garlic*
> *½ cup good-quality olive oil*
> *1 cup grated Parmesan cheese*
> *¾ cup whipping cream*
> *½ cup finely ground walnuts*
> *¼ cup minced green onions*
> *Salt and freshly ground pepper, to taste*
> *1 tablespoon milk or water (optional)*

1. In a blender combine watercress, basil, garlic, olive oil, and Parmesan; blend to form a paste. Add cream and blend only until mixed; do not overblend.

2. Transfer mixture to a bowl and stir in walnuts and green onion. Season with salt and pepper. Mixture will thicken as it stands. If desired, add a tablespoon of milk or water to thin it out before serving. Mixture will keep up to 10 days, refrigerated.

Makes 2 cups.

GUACAMOLE WITH TOMATILLOS

The unusual lemony flavor of tomatillos and the cilantro give this favorite Mexican dip a new slant. Tomatillos resemble little green tomatoes. They're turning up more and more in specialty produce stores and well-stocked supermarkets. They are also sold canned if you can't find them fresh.

> *4 or 5 fresh or canned tomatillos*
> *3 canned green chiles, seeded*
> *2 large ripe avocados*
> *1 tablespoon minced onion*
> *Salt and freshly ground pepper, to taste*
> *¼ cup cilantro leaves, minced, for garnish*

1. If using fresh tomatillos, discard husks and wash the tomatillos. Boil in a small amount of water until just tender (about 5 minutes); drain.

2. Combine tomatillos and chiles in a food processor or blender; process until smooth.

3. Halve the avocados and remove seeds. Scoop out pulp and mash with a fork. Stir in tomatillo mixture and onions. Season with salt and pepper. Spoon into a serving bowl and sprinkle with cilantro.

Makes 2½ cups.

Fresh basil gives this Watercress Dip With Basil and Pecans its lovely aroma and color. Serve with a basket of assorted crudités.

FEATURE

WING IT

Many supermarkets are now selling what look like tiny chicken legs, called "drummettes." These are not legs from mini chickens, but chicken wings with the wing tips removed, something you can do yourself if you prefer. They have great charm because they are so small, and are perfect finger food—gone in a bite or two and easy to pick up and hold. In fact, they are so appealing you might want to prepare an extra batch; they disappear like popcorn. The following are some tasty ideas for preparing wing drummettes in the oven, under a broiler, or on the grill.

SESAME WINGS

These nibbles develop a rich, teriyaki-type glaze as they broil, while the toasted sesame seed adds a nutty flavor. They really won't last long; they're that good.

- ½ cup vegetable oil
- ½ cup sherry
- ¼ cup soy sauce
- ¼ cup lemon juice
- 2 cloves garlic, minced
- ¼ cup toasted sesame seeds
- 2 pounds chicken drummettes
  Salt, to taste

1. In a blender, combine oil, sherry, soy sauce, lemon juice, garlic, and sesame seed; process until smooth.

2. Salt drummettes lightly. Place in a large bowl and cover with marinade; refrigerate for at least 1 hour.

3. Preheat broiler. Broil drummettes 5 inches from heat for 7 minutes per side, basting once on each side with marinade.

Makes about 20 drummettes.

PIQUANT WINGS

Let the chicken soak up this spicy, sweet-and-tangy marinade, then cook in any of three ways: baking, broiling, or grilling. Baking instructions are given below; broiling takes about 5 to 6 minutes. Perhaps the tastiest results come from the charcoal grill, where the chicken can be cooked and basted for 12 to 15 minutes, until it is crisp and richly browned.

- ½ cup dry sherry
- 2 tablespoons sherry vinegar
- 2 tablespoons lemon juice
- 1 tablespoon tomato paste
- 1 tablespoon sugar
- 2 tablespoons minced garlic
- 2 teaspoons salt
- 2 tablespoons ground cumin
- ½ teaspoon cayenne pepper
- 24 chicken drummettes
- 2 tablespoons chopped cilantro,
    for garnish

1. In a stainless steel, glass, or ceramic bowl, combine sherry, vinegar, lemon juice, tomato paste, sugar, garlic, salt, cumin, and cayenne. Marinate chicken in mixture for at least 4 hours or overnight.

2. Preheat oven to 350° F. Bake uncovered for 45 minutes. Serve hot, garnished with chopped cilantro.

Makes 2 dozen drummettes.

LOW-CAL MUSTARD WINGS

These wings are brushed with a sweet and spicy mixture of cayenne pepper, mustard, garlic, and honey; then they're baked to a crunchy turn.

- 12 chicken drummettes
   Freshly ground pepper, to taste
- 1 tablespoon honey
   Cayenne pepper, to taste
- 1 clove garlic, finely minced
- 2 teaspoons Dijon-style mustard
   Whole wheat bread crumbs,
     very finely ground

1. Preheat oven to 400° F. Lightly oil a baking sheet. Remove as much skin as possible from drummettes. Sprinkle chicken with pepper.

2. Combine honey, cayenne, garlic, and mustard. Brush mixture onto chicken, coating all sides lightly and evenly, then dip in bread crumbs.

3. Place on prepared baking sheet and bake until light brown (about 30 minutes). Serve hot.

Makes 12 drummettes.

BAKED BUFFALO WINGS

The original recipe of this popular hors d'oeuvre is the specialty of a bar in Buffalo, New York. That version is deep-fried, but in this healthier rendition the chicken is baked. Serve hot from the oven with celery sticks and Roquefort Dressing. You can prepare the dressing with low-fat sour cream and mayonnaise if you prefer.

> 2 tablespoons melted butter
> ¼ cup hot-pepper sauce
> 2 tablespoons rice vinegar
> 30 chicken drummettes
> Paprika, for sprinkling
> Celery sticks, for accompaniment

Roquefort Dressing

> 6 ounces Roquefort cheese
> 1 cup sour cream
> 2 tablespoons mayonnaise
> Freshly ground pepper, to taste

1. Preheat oven to 350° F. Lightly oil a baking sheet. Mix together butter, hot-pepper sauce, and vinegar. Dip chicken into mixture, then place on prepared baking sheet. Sprinkle lightly with paprika.

2. Bake until crisp and brown (about 30 minutes). Serve with celery sticks and Roquefort Dressing.

Makes 30 drummettes.

Roquefort Dressing   Mix Roquefort, sour cream, and mayonnaise together. Season with pepper.

Makes about 1¼ cups.

PICK-UPS

The following hors d'oeuvres are savory mouthfuls that are easily managed by guests: no dripping or crumbs, no decisions as to how much to take. They're already in bite-sized pieces—just pick one up, eat, and enjoy. Some are served hot, right after cooking; others can be made in advance and set out when you need them because they are meant to be eaten at room temperature or cold.

BAKED POTATO CRISPS

These crusty baked skins are utterly addictive, either on their own or with sour cream and snipped fresh chives. You can store the peeled potatoes in ice water for a day or two, then use them in any potato recipe.

> Approximately 2 cups potato peelings, preferably with some potato "flesh" left on them
> 2 tablespoons unsalted butter

Preheat oven to 450° F. Place skins on lightly oiled or buttered baking sheet. Dot with butter. Bake until skins are quite golden and crisp (about 20 minutes). Drain on paper towels and serve immediately.

Makes about 6 dozen potato "crisps."

BALSAMIC ONION AND CHEESE PICKS

Tiny pearl onions turn sweet and soft when roasted with oil and vinegar, especially a vinegar as mellow and rich as Italian balsamic. The onions can be roasted a few days ahead; the cheese can be cubed and wrapped in plastic a day in advance. The cheese will cube better if cold, but both onions and cheese taste better at room temperature.

> 1½ pounds pearl onions
> ⅓ cup olive oil
> ¼ cup balsamic vinegar
> Salt and freshly ground pepper, to taste
> ¾ pound Italian fontina cheese, cut into ⅓-inch cubes
> 24 to 30 cocktail skewers

1. Preheat oven to 375° F. Blanch onions in boiling, salted water 30 seconds; drain. Slice off the root end. "Peel" the onions by pressing them slightly between your fingers; the inner part will slip out of the papery skin.

2. Whisk together oil, vinegar, salt, and pepper. Put onions in a roasting pan, add oil-vinegar mixture, and toss to coat well. Bake until tender (about 25 minutes). Remove from oven and let cool in pan. Taste; adjust seasoning as necessary.

3. To serve, place 2 onions and 1 cheese cube on each cocktail skewer.

Makes 24 to 30 skewers.

Roasting brings out the earthy sweetness of pearl onions for these Balsamic Onion and Cheese Picks.

MUSHROOM PÂTÉ EN BAGUETTE

Mushrooms and herbs are blended into a savory pâté and stuffed into a hollowed-out loaf of French bread. To serve, slice into thin rounds, revealing a circle of bread surrounding a disc of pâté.

    ½ cup chopped onion
    1 tablespoon olive oil
    ¼ cup sake or dry sherry
    ½ cup chopped green onions,
        including green tops
    2 teaspoons minced garlic
    1½ cups sliced mushrooms
    ½ cup minced celery
    ½ cup almonds or walnuts,
        minced
    ½ cup minced parsley
    1 cup rye bread crumbs
    1 teaspoon ground dried rose-
        mary
    1 teaspoon dried thyme
    1 tablespoon soy sauce
    1 teaspoon salt
    ½ teaspoon dried basil
    ¼ teaspoon dried oregano
    1 baguette

1. In a large skillet over medium-high heat, sauté onion in olive oil and sherry until soft but not browned. Add green onions, garlic, and mushrooms, and continue to cook for 5 minutes.

2. When mushrooms begin to release their juice, add celery, walnuts, and parsley, and cook 3 minutes longer.

3. Spoon sautéed vegetables into a large bowl. Add rye bread crumbs, rosemary, thyme, soy sauce, salt, basil, and oregano. Purée half of mixture in a blender and mix well with pâté remaining in bowl until it reaches a paste-like consistency.

4. Cut baguette in half lengthwise and slice off each end. With your fingers, remove the soft center of the loaf, hollowing out top and bottom sections. Stuff pâté into the cavity, wrap in plastic wrap, and chill for 2 hours or more. To serve, slice baguette into rounds.

Makes about 2½ dozens rounds.

PEANUT-CHICKEN SKEWERS

Strips of chicken flavored with a sweet and peppery peanut sauce are threaded on skewers with red peppers and grilled until crisp and juicy. Note that the chicken must marinate in the sauce overnight.

    6 chicken breast halves, boned
        and skinned
    1 cup crunchy peanut butter
    ⅓ cup chopped cilantro
    ½ cup bottled chili sauce
    1 tablespoon salt
    ½ teaspoon cayenne pepper
    ½ teaspoon freshly ground black
        pepper
    ¼ cup lemon juice
    ¼ cup firmly packed brown sugar
    ½ cup soy sauce
    8 green onions, minced
    3 tablespoons minced garlic
    2 sweet bell peppers, red or green,
        cut into ½-inch cubes
    2 dozen 6- to 8-inch bamboo
        skewers
    Minced parsley, for garnish

1. Slice each breast half into four lengthwise strips; set aside.

2. In a stainless steel, glass, or ceramic bowl, combine peanut butter, cilantro, chili sauce, salt, cayenne, black pepper, lemon juice, sugar, soy sauce, green onion, and garlic. Add chicken strips, cover, and let marinate overnight or up to 2 days.

3. Soak bamboo skewers in water for 30 minutes. Preheat broiler or prepare a charcoal fire. Thread chicken strips on the skewers like serpents, with pepper cubes interspersed. Broil or grill for 5 to 6 minutes, turning once. Serve garnished with minced parsley.

Makes 2 dozen skewers.

A savory filling complements the goodness of French bread in this Mushroom Pâté en Baguette.

Peanut-Chicken Skewers combine cubes of sweet peppers and strips of chicken marinated in a sweet and peppery peanut sauce.

MENU

A PRE-GAME TAILGATE WARM-UP

For 12

Artichokes With Spicy Crab
New Potatoes With Caviar
Walnut Gorgonzola Bites
Antipasto Skewers
Panbalie
Lasagne With Three Cheeses (double recipe; see page 99)
Garden Salad
Crusty Bread
Fudge Brownies (double recipe; see Brownie à la Mode, page 125)

This menu can be either a pre-game or a post-game collation, or, if you prefer, serve the hors d'oeuvres before and save the rest for later. Lasagne, well wrapped in foil and a bath towel "cozy," will keep warm for several hours. Store the salad in plastic bags and dress it just before serving. For fudge brownies, prepare only the brownie portion of Brownie à la Mode.

ARTICHOKES WITH SPICY CRAB

In this case, "spicy" does not mean hot; it means "well seasoned"–with mustard, green onions, capers, and more.

> 24 baby artichokes
> 1 lemon
> ¾ pound fresh cooked crabmeat
> ¼ cup whipping cream
> 1 tablespoon capers
> ¼ cup finely chopped green pepper
> 2 tablespoons minced green onion
> 2 teaspoons Dijon-style mustard
> 1 tablespoon butter
> 1 teaspoon olive oil
> 3 tablespoons minced shallot
> 2 tablespoons white wine
> Salt and freshly ground pepper, to taste
> Worcestershire sauce, to taste
> Minced fresh parsley, for garnish

> *Lemon wedges, for accompaniment*

1. Pull off dark green outer leaves of artichokes until you reach the pale green "heart." Cut ½ inch off top and trim stem end down to the pale green part. Rub artichoke hearts well with lemon and cook in boiling salted water until tender. Drain and pat dry. Pull out some of the innermost leaves and spread the hearts open slightly.

2. In a bowl combine crabmeat, cream, capers, green pepper, green onion, and mustard. In a small skillet over moderate heat, heat butter and oil. Add shallots and cook until translucent (4 to 5 minutes). Add wine and cook until mixture is reduced to a glaze. Cool slightly and add to crab mixture. Season with salt, pepper, and Worcestershire sauce.

3. Stuff artichoke hearts with crab mixture. Pack into a tightly sealed container along with a plastic bag of minced parsley and the lemon wedges. At serving time, garnish hearts with minced parsley and serve with lemon wedges.

Serves 12.

NEW POTATOES WITH CAVIAR

Don't blanch: The caviar need not be expensive imported sturgeon roe (although it can be!). Let your budget be your guide in selecting from among the variety of colorful caviars on the market, then pack them in ice for the trip. The contrast of warm potato with sour cream and ice-cold caviar makes a memorable mouthful. The foil will keep the potatoes warm for several hours, but you may want to pack them in an insulated carrier as well.

> 3 dozen tiny red-skinned new potatoes
> Olive oil, for drizzling
> Salt, for seasoning
> Juice of 1 lemon, for seasoning
> 12 ounces assorted caviar (golden, red, and black), for filling
> Sour cream or crème fraîche, for topping
> Lemon wedges, for accompaniment

1. Steam potatoes over boiling salted water until they are just tender when pierced. Dry them well; drizzle them while hot with olive oil, then sprinkle with salt and lemon juice. Cut off the top of each potato about ¼ inch down; scoop out and discard some of the inside pulp, leaving a firm, thick-sided shell. Wrap potatoes in aluminum foil and place in a tightly sealed container.

2. At serving time, set out potato "shells," caviars, sour cream, lemon wedges, some tiny serving spoons, and plenty of napkins. Guests can fill their potato "shells" with sour cream and the caviar of their choice, with a little lemon juice squeezed over the top.

Serves 12.

WALNUT GORGONZOLA BITES

While you're readying the rest of the hors d'oeuvres, pass these toasted walnut "bites."

> 72 perfect walnut halves
> ⅓ pound ripe Gorgonzola cheese, at room temperature
> 3 tablespoons unsalted butter, softened

1. Preheat oven to 350° F. Toast walnut halves on a cookie sheet until they are fragrant and lightly browned (5 to 10 minutes). Cool completely.

2. In a small bowl work cheese and butter together with a wooden spoon. Sandwich two nut halves with a dab of the cheese mixture. Refrigerate briefly to firm the cheese. Serve cool but not cold.

Makes 3 dozen "bites."

ANTIPASTO SKEWERS

Olives and cheese, prosciutto and melon come together on these colorful skewers. It's an antipasto platter made into finger food, and it's open to dozens of variations: shrimp, feta cheese, and Greek olives? mozzarella, cherry tomatoes, and rolled anchovies? You decide.

> 1 large or 2 small seasonal melons, peeled and cut into 36 cubes
> ½ pound prosciutto, sliced paper-thin

1 pound Italian fontina cheese,
cut into 36 cubes
36 best-quality black olives
Olive oil, for drizzling
Freshly ground pepper, for
garnish

1. Wrap each cube of melon in a piece of prosciutto.

2. On each of 36 skewers, thread a cube of cheese, an olive, and a prosciutto-melon cube. Place skewers in a tightly sealed container.

3. At serving time, drizzle with olive oil and dust with pepper.

Makes 3 dozen skewers.

PANBALIE

A juicy shrimp sandwich from the French Mediterranean, *panbalie* tastes better when the filling has had time to blend and soak into the bread. On game day, pack the sandwiches into your basket first and weight them down with the rest of the tailgate goodies. They'll be all the better for it! The shrimp mixture may be made a day ahead and stored in the refrigerator.

1 pound cooked tiny shrimp
2 red onions, coarsely chopped
¼ cup olive oil
3 tablespoons lemon juice
1 tablespoon minced fresh
oregano

Salt and freshly ground pepper,
to taste
6 six-inch, day-old French rolls
3 ripe tomatoes, thinly sliced

1. In a small bowl combine shrimp, onions, 2 tablespoons of the olive oil, lemon juice, oregano, and salt and pepper.

2. Slice rolls in half lengthwise. Moisten each half with a little of the remaining olive oil. Arrange tomato slices on the bottom half. Spread shrimp mixture over tomato slices and add top half of roll. Wrap each sandwich tightly in foil. At serving time, slice each sandwich in half or thirds.

Serves 12.

POLYNESIAN PRAWNS

A zesty sweet-and-sour plum sauce is the partner for these prawns. Serve with chilled beer—or Mai Tais for a Hawaiian island flavor.

3 pounds large prawns, boiled and shelled
2 tablespoons minced parsley
1 teaspoon grated lemon peel

Plum Sauce

2 pounds purple plums
¼ cup lemon juice
½ cup red wine vinegar
¼ cup Japanese plum wine or sake
1 tablespoon Dijon-style mustard
Cayenne pepper, to taste
Salt, to taste

Arrange prawns on a serving platter. Combine parsley and lemon peel and sprinkle over prawns. Serve with Plum Sauce and cocktail picks.

Serves 10.

Plum Sauce   Cut a cross in the bottom of each plum. Plunge into boiling water briefly, then into a bowl of ice water. Peel the plums (skins should peel off easily) and pit them. In a food processor or blender, combine plums and lemon juice and process until smooth. Stir in vinegar, plum wine, and mustard. Season with cayenne and salt.

INDONESIAN CORN-SHRIMP FRITTERS

Wherever you wander in Indonesia, you never seem to escape the tantalizing and seductive aroma of frying fritters. This corn fritter with shrimp and Indonesian spices makes an exciting appetizer.

3 large ears corn, scraped and coarsely chopped (about 2 cups), or 1 package (10 oz) frozen corn, thawed
½ pound shrimp, shelled, deveined, and cut into ½-inch pieces
½ teaspoon chopped garlic
4 green onions, chopped (about ½ cup)
2 stalks celery, finely chopped (about ½ cup)
1 teaspoon ground coriander
½ teaspoon ground cumin
2 tablespoons chopped fresh cilantro
3 tablespoons flour
1 teaspoon salt
2 eggs, beaten
Peanut or vegetable oil, for frying
Bottled chili sauce, for dipping

1. In a large bowl, combine corn, shrimp, garlic, green onion, celery, coriander, cumin, cilantro, flour, salt, and eggs. Mix thoroughly.

2. In a preheated medium skillet or wok, add peanut or vegetable oil to a depth of 1 inch; heat oil over medium-high heat to 375° F. Add corn mixture in ¼-cup batches, leaving ½ inch space between fritters. Fry fritters until golden brown and crisp (about 2 minutes per side). Remove, drain on paper towels, and keep warm while frying remaining mixture. Serve hot or at room temperature with chile sauce.

Makes twelve 2½-inch fritters.

BAKED ARTICHOKE SAVORIES

Guests will devour these rich-tasting, melt-in-your-mouth pastries, so make plenty. Use marinated artichokes for the best flavor, and low-fat cheeses for the best nutritional value. This recipe can be made up to three weeks ahead of time and frozen until ready to bake and serve.

2 tablespoons chopped onion
1 teaspoon minced garlic
⅓ cup dry sherry
3 egg whites
1 whole egg
¼ cup bread crumbs
3 tablespoons minced parsley
¼ teaspoon dried dill
⅛ teaspoon cayenne pepper
1 cup grated low-fat mozzarella cheese
½ cup low-fat ricotta cheese
10 ounces marinated artichoke hearts, drained and chopped

1. Preheat oven to 350° F. Lightly oil an 8-inch square baking pan.

2. In a medium skillet over medium-high heat, sauté onion and garlic in sherry until soft but not browned. Lightly beat egg whites until soft peaks form. Spoon into a bowl and mix with whole egg, bread crumbs, parsley, dill, cayenne, cheeses, and artichokes. Add sautéed onion and garlic. Pour into prepared baking pan.

3. Bake until set (about 30 minutes). Let cool, then cut into about 25 squares. Serve warm or cold.

Makes about two dozen pieces.

These tantalizing Indonesian fritters, made of corn, shrimp, and green onion, make exciting appetizers.

This French Celery Root Salad with its creamy mustard-shallot dressing makes an elegant first course.

FIRST COURSE

SOUPS AND SALADS

F irst course" implies that there is more to come. The light soups and salads in this chapter are perfect opening acts. They ease us into the meal by tempting our palates without making us too full for what is to follow. When your appetite is on the light side, you might find them just right for a simple lunch or supper, served with crackers or bread, cheese, or fruit. On the following pages you'll also learn how to make the perfect salad crouton and your own vinaigrette dressing. And you'll flash back to the Fifties with a nostalgic meal that begins with a favorite comfort food—homemade alphabet soup.

SOUPS TO START

A first-course soup should be light—just enough to stimulate the appetite for what comes next. That doesn't mean it must be bland or boring, as this diverse collection of delicious yet easy to prepare soup recipes demonstrates. Straw and Hay Soup (see page 28), a simple concoction of ribbons of spinach and egg pasta in a flavorful beef stock, proves that less is definitely more. Spring Green Soup with Puff Pastry Cap (see page 28) celebrates the arrival of spring's first delicate stalks of asparagus. Double Mushroom Soup with Barley (see page 31) gets special flavor from exotic Japanese mushrooms and a hint of fresh ginger.

ITALIAN RICE AND CHARD SOUP

This light vegetable soup is a good start to a menu of grilled chicken or sausages. Short-grained Arborio rice is imported from Italy and can be found in most specialty markets.

> 2 large bunches fresh green or red chard
> ¼ cup olive oil
> ¼ cup minced onion
> 3 cups (approximately) chicken stock
> ½ cup Arborio rice
> ⅓ cup fresh basil leaves, for garnish
> Grated Parmesan cheese, for garnish

1. Wash chard well. Remove stems and cut them into ¼-inch pieces. Bring a large pot of salted water to a boil and blanch the chard leaves for 10 to 15 seconds. Transfer them with a large slotted spoon to ice water, then drain, squeeze dry, and chop coarsely. Blanch the stems in the same boiling water, refresh them in ice water, then drain and dry.

2. Heat oil in a large pot over moderate heat. Add onion and sauté until translucent and soft (3 to 5 minutes). Add chard stems and stir to coat with oil. Add chicken stock and rice and bring to a simmer. Cover and simmer gently 15 minutes or until rice is just cooked. Add chopped chard and heat through gently.

(continued on page 28)

Basics

STOCKING UP ON STOCKS

Homemade stocks add a special dimension to cooking. A supply of the following basic stocks, stored in serving-sized portions in the freezer, will simplify meal preparation, as well as improve flavor. Beef and veal bones are available from butcher shops and at many supermarkets. Chicken wings or necks are found in almost every supermarket; poultry bones and carcasses left over from other preparations can be frozen for later use in stock. Fish bones for stock can be obtained at seafood markets.

Canned broth is often excessively salty and will never have the same taste as homemade stock; however, it is convenient. Dilute canned broth with an equal part water to make it more palatable. Canned chicken stock can be improved by simmering 5 cups stock with 4 green onions (cut in pieces), 1 clove garlic, 1 carrot (cut in pieces), 1 sprig parsley, and 1 bay leaf for 20 minutes. Strain before using.

BEEF STOCK

The bones and vegetables in this recipe are first roasted to give the stock a brown color and rich taste. For the best flavor, use knuckle bones with some meat attached. If possible, include a mixture of beef soup bones and veal knuckle bones; the combination will make a more flavorful stock, with the veal bones also serving as a natural thickener. Or, if desired, use only veal bones (see Brown Veal Stock, at right). Meat scraps, completely trimmed of fat, can be added to the stock during the last hour of cooking time.

> 4 pounds beef soup bones, chopped in a few pieces by butcher
> 2 medium onions, unpeeled, root end cut off, and quartered
> 2 medium carrots, scrubbed but not peeled, and quartered
> 2 stalks celery, cut in 2-inch pieces
> 2 bay leaves
> 10 stems parsley, leaves removed
> 4 cloves garlic, unpeeled
> ½ teaspoon black peppercorns
> ½ teaspoon dried thyme
> 16 cups (approximately) cold water

1. Preheat oven to 450° F. Place bones in a roasting pan; roast, turning occasionally with a slotted metal spatula, until they begin to brown (about 30 minutes). Add onions, carrots, and celery; roast until browned (about 30 minutes).

2. Drain off fat. With a slotted spatula transfer bones and vegetables to a stockpot, kettle, or other large pot. To ingredients in stockpot add bay leaves, parsley stems, garlic, peppercorns, thyme, and enough of the cold water to cover.

3. Bring just to a boil. Add a little more of the cold water to reduce to below boiling; stir once. Bring back just to a boil and reduce heat to very low so that liquid bubbles very gently. Skim off foam that collects on surface. Partially cover and cook, skimming foam and fat occasionally, for 4 to 6 hours. During first 2 hours of cooking, add hot water as needed to keep ingredients covered.

4. Strain stock through a colander lined with several thicknesses of dampened cheesecloth, discarding solids. If stock is not to be used immediately, cool to lukewarm. Refrigerate until fat rises to surface and congeals (about 8 hours). If stock will be used within 3 to 5 days, leave fat; skim fat when ready to use stock. If stock is to be frozen, skim fat before freezing.

Makes about 8 cups.

Brown Veal Stock Substitute veal bones, preferably knuckle bones, for the beef bones.

CHICKEN STOCK

Chicken and turkey are most common in poultry stock, but other fowl, such as duck or pheasant, are also used. The process for making poultry stock is the same regardless of which bird is the main ingredient. The most flavorful result is produced from an older bird such as a stewing hen. Use whatever parts are available–carcass, cooked scraps, wing tips, giblets (excluding livers), skin, or any leftovers. For more flavor, roast bones, carcass, necks, and back in a 450° F oven until brown (15 to 30 minutes); watch carefully, turn occasionally, and drain off all fat.

> 3 *pounds chicken wings, chicken backs, or a mixture of wings, backs, necks, and giblets (excluding livers)*
> 16 *cups (approximately) cold water*
> 2 *medium onions, peeled and quartered*
> 2 *medium carrots, peeled and quartered*
> 2 *bay leaves*
> 10 *stems parsley, leaves removed*
> ½ *teaspoon black peppercorns*
> ½ *teaspoon dried thyme*

1. Put chicken in a stockpot, kettle, or other large pot. Add enough of the cold water to cover. Bring just to a boil. Add a little more of the cold water to reduce to below boiling; stir once. Bring back just to a boil and reduce heat to very low so that liquid bubbles very gently. Skim off foam that collects on surface.

2. Add onions, carrots, bay leaves, parsley stems, peppercorns, and thyme. Adjust heat to keep surface just breaking with bubbles, but not boiling. Partially cover and cook for 2 to 3 hours, skimming foam and fat occasionally.

3. Strain stock through a colander lined with several thicknesses of dampened cheesecloth, and discard solids. If stock is not to be used immediately, cool to lukewarm. Refrigerate until fat rises to surface and congeals (about 8 hours). If stock will be used within 3 to 5 days, leave fat; skim fat when ready to use stock. If stock is to be frozen, skim fat before freezing.

Makes about 10 cups.

Rich Chicken Stock For a more strongly flavored stock, add beef, pork, or veal bones and trimmings. Increase the simmering time by 1 hour or more to

extract additional flavor and body. Or, follow the recipe for Chicken Stock, but begin with a previous batch of stock in place of the water. The resulting "double stock" will make an excellent soup. Adding cut-up chicken regularly is a good way to keep a batch of stock fresh, and it gets richer with each extraction. Rich stock can always be diluted with water when a basic or thin stock is needed.

FISH STOCK

The best bones for fish stock come from mild fish, such as sea bass or halibut. Do not use bones from strong-flavored fish, such as tuna or mackerel.

> 2 *pounds fish bones, tails, and heads*
> 1 *tablespoon unsalted butter*
> 1 *medium onion, sliced*
> ½ *cup dry white wine*
> 7 ½ *cups cold water*
> 1 *stalk celery, cut in 2-inch pieces*
> 1 *bay leaf*
> 8 *stems parsley, leaves removed*
> ½ *teaspoon dried thyme*

1. Put fish bones in bowl in sink. Let cold water run over bones for 5 minutes.

2. In a stockpot, kettle, or large saucepan over low heat, melt butter. Add onion and cook, stirring often, until soft but not brown (about 10 minutes).

3. Add fish bones, wine, the water, celery, bay leaf, parsley, and thyme. Mix well. Bring just to a boil and skim thoroughly to remove foam. Reduce heat to low and simmer, uncovered, skimming occasionally, for 20 minutes.

4. Drain contents of pot by pouring through a fine wire-mesh strainer into a bowl without pressing down on the mass; discard solids. (Pressing down on solids will cloud liquid, making it unsuitable for an aspic or a clear sauce.)

5. If not using stock immediately, cool to room temperature. Pour into 1- to 2-cup containers. Refrigerate, covered, up to 2 days or freeze up to 3 months.

Makes about 6 cups.

(continued from page 26)

If rice has absorbed most of stock, add a little more, but soup should be thick.

3. To serve, cut the basil into fine julienne. Divide soup among warm bowls and garnish with julienned basil and Parmesan.

Makes 6 to 8 servings.

STRAW AND HAY SOUP

In Italy, when egg pasta and spinach pasta are tossed in a cream sauce with peas and prosciutto, the dish is known as *paglia e fieno*—"straw and hay." The same combination of yellow and green produces a striking first-course soup, the colorful noodles afloat in a rich meat broth. It makes an elegant introduction to almost any main course.

    4 cups beef or chicken stock
    3 ½ ounces fresh spinach fettuccine,
        cut in 6-inch lengths
    3 ½ ounces fresh egg fettuccine, cut in
        6-inch lengths
    Salt, to taste
    2 ounces grated Parmesan cheese,
        for garnish

1. Bring stock to a simmer in a large pot over medium-low heat. In a separate pot, bring a large amount of salted water to a boil over medium-high heat. Add both spinach and egg fettuccine to water and cook until just wilted (20 to 25 seconds). Drain and run under cold water to remove any starch. Transfer pasta to the simmering stock and simmer until pasta is just tender. Season broth with salt.

2. Ladle soup into warm serving bowls and top each serving with grated Parmesan.

Makes 4 to 6 servings.

ROASTED EGGPLANT SOUP

Storebought sesame crackers or Armenian *lahvosh* (cracker bread) complement mugs of steaming eggplant soup.

    2 large eggplants (12 to 14 oz
        each), peeled
    ¼ cup olive oil
    2 tablespoons butter
    ¼ cup minced shallot

    ½ cup minced carrot
    1 tablespoon minced garlic
    1 cup peeled, seeded, and diced
        tomato, fresh or canned (see
        page 56)
    1 teaspoon dried marjoram
    2 bay leaves
    8 cups chicken stock
    Salt and freshly ground pepper, to
        taste
    1 tablespoon lemon juice

Yogurt Topping

    ½ cup plain yogurt
    Grated peel of 1 lemon
    2 tablespoons minced chives
    Salt and freshly ground pepper, to
        taste

1. Preheat oven to 375° F. Cut eggplants into quarters and brush cut surfaces with 2 tablespoons of the oil. In a roasting pan place eggplants and bake until soft (about 30 minutes).

2. In a large saucepan over moderate heat, warm remaining 2 tablespoons oil and butter. Add shallot, carrot, and garlic, and sauté 2 minutes. Add tomato and simmer 5 minutes. Add marjoram, bay leaves, roasted eggplant, and stock. Bring to a simmer and cover; reduce heat to maintain a simmer and cook 20 minutes.

3. Remove bay leaves. Transfer soup to a blender or food processor and purée. The soup can be made 1 day ahead to this point, covered, and refrigerated. Reheat slowly; add salt, pepper, and lemon juice. Garnish each serving with Yogurt Topping.

Makes about 8 servings.

Yogurt Topping   In a small bowl stir together yogurt, lemon peel, and chives. Season with salt and pepper.

Makes about ½ cup.

ALLIUM BISQUE

Chives, garlic, leeks, onions, and shallots are members of the *allium* family. These bulblike roots are also related to the lily. When they are cooked, they develop a delicious sweetness.

    4 onions
    4 leeks
    4 potatoes
    2 tablespoons butter
    2 tablespoons oil
    10 cloves garlic, minced
    4 shallots, minced
    6 cups chicken stock
    Salt, to taste
    1 teaspoon dried basil
    1 bay leaf
    1 teaspoon dried oregano
    ½ teaspoon dried marjoram
    Minced chives, for garnish

1. Cut onions into large dice. Clean leeks as follows: cut off root ends; remove and discard coarse outer leaves; discard green tops. Split lengthwise, cutting to within 1 inch of root end. Soak in cold water for several minutes; separate leaves under running water to rinse away any dirt. Cut leeks into ¼-inch slices. Peel potatoes and cut into ½-inch cubes.

2. In a large saucepan, heat butter and oil. Add onions, garlic, shallots, and leeks. Cook slowly over low heat until lightly browned. Add potatoes, stock, salt to taste, basil, bay leaf, oregano, and marjoram. Bring to a boil, reduce heat to simmer, and cook 40 minutes. Serve immediately or refrigerate and warm before serving. Garnish with minced chives.

Makes 6 to 8 servings.

SPRING GREEN SOUP WITH PUFF PASTRY CAP

This elegant soup will always impress, but couldn't be easier to make. Prepared puff pastry can be found in the frozen food section of most supermarkets.

    3 leeks
    4 green onions
    ½ pound shiitake or domestic
        mushrooms
    1 pound thin asparagus (about
        24 spears)
    ¼ pound sugar snap peas or
        ¾ pound fresh peas
    2 tablespoons butter
    6 cups chicken stock
    ¼ teaspoon salt

⅛ teaspoon white pepper
½ pound prepared puff pastry
        (thawed if frozen)
1 egg
1 tablespoon water

1. Clean leeks (see step 1, Allium Bisque, page 28); slice crosswise into ¼-inch-thick pieces. Trim green onions and slice diagonally into 1-inch pieces. Wash mushrooms, trim and discard stems, and slice into strips about ¼ inch wide. Wash asparagus, discard any dry, tough ends, and slice on diagonal into 1-inch pieces. Remove stems from snap peas.

2. Heat butter in a large saucepan. Add leeks and cook over medium heat, stirring occasionally, until tender (about 8 minutes). Add mushrooms and cook for 5 minutes. Stir in onions and cook 1 minute. Add stock, salt, and pepper. Bring to a boil, reduce heat, and simmer 10 minutes. Add asparagus and peas; turn off heat.

3. Pour into 2-quart soufflé dish. Cool slightly, then refrigerate until well chilled.

4. Cut puff pastry into a circle 2 inches larger than soufflé dish. Place pastry over top of dish and press onto sides, smearing edges of puff pastry slightly to adhere to dish. Refrigerate until 45 minutes before serving time.

5. Preheat oven to 400° F. Mix egg and water and brush on puff pastry. Bake until pastry is golden brown and crisp (about 40 minutes). Serve immediately: cut puff pastry open at the table, ladle a piece of pastry and a serving of soup into individual bowls.

Makes 6 servings.

MINTY GAZPACHO

This version of a refreshing summer favorite is loaded with fresh mint and tangy tomatoes. To turn this soup into a main course, serve it with grilled tiger prawns—colorful freshwater shellfish with distinctive dark stripes across their tails. (If these prawns are unavailable, any prawns can be substituted.)

3 large, ripe tomatoes, diced
        (3½ cups)
1 English cucumber, diced
1 large green bell pepper, diced
3 stalks celery, diced
1 large red onion, diced
1 bunch green onions, diced
3 cloves garlic, minced
1 ½ cups minced parsley
3 cups minced fresh mint
½ cup white wine vinegar
½ cup extra virgin olive oil
5 cups tomato juice
1 teaspoon salt
½ teaspoon freshly ground pepper

In a 4-quart serving bowl, stir together all ingredients. Let mixture marinate in refrigerator for 1 to 24 hours. Serve chilled, but not ice-cold.

Makes 8 servings.

For an impressive, aromatic presentation, break the puff pastry on this Spring Green Soup With Puff Pastry Cap at the table.

Vine-ripened tomatoes and fresh mint make Minty Gazpacho a delightful first course. The addition of grilled tiger prawns turns the soup into a flavorful main course.

TAXCO MINERS' SOUP

Hot, crisply fried tortilla strips sizzle as this zesty Mexican soup is ladled over them. After the soup, serve grilled snapper or shrimp with garlic butter, and a green vegetable.

    4 *corn tortillas, cut in halves, then into ½-inch-wide strips*
      Salt, to taste
    1 *tablespoon olive oil*
    1 *medium onion, thinly slivered*
    1 *small clove garlic, minced*
    ½ *teaspoon ground cumin*
    2 *canned green chiles, finely chopped*

    1 *large can (15 oz) tomato sauce*
    2 *cups chicken stock*
    1 *cup water*
    ¼ *pound Monterey jack cheese, cut in ½-inch cubes (about 1 cup)*
    Sour cream, for garnish (optional)

1. Fill a deep, heavy skillet with about ½ inch of vegetable oil. Heat oil to 350° to 375° F. Fry tortilla strips, about a third at a time, until crisp and lightly browned (about 2 minutes). Remove with slotted spoon to paper towels to drain; salt lightly.

2. In a medium saucepan, heat olive oil over medium heat. Add onion and sauté until soft, but not browned. Mix in garlic and cumin; then add green chiles, tomato sauce, stock, and water. Bring to a boil, cover, reduce heat, and simmer for 10 minutes.

3. Meanwhile, bake fried tortilla strips in a single layer in a preheated 325° F oven 8 to 10 minutes. Place heatproof soup bowls on baking sheet in oven during last 5 minutes.

4. Remove hot soup bowls to a heatproof tray. Working quickly, divide hot tortilla strips among the bowls. Top with cheese cubes. Ladle hot soup over tortillas and cheese and serve at once.

5. Spoon in a little sour cream at the table, if desired.

Makes 4 servings.

Crisp tortilla strips still hot from the frying pan are a sizzling complement to spicy Taxco Miners' Soup.

DOUBLE MUSHROOM SOUP WITH BARLEY

Fresh ginger hints of the Orient in this easy soup that combines Japanese tree oyster mushrooms with the more familiar cultivated variety.

    ¼ cup butter
    1 package (4 oz) fresh tree oyster
        or other Japanese-type
        mushrooms (use small
        mushrooms whole, larger
        ones sliced)
    ¼ pound cultivated mushrooms,
        thinly sliced
    ¼ cup pearl barley, rinsed and
        drained
    1 small clove garlic, minced
    3 ½ cups beef stock
    1 teaspoon grated fresh ginger or
        ¼ teaspoon ground ginger
        Salt and white pepper, to taste
    2 green onions, thinly sliced on
        the diagonal

1. In a heavy, 2- to 3-quart saucepan over medium heat, melt butter. Add both kinds of mushrooms and cook, stirring occasionally, until they are lightly browned and any liquid has cooked away. Add barley and garlic, stirring to coat barley with mushroom mixture.

2. Mix in 1 cup of stock. Bring to a boil, cover, reduce heat, and simmer until barley is tender (about 45 minutes).

3. Stir in ginger and remaining stock. Cook, uncovered, over medium heat until soup is hot. Taste, season with salt if needed, and add pepper to taste. Just before serving, stir in green onions.

Makes 4 servings.

HOT AND SOUR SOUP

It is surprisingly easy to reproduce this restaurant favorite at home. If you like greens in your soup, stir in 2 cups fresh raw spinach leaves with the mushrooms.

    8 cups chicken stock
    ½ cup dried black mushrooms,
        such as Japanese shiitake
    1 teaspoon sesame oil
    1 tablespoon sake
    ¼ cup minced onion
    8 ounces firm tofu, cubed
    3 tablespoons arrowroot mixed
        with ½ cup cold water
    3 ½ tablespoons rice vinegar
    1 beaten egg
    3 tablespoons soy sauce
    ¼ teaspoon cayenne pepper
    ⅛ teaspoon freshly ground
        black pepper

1. Put stock in a large pot and bring to simmer over medium-low heat. Add dried mushrooms and simmer 15 minutes.

2. Strain out mushrooms, leaving stock simmering on stove. Cut off and discard mushroom stems. Slice tops thinly and return to stockpot.

3. In a small skillet, heat sesame oil and sake; add onion and sauté slowly until onion is very soft. Add onion and any pan liquor to stock in pot.

4. Stirring constantly, mix in tofu, arrowroot mixture, vinegar, egg, soy sauce, cayenne, and black pepper; cook until egg forms into ribbons and soup thickens slightly from arrowroot (about 1 minute). Serve hot.

Makes 8 servings.

CREAMY CARROT SOUP

You could call this "Quick Cream of Anything Soup." It's a versatile recipe that should be in everyone's file. Make it with carrots, or substitute cauliflower or broccoli. It will keep up to one month in the freezer.

    1 pound carrots, peeled and
        coarsely chopped
    1 medium potato, peeled and
        coarsely chopped
    ½ cup unsalted butter
    1 teaspoon salt
    ¼ teaspoon freshly ground pepper
    3 cups chicken stock
    ¼ cup sour cream, for garnish
    4 to 6 sprigs fresh oregano, for
        garnish

1. In a medium saucepan over medium-low heat, place carrots and potatoes and add water to cover; simmer until vegetables are easily pierced with a sharp knife (about 25 minutes).

2. Purée carrots and potato in a blender or food processor with butter, salt, and pepper. Return to saucepan and stir in stock. Place over medium heat and cook until warm. Serve immediately. Garnish each serving with a tablespoon of sour cream and a sprig of fresh oregano.

Makes 4 to 6 servings.

SUMMER CURRIED PEA SOUP

Try to make this soup with fresh peas when they are in season, especially if you have a volunteer to shell them. Frozen peas are an acceptable substitute if fresh ones are unavailable.

    1 cup chopped onion
    2 teaspoons dark sesame oil
    ¼ cup dry sherry
    1 tablespoon minced garlic
    1 tablespoon curry powder
    ½ cup chopped carrots
    3 cups peas, fresh or frozen
    2 tablespoons flour
    3 cups chicken stock
        Salt and freshly ground pepper, to
        taste
        Minced green onion and plain
        nonfat yogurt, for garnish

1. In a large pot over medium-high heat, sauté onion in oil and sherry until soft (8 to 10 minutes). Add garlic, curry powder, carrots, and peas, and continue to cook, stirring frequently, for 5 minutes.

2. Add flour and cook 2 minutes, stirring constantly (do not let flour brown). Add stock and bring to a boil.

3. Lower heat and simmer soup, uncovered, 10 to 12 minutes. In a food processor or blender, purée half the soup at a time, and then return to pot. Heat through. Adjust seasonings, if needed, and serve hot, garnished with green onions and yogurt.

Makes 6 servings.

VERSATILE SALADS

In many European countries, salad is usually served after the main course to refresh and clear the palate. A salad bowl is filled with crisp butter lettuce and perhaps some curly endive, and then drizzled with vinegar, oil, salt, and pepper. There are fewer rules in the United States about when salad appears on the table, whether before the main course, as an accompaniment to it, or afterward. Salads are often more than just fresh greens. Greek Orzo Salad (see page 32) mixes rice-shaped pasta with tomatoes, cucumbers, olives, and tangy feta cheese, all tossed in a wine vinaigrette. Barley, brown rice, and wild rice combine with a minty dressing for substantial, cool-weather Mixed-Grains Salad (see page 33). Tricolor Salad (see page 39) is a lovely composition of tapered leaves of Belgian endive, fresh tangy orange and grapefruit sections, and pungent watercress.

PANZANELLA

This robust salad is a great way to use slightly stale French or Italian bread. Substitute crunchy red bell peppers when tomatoes are out of season.

> 20 slices (about 1 lb) slightly stale
>   French or Italian bread
> 1 cup olive oil
> 3 ripe tomatoes
> 2 green bell peppers
> 1 red onion, chopped
> 2 cloves garlic, minced
> 1 cup (6 oz) black olives, pitted
> ¼ cup vinegar
> 1 tablespoon salt
> 2 teaspoons dried basil
> ½ teaspoon freshly ground pepper

1. Preheat oven to 350° F. Brush bread slices with ½ cup of the olive oil. Place on a baking sheet and toast in oven until crisp and lightly browned (about 10 minutes).

2. Dice tomatoes and bell peppers into 1-inch cubes. In a 4-quart bowl toss together tomatoes, bell peppers, remaining olive oil, onion, garlic, black olives, vinegar, salt, basil, and pepper.

3. Cover with plastic wrap and set aside to marinate 30 minutes at room temperature or up to 3 hours in the refrigerator. Bring to room temperature to serve.

4. About 1 hour before serving, break toasted bread into roughly 1-inch cubes. Toss with marinated vegetables. Transfer to a serving bowl; set aside until ready to serve.

Serves 8.

GREEK ORZO SALAD

Orzo, sometimes called *riso,* is a pasta that, when cooked, resembles rice. It is an excellent accompaniment to grilled lamb. Note that the pasta marinates at least two hours, or as long as overnight.

> 1 cup orzo
> 6 tablespoons olive oil
> 5 tablespoons red wine vinegar
> 1 small red onion, minced
> 1 ½ teaspoons salt
> ½ teaspoon freshly ground pepper
> 1 teaspoon dried oregano
> ¼ cup minced parsley
> 2 large tomatoes, diced
> 1 English cucumber, diced
> 12 to 18 Greek olives, halved and
>   pitted
> 6 ounces feta cheese

1. In a medium saucepan, bring 2 quarts water to a vigorous boil. Add orzo and cook until slightly *al dente* (8 to 10 minutes). Drain, place in a 2-quart serving dish, and toss with 1 tablespoon olive oil.

2. Whisk together remaining olive oil, vinegar, onion, salt, pepper, oregano, and parsley. Pour over orzo and let marinate for 2 to 24 hours.

3. At serving time, toss tomatoes, cucumber, olives, and feta with marinated orzo. Season again if necessary. Serve immediately.

Serves 8.

A zesty marinade gives the rice-shaped pasta for this Greek Orzo Salad a flavor that goes well with grilled lamb.

BISTRO LENTIL SALAD

Lentils cook quickly and make an unusual salad accompaniment to ham or even corned beef. This is classic French bistro fare. Serve this salad hot—mixed as soon as the lentils are cooked and drained—or at room temperature.

    1 cup dried lentils, rinsed and
        drained
    ½ teaspoon salt
    1 bay leaf
    ¼ teaspoon dried thyme
    1 carrot, shredded
    3 cups water
    3 tablespoons tarragon vinegar
    1 tablespoon coarse-grained Dijon-
        style mustard
    1 clove garlic, minced
    ¾ teaspoon salt
    2 tablespoons olive oil
    ¼ cup vegetable oil
    1 small red onion, finely chopped
    ¼ cup chopped parsley
        Butter or Boston lettuce leaves

1. In a large saucepan, combine lentils, salt, bay leaf, thyme, carrot, and water. Bring to a boil, cover, reduce heat, and boil gently until lentils are tender (25 to 30 minutes). Drain thoroughly; discard bay leaf.

2. To make dressing, in a small bowl mix vinegar, mustard, garlic, and salt. Using a whisk or fork, gradually beat in oils until well blended and slightly thickened.

3. Mix lentils, onion, parsley, and dressing. If not serving immediately, cover salad and refrigerate 1 to 3 hours or overnight to blend flavors. Serve on lettuce leaves.

Serves 4 to 6.

MIXED GRAINS SALAD

Mixing costly wild rice with inexpensive grains adds a luxurious touch to a menu at modest expense. This salad travels well, so take it to a picnic or a tailgate party.

    ¾ cup each barley, brown rice, and
        wild rice
    ⅓ cup minced red onion
    ½ cup minced celery
    ⅓ cup chopped toasted walnuts
        (optional)

(continued on page 34)

BASICS

MAKE YOUR OWN CROUTONS

Making your own salad croutons is simple—all it takes are a few slices of day-old (or older) bread. They can accent many types of salads and homemade croutons are much fresher and more flavorful than the packaged kind. Once you have tasted any of the following, you will never again spend money on store-bought croutons. Any croutons that aren't used within a day or two should be stored in a cool place in an opaque, airtight container. They can also be frozen.

Garlic Croutons Cut crusts from 5 slices firm white bread or 6 slices French bread. Dice bread into ½-inch cubes. In a large frying pan over medium heat, heat 2 tablespoons each butter or margarine and olive oil or vegetable oil. Mix in 1 clove garlic, minced. Add bread cubes, stirring until well coated with butter mixture. Transfer bread cubes to a rimmed baking sheet and spread in a single layer. Bake in a 300° F oven until lightly browned and crisp (25 to 30 minutes). Cool. Makes about 2 cups.

Parmesan Croutons Prepare as for Garlic Croutons. To butter mixture add ¼ teaspoon paprika. Add ¼ cup grated Parmesan cheese with bread cubes.

Herbed Croutons Prepare as for Garlic Croutons. To butter mixture add ¼ teaspoon each dried oregano, thyme, crumbled rosemary, and basil.

Sesame Croutons Prepare as for Garlic Croutons, omitting garlic. Substitute 1 tablespoon Asian sesame oil for 1 tablespoon of the olive oil or vegetable oil with bread cubes. Add 1 tablespoon sesame seed with bread cubes.

Bacon-Onion Croutons Prepare as for Garlic Croutons, omitting garlic. Substitute 2 tablespoons bacon drippings for butter or margarine. To oil mixture add ½ teaspoon onion powder and 1 teaspoon poppy seed.

Dilled Rye Croutons Substitute 6 slices oval or round rye bread for the white or French bread. To butter mixture add 1 teaspoon dried dill weed.

(continued from page 33)

    2 *tablespoons apple cider vinegar*
    3 *tablespoons lemon juice*
    ¾ *cup olive oil*
    1 *tablespoon each minced fresh*
       dill, mint, cilantro, and
       parsley
       Salt and freshly ground pepper, to
       taste

1. In a medium saucepan over high heat, bring 2 cups lightly salted water to a boil. Add barley, cover, reduce heat to low, and cook 30 minutes. Set aside 5 minutes, then uncover and transfer to a bowl to cool.

2. In a medium saucepan over high heat, bring 2 ½ cups lightly salted water to a boil. Add brown rice, cover, reduce heat to low, and cook for 40 minutes. Set aside 5 minutes, then uncover and transfer to a bowl to cool.

3. In a medium saucepan over high heat, bring 2 cups lightly salted water to a boil. Add wild rice, cover, reduce heat to low, and cook 40 minutes. Set aside 5 minutes, then uncover and transfer to a bowl to cool.

4. In a large bowl, combine cooled barley, brown rice, wild rice, onion, celery, and walnuts (if used). In a small bowl whisk together vinegar and lemon juice; whisk in oil gradually, then add dill, mint, cilantro, and parsley. Season with salt and pepper. Pour dressing over grains and toss to coat well. Serve at room temperature.

Serves 8.

ASIAN BLACK BEAN-ASPARAGUS SALAD

Asparagus epitomizes spring produce: short-lived, bright, and subtle. The Asian ingredients used in this spicy, richly flavored dressing are available at Asian markets and in well-stocked supermarkets.

    1 *cup cooked black beans*
    ¼ *small red onion, diced*
    ¼ *cup minced cilantro*
    1 *tablespoon rice wine vinegar*
    1 *teaspoon soy sauce*
    1 *teaspoon Asian hot oil*
    ⅛ *teaspoon Asian sesame oil*
    1 *pound asparagus*
    4 *lettuce leaves*

1. Place cooked beans in a small bowl. Stir red onion, cilantro, vinegar, soy sauce, hot oil, and sesame oil into beans. Marinate 20 to 30 minutes at room temperature.

2. Bring 2 quarts of water to a boil. Trim dried, tough ends from asparagus stalks. Slice asparagus on the diagonal. Blanch in boiling water for 3 minutes. Remove from water, drain, and toss with marinated beans.

3. To serve, place each lettuce leaf on a chilled salad plate. Divide salad evenly among lettuce leaves.

Serves 4.

INSALATA CAPRICCIOSA

This Italian classic is a salad for summer, when the tomatoes and basil are at their best. Use only sweet, vine-ripened tomatoes, and visit a cheese merchant for the finest whole-milk mozzarella. A hot loaf of crusty bread should be on the table, too.

    8 *ounces fresh whole-milk moz-*
       zarella or imported buffalo-
       milk mozzarella, at room
       temperature
    4 *tomatoes, at room temperature,*
       cored and thinly sliced
    ½ *cup extra virgin olive oil*
       Juice of 1½ large or 2 small
       lemons
    ¼ *cup shredded fresh basil leaves*
       Coarse salt and freshly ground
       pepper, to taste
       Additional basil sprigs, for
       garnish

1. Slice cheese into rounds about ⅛ inch thick. On a large serving platter or on individual salad plates, arrange alternate slices of cheese and tomato in a concentric pattern.

2. In a small bowl, combine olive oil, lemon juice, and basil. Whisk well. Spoon dressing over salad. Season with salt and pepper. Garnish with basil sprigs and serve immediately.

Serves 4.

Dijon mustard vinaigrette and pecans add a sharpness and crunch to this unusual Beet Salad With Pecans and Mixed Greens.

BEET SALAD WITH PECANS AND MIXED GREENS

Beets keep all their flavor when steamed. Their delicate sweetness is a wonderful complement to the slight bitterness of the greens and the sharpness of the mustard dressing in this recipe. Remember this salad for your next special-occasion dinner.

> 5 small beets (about 1½ inches in diameter)
> 2 teaspoons Dijon-style mustard
> 2 tablespoons red wine vinegar
>   Salt and freshly gound pepper, to taste
> 6 tablespoons vegetable oil
> ¾ pound Belgian endive
> 12 leaves romaine lettuce, cut in ½-inch-wide strips
> ½ cup pecan pieces

1. Rinse beets, taking care not to pierce the skin. In base of a steamer over medium-high heat, bring at least 1 inch of water to a boil (boiling water should not reach holes in upper part of steamer).

2. Place beets in steamer top above boiling water. Cover tightly and steam over high heat, adding boiling water occasionally as needed, until beets are tender (about 50 minutes).

3. Remove beets and let cool. Peel beets while holding them under cold running water.

4. To make dressing, whisk mustard, vinegar, salt, and pepper in a small bowl. Gradually pour in oil in a fine stream, whisking constantly. Taste and add more salt and pepper, if needed.

5. Wipe endive and trim bases. Cut leaves in fairly thin slices crosswise. In medium bowl, combine endive with vinaigrette and toss; let marinate 5 minutes.

6. Just before serving, dice beets and add to endive mixture. Add strips of lettuce and toss gently. Taste and add more salt and pepper, if needed. Sprinkle with pecans and serve.

Serves 6.

TOMATOES, GREEN PEPPER, AND CUCUMBERS

There's lots of color and crunch in this refreshing salad, yet it's extremely simple to toss together. Serve it with any grilled meat or poultry.

> 3 medium ripe tomatoes, diced
> 1 small green pepper, diced
> 2 medium cucumbers, pared and very thinly sliced
> ½ cup minced parsley
> ¼ cup minced fresh mint leaves (optional)
> 3 green onions, including some crisp green parts, thinly sliced
> ¼ cup lemon juice
> ¼ cup olive oil
> 1½ teaspoons salt

Place tomatoes, pepper, cucumber, parsley, mint (if used), and green onion in a salad bowl. Beat together lemon juice, olive oil, and salt; pour over vegetables, toss, and serve.

Serves 4.

Simple to prepare and delightful to look at, this colorful salad of Tomatoes, Green Pepper, and Cucumbers is a fine accompaniment to grilled meats or poultry.

BASICS

VINAIGRETTE

Vinaigrette is the traditional French salad dressing. Blends of oil (usually olive, safflower, peanut, or walnut) and wine vinegar, with minced herbs added to taste, vinaigrettes dress everything from simple lettuce salads to elaborate combinations of meats and vegetables. Some cooks add a touch of cream to their vinaigrette, but creamy dressings in the American style are rare in France.

Leftover vinaigrette may be stored at room temperature for up to a day or refrigerated in an airtight jar for up to three days. Whisk, taste, and adjust seasoning before using.

BASIC VINAIGRETTE

¼ cup red wine vinegar
    Salt and freshly ground pepper,
        to taste
¾ cup olive oil

In a small bowl, combine vinegar, salt, and pepper. Whisk in oil and let stand 5 minutes. Whisk again, then taste and adjust seasoning.

Makes 1 cup.

Garlic Vinaigrette Cover ½ table-spoon minced garlic with ¾ cup olive oil and let stand overnight. Substitute the resulting flavored olive oil for regular olive oil.

Lemon-Chive Vinaigrette
Substitute ¼ cup lemon juice for wine vinegar. Add grated peel of ½ lemon and 2 tablespoons minced chives.

Mustard Vinaigrette Add 2 tea-spoons prepared Dijon-style mustard to wine vinegar before adding oil.

Tarragon Vinaigrette Add 1 table-spoon minced fresh tarragon and substitute white wine vinegar for red wine vinegar.

CELERY ROOT SALAD

The unglamorous celery root, when peeled and shredded, can be transformed into an elegant salad, often served as a first course in French restaurants. A creamy dressing made of mustard and shallot coats the crunchy pieces. Use a food processor, if you have one, fitted with a shredding disk, for the tedious shredding job. A food processor also makes quick work out of emulsifying the ingredients for the piquant dressing.

1 large (1 to 1½ lb) celery root
2 tablespoons lemon juice
1 egg yolk
2 tablespoons tarragon wine
    vinegar
1 tablespoon Dijon-style mustard
½ teaspoon salt
    Pinch cayenne pepper
1 shallot, finely chopped
¼ cup each olive oil and vegetable
    oil
    Butter or Boston lettuce leaves
    Chopped parsley, for garnish

1. Peel celery root thoroughly, cutting out any deep bits of peel. Shred quickly, using a food processor or grater (you should have 5 to 6 cups). Immediately mix well with lemon juice to prevent discoloration. Cover and refrigerate for about 1 hour.

2. In a medium bowl, beat egg yolk with vinegar, mustard, salt, cayenne, and shallot. Using a whisk or fork, gradually beat in oils, a small amount at a time, until dressing is thick and creamy. Or in a food processor, use metal blade to process egg yolk, vinegar, mustard, salt, cayenne, and 1 tablespoon oil for 1 minute. Slowly add remaining oil. Add shallot and process 10 seconds more.

3. Shortly before serving, mix celery root lightly with dressing to coat. Serve mixture on lettuce leaves, sprinkled with parsley.

Serves 6.

WATERCRESS AND MUSHROOM SALAD

The singular texture of sliced fresh mushrooms contrasts nicely with sprigs of watercress in a mustard-and-tarragon-flavored dressing. This salad would be an elegant introduction to a multicourse dinner.

- 1 bunch watercress (about 6 oz)
- ½ pound mushrooms, thinly sliced
- 1 tablespoon each red wine vinegar and lemon juice
- 1 shallot, finely chopped, or 1 tablespoon finely chopped red onion
- 1 tablespoon Dijon-style mustard
- ¼ teaspoon each salt and sugar
- ⅛ teaspoon dried tarragon
  Dash white pepper
- 1 tablespoon olive oil
- ¼ cup vegetable oil
- 1 tablespoon each chopped parsley and minced chives

1. Remove leaves from watercress, using only tender stems; discard coarse stems. You should have about 3 cups leaves and stems. Combine with mushrooms in a medium bowl. If done ahead, cover and refrigerate.

2. In a small bowl, mix vinegar, lemon juice, shallot, mustard, salt, sugar, tarragon, and pepper. Using a whisk or fork, gradually beat in oils until slightly thickened and well combined. Mix in parsley and chives.

3. Toss watercress mixture lightly with dressing and serve immediately.

Serves 4 to 6.

SPICY FRUIT-AND-VEGETABLE SALAD

Fruit salads do not have to be sweet, as this spicy salad attests, nor do they have to be all fruit. This vibrant, exotic, international mixture combines tropical fruits and garden vegetables. The result is outstanding. Note that the salad must chill 4 to 8 hours before serving.

- 1 seedless English cucumber or regular cucumber
- 3 medium tomatoes, cored
- ½ bunch (¾ cup) cilantro
- ½ pineapple, peeled
- ½ honeydew melon, peeled and seeded
- ½ papaya, peeled, seeded, and cubed
- 1 red onion, diced
- 1 jalapeño chile, minced
- 1 tablespoon vegetable oil
- 2 tablespoons white wine vinegar
- ⅛ teaspoon salt

1. If using a seedless cucumber, it is not necessary to peel or seed it. Peel other types of cucumber, remove seeds, and discard peel and seeds. Cut cucumber into ½-inch-thick slices. Cut each cored tomato into pieces about ½-inch square. Reserve 6 sprigs of cilantro for garnish, and mince the rest. Cut pineapple and honeydew melon into 1 ½-inch cubes.

2. Place pineapple, papaya, honeydew, red onion, cucumber, tomatoes, jalapeño chile, and minced cilantro in a medium bowl. Toss together with oil, vinegar, and salt. Chill 4 to 8 hours. Remove from refrigerator 30 minutes before serving. Garnish with reserved cilantro sprigs.

Serves 8 to 10.

CHINESE POTATO SALAD

Potato salad, that American picnic staple, is going cross-cultural these days. This dressing uses Chinese flavors—rice vinegar, sesame oil, and fresh ginger—and can be made up to 5 days ahead and refrigerated until needed. Plan enough time to chill the potatoes after cooking. Hoisin sauce is available at Asian markets and at well-stocked supermarkets.

- 3 cups cubed red potatoes, skin intact
- ¾ cup minced red bell pepper
- ½ cup minced celery
- ¼ cup finely chopped green onions
- ¼ cup rice wine vinegar
- 2 tablespoons dark sesame oil
- 1 teaspoon grated fresh ginger
- 1 teaspoon honey
- 1 tablespoon lemon juice
- 1 tablespoon hoisin sauce
- ¼ teaspoon cayenne pepper, or more, to taste

1. In a large pot over medium-high heat, cook potatoes until tender (about 20 minutes). Drain and chill for 20 minutes.

2. In a serving bowl, combine red bell pepper, celery, green onions, vinegar, sesame oil, ginger, honey, lemon juice, hoisin sauce, and cayenne. Add chilled potatoes and toss well. Cover with plastic wrap and set aside to marinate at room temperature for 20 minutes more. Serve at room temperature.

Serves 4.

JAMAICAN PAPAYA SALAD

Not only does this dressy salad taste wonderful and look beautiful, it has only 87 calories per serving and very little fat.

- 1 cup watercress
- 2 cups peeled, seeded, and thinly sliced papaya
- ¼ cup thinly sliced avocado
- 1 cup canned hearts of palm, drained and sliced
- 1 cup thinly sliced tomato
- 2 tablespoons lime juice
- 2 tablespoons chopped cilantro
- ¼ teaspoon salt
- ⅛ teaspoon ground coriander
- ⅛ teaspoon ground allspice

1. Arrange watercress on 4 small salad plates. Layer slices of papaya, avocado, hearts of palm, and tomato on top.

2. Stir together lime juice, cilantro, salt, coriander, and allspice. Drizzle over salads. Cover with plastic wrap and chill 30 minutes before serving.

Serves 4.

A savory lime juice dressing gives this low-calorie, low-fat Jamaican Papaya Salad a Caribbean touch.

TRICOLOR SALAD

Tangy oranges and grapefruit are flavorful enough to complement the hearty vinaigrette dressing. Watercress and endive lend their peppery and slightly bitter flavors to this composed salad. For an alternative presentation, simply toss the vinaigrette, greens, and fruit together.

1 pomegranate
2 oranges
1 grapefruit
2 heads Belgian endive
2 bunches watercress
3 cloves garlic, minced
1 tablespoon Dijon-style mustard
½ teaspoon salt
3 tablespoons balsamic vinegar
7 tablespoons vegetable oil
1 tablespoon parsley
1 tablespoon chives
3 to 4 leaves fresh basil
Freshly ground pepper, to taste

1. Pull open pomegranate and reserve seeds. Peel and section oranges and grapefruit. Separate endive leaves. Arrange watercress in center of a 12- to 15-inch platter. Place endive leaves around perimeter like spokes in a wheel. Place a section of grapefruit and a section of orange between endive spokes.

2. Whisk together garlic, mustard, salt, vinegar, oil, parsley, chives, basil, and pepper. Drizzle dressing over salad and dot with pomegranate seeds. If making dressing ahead, chill and whisk again before serving.

Serves 6.

This lovely Tricolor Salad features pomegranate, orange, and grapefruit artfully arranged with watercress and endive.

MENU

FARE FROM THE FIFTIES

For 8

Alphabet Soup
Dagwood Sandwiches
Rings 'n' Strings
Kosher Dill Pickles
Triple Chocolate Pudding
Malteds and Cherry Colas

The sounds of golden oldies fill your ears while your eyes take in stacks of fresh bread and slices of ham, turkey, cheese, and more for mile-high Dagwood Sandwiches. The sight of alphabet letters floating in soup and a whiff of Rings 'n' Strings put you right back in the era of bobby sox and T-birds. A fitting finale is a fabulous chocolate pudding. Most supermarkets carry malted milk powder for adding to milk shakes to create malteds; to make cherry colas, mix equal parts (or to taste) cherry soda and cola.

ALPHABET SOUP

The canned version may hold the memories, but this one is chock-full of homemade flavor. Check the pasta section of the supermarket for dried alphabet pasta.

> ¼ *cup olive oil*
> 2 *medium boiling potatoes, peeled and diced*
> 1 *cup peeled and diced carrot*
> ¾ *cup minced onion*
> 1½ *quarts chicken stock*
> 2 *tablespoons minced fresh basil*
> 1 *teaspoon minced fresh oregano*
> 3 *cups diced zucchini*
> 3 *cups peeled, seeded, and diced tomatoes, fresh or canned*
> 1½ *cups dried alphabet pasta*
> ½ *cup cooked peas*

> *Salt and freshly ground pepper, to taste*
> *Grated Parmesan cheese, for accompaniment*

In a large pot over moderate heat, warm olive oil. Add potatoes, carrot, and onion and sauté 5 minutes. Add chicken stock, basil, and oregano. Bring to a boil, reduce heat to maintain a simmer, and simmer 15 minutes. Add zucchini and 1 cup of the tomatoes. Simmer 10 minutes. Add pasta, peas, and remaining 2 cups tomatoes; simmer until pasta is cooked through. Season with salt and pepper. Serve immediately and pass a bowl of Parmesan.

Makes about 16 cups.

DAGWOOD SANDWICHES

Dagwood Bumstead, of comic strip fame, is known for taking everything out of the refrigerator and piling it high between slices of bread. This sandwich is more highly designed, but it's still a double-decker construction for hearty eaters. Variations are absolutely encouraged. You will need 16 eight-inch bamboo skewers to hold the sandwiches together.

> *Dijon-style mustard*
> 1 *loaf best-quality sliced whole-grain bread*
> *Dressing from Celery Root Salad (see page 36)*
> 1 *cup mayonnaise*
> 1½ *tablespoons minced fresh basil*

1 loaf best-quality sliced sourdough bread

½ pound each smoked turkey, and imported Emmenthaler or Jarlsberg cheese, sliced paper-thin

1 bunch fresh spinach, washed, dried, and stems removed

1 head romaine lettuce, washed and dried

½ pound ham, sliced paper-thin

To make one sandwich, spread mustard on one side of a slice of whole-grain bread. Spread salad dressing on one side of a second slice of whole-grain bread. Combine mayonnaise and basil; spread on both sides of a slice of sourdough bread. Put a slice of turkey, a slice of cheese, and two spinach leaves on one whole-grain slice. Top with sourdough bread. Stack a leaf of romaine and a slice of ham on top of that. Cover with remaining slice of whole-grain bread. Secure with two bamboo skewers and slice.

Makes 8 double-decker sandwiches.

RINGS 'N' STRINGS

French-fried onion rings and potatoes must be cooked at the last minute, but it would hardly be a Fifties party without them. Line baskets with brightly colored paper napkins and pile them high with hot-from-the-fryer Rings 'n' Strings.

2 cups flour

2 cups flat beer

2 teaspoons salt, plus salt to taste

2 pounds sweet red onion, in ¼-inch-thick slices

2 pounds baking potatoes, peeled Vegetable oil, for deep-frying

1. Whisk together flour, beer, and 2 teaspoons of the salt and let stand, covered, 3 hours. Soak onion slices in ice water while beer batter rests.

2. Using a mandoline, a sharp knife, or a shoestring-potato cutter, cut potatoes into thin strips about 5 inches long and ⅛ inch thick. Transfer strips to ice water as they are cut and soak 30 minutes.

3. In a deep kettle heat at least 3 inches of vegetable oil to 375° F. Drain potato strips well and pat thoroughly dry. Fry until golden brown (about 2 to 3 minutes). Use a large wire-mesh spoon to transfer potatoes to paper towels to drain. Salt lightly.

4. Drain onions well and pat thoroughly dry. Dip in batter, letting excess drip off. Fry until golden on both sides, turning once. Drain on paper towels and salt lightly.

Serves 8.

TRIPLE CHOCOLATE PUDDING

Instant pudding from a package can't compare with this rich and creamy homemade version. Use premium-quality chocolate for best results.

4½ cups milk

½ cup plus 1 teaspoon unsweetened cocoa

1 cup sugar

¼ cup cornstarch

3 eggs

4 egg yolks

5 ounces each grated bittersweet and grated semisweet chocolate

1 teaspoon vanilla extract

½ teaspoon almond extract

¼ cup unsalted butter, softened

1 cup whipped cream

2 ounces grated white chocolate, for garnish

1. In a large saucepan combine milk, ½ cup of the cocoa, and sugar. Bring to a simmer over moderate heat, stirring constantly. Set aside.

2. In a small bowl whisk together cornstarch and ½ cup of the hot chocolate-milk mixture. In a separate bowl whisk together eggs and egg yolks. Add some of the hot chocolate-milk mixture from the saucepan to eggs to warm them, then add all of egg mixture to saucepan. Cook over moderate heat, stirring constantly, 1 minute; do not allow mixture to boil. Stir in cornstarch mixture and cook, stirring, until mixture comes to a simmer. Simmer 1 minute.

3. Strain mixture through a fine sieve into a clean saucepan. Stir in chocolates, vanilla and almond extracts, and butter. Spoon mixture into 8 dessert glasses arranged on a tray; cover glasses with plastic wrap to prevent a skin from forming on the tops of the puddings. Cool slightly, then refrigerate until thoroughly chilled (about 4 hours).

4. To serve, sift remaining 1 teaspoon cocoa over whipped cream. Fold in gently. Garnish puddings with cocoa-flavored whipped cream and white chocolate.

Serves 8.

Whole wheat pasta with julienned carrots and green and yellow zucchini create visual interest in this flavorful Vegetable Spaghetti.

LIGHT MEALS

E very recipe collection needs a file of favorite hearty soups, substantial salads, pastas, and eggs for those times when a traditional multi-course meal is more than anyone has room for. These kinds of dishes epitomize the do-ahead dinner because many can be prepared in part or completely ahead. They're also great ways to recycle leftovers or to plan menus that are pulled from what is stocked in your pantry. This chapter will add to your file if it's already started or get the file going. Suggestions for an entire meal are international—an Italian Soup Supper (see page 46) and a Brittany Brunch (see page 60).

SOUPS THAT MAKE A MEAL

These soups can be satisfying dinners when paired with a good, flavorful bread and a salad, and followed by homemade cookies or an ice cream sundae. They are more substantial than those used as a first course because the ingredients are actually a mini-meal: bits of poultry, fish, or meat; chunks of vegetables; appetite-appeasing grains, beans, and pasta. Some of the recipes, like Minnesota Chicken and Wild Rice Soup (see below) or Creamy Salmon Chowder (see page 45), are short-order–quick to prepare and quick to the table. A few, such as Chili Bean Soup (see page 51), demand longer cooking times to develop their flavor, but not much of your time for preparation.

Simple-to-make Minnesota Chicken and Wild Rice Soup makes a delicious meal when served with French bread and a crisp green salad.

MINNESOTA CHICKEN AND WILD RICE SOUP

Living in a state famous for blue lakes and blue skies, Minnesotans enjoy yearly harvests of vitamin-rich wild rice–the meaty, chewy grain that grows in the northern lake country. This rich soup combines a hearty chicken broth studded with vegetables, chunks of white-meat chicken, and rice. Accompany each serving with French bread and a green salad to make a meal.

- ½ cup chopped onion
- 2 teaspoons olive oil
- ¼ cup dry sherry
- ½ cup chopped celery
- ½ cup chopped carrots
- ½ cup chopped spinach
- 2 cups diced, cooked chicken, skin removed
- 1 cup wild rice
- 5 cups chicken stock
- ½ teaspoon dried thyme
- ½ teaspoon dried marjoram
  Pinch of ground ginger
- ⅛ teaspoon ground cumin
  Salt and freshly ground pepper, to taste
- 2 tablespoons soy sauce

1. In a large pot over medium-high heat, sauté onion in oil and sherry until soft but not browned. Add celery, carrots, and spinach, and continue cooking for 5 minutes, stirring frequently.

2. Add chicken, wild rice, stock, thyme, marjoram, ginger, and cumin, and bring to a boil. Lower heat, cover, and simmer until rice is tender (30 to 35 minutes). Before serving, season with salt and pepper; stir in soy sauce.

Makes 8 servings.

CHICKEN AND ESCAROLE SOUP

This is a main-dish version of an Italian soup that generally is served as a first course. Make it a meal by adding a generous quantity of chicken and serving with bread sticks and vegetable relishes.

> 1 frying chicken (3 ½ to 4 lbs), cut up
> 1 large onion, finely chopped
> 1 small carrot, thinly sliced
> 1 sprig parsley
> 1 bay leaf
> 1 stalk celery, chopped (including leaves)
> 2 teaspoons salt
> ⅛ teaspoon each ground nutmeg and white pepper
> ¼ teaspoon dried thyme
> 4 cups water
> ¼ cup tiny shell macaroni
> 2 tablespoons butter
> 2 cups escarole, inner leaves only, thinly sliced
> Salt, to taste
> Grated Parmesan cheese, for garnish

1. In a large pot or Dutch oven, combine chicken pieces, onion, carrot, parsley, bay leaf, celery, salt, nutmeg, pepper, thyme, and water. Bring to a boil over medium-high heat, reduce heat to medium-low, cover, and simmer for about 2 hours, until chicken is very tender. Strain broth; remove and discard skin and bones from chicken. Cut chicken into large pieces. Discard vegetables and whole seasonings. Return chicken to broth. (This much can be prepared ahead, if you wish, and reheated later.)

2. Reheat soup to a gentle boil. Add macaroni and cook, uncovered, until just tender (see package directions for macaroni cooking time).

3. Meanwhile, in a medium skillet, over medium heat, melt butter; cook escarole in butter, stirring until it is wilted and bright green (about 3 minutes). Stir escarole mixture into soup. Season with salt. Serve in broad soup bowls sprinkled with Parmesan cheese.

Makes 4 servings.

CREAMY SALMON CHOWDER

The line separating a soup from a stew becomes very thin where fish is involved, as this robust salmon chowder attests. It makes a fine main course when paired with a salad of mushrooms and young greens, followed by a nut ice cream and crisp cookies for dessert.

> 3 tablespoons butter
> 4 shallots, slivered (about ¾ cup)
> 1 teaspoon dried tarragon
> 3 medium smooth-skinned potatoes (about 1 ½ lbs), thinly sliced
> ½ teaspoon salt
> ⅛ teaspoon white pepper
> 2 cups fish stock or chicken stock
> 1 ½ pounds salmon steaks, ¾ to 1 inch thick
> 1 lemon, thinly sliced
> 1 bay leaf
> 1 cup dry white wine
> ¼ pound sliced bacon, cut in ½-inch-wide pieces
> Half a small cabbage, cored and thinly shredded (about 4 cups)
> 1 cup whipping cream

1. In a large pot or Dutch oven over medium heat, melt butter; add shallots and cook, stirring, until soft but not browned. Mix in tarragon.

Savory Chicken and Escarole Soup is a classic Italian dish that makes a light but satisfying meal.

2. Add potatoes. Sprinkle with salt and pepper. Add broth and bring to a boil over medium-high heat. Cover, reduce heat to medium, and boil gently 15 minutes.

3. Add salmon steaks in a single layer; cover with lemon slices, then add bay leaf. Pour in wine. Cover again and cook over low heat until salmon flakes when tested with a fork and potatoes are tender (10 to 12 minutes). Meanwhile, in a medium skillet, cook bacon in its own drippings until lightly browned. Remove from heat, drain on paper towel, and keep warm.

4. Remove and discard bay leaf and lemon slices. Remove salmon steaks; discard salmon bones and skin and divide salmon into chunks. Add cabbage and cream to soup. Stir occasionally over medium heat until cabbage is wilted and bright green (3 to 5 minutes). Gently mix in salmon. Taste, and add salt if needed.

5. Serve chowder hot, spooning several pieces of bacon into each bowl.

Makes 4 to 6 servings.

MENU

ITALIAN SOUP SUPPER

For 8

Tuna Toasts
Apéritifs
Minestrone Milanese
Bread Sticks
Pears or Fresh Figs
Cheeses
Spiced Nut Cookies
Red Wine
Espresso Coffee

This minestrone is smoky with ham and thick with rice in the style of Milan. For wine, select a light Zinfandel or a Chianti.

Serve cheeses that go well with pears or figs, such as Taleggio (a creamy, Brie-like soft cheese), rich Fontina, and a nutty (not too dry) Parmesan. With coffee, enjoy the chewy cookies, known as *quaresimali* in Italy.

TUNA TOASTS

These crisp little herbed toast rounds are called *crostini* in Italy where they are a favorite first course. They are normally enjoyed with apéritifs such as Campari, Cynar, or vermouth.

The spread served with these toasts is usually a purée of savory chicken livers, but here it is a tuna mixture.

  1 large can (12 ½ oz) oil-packed
      tuna, drained
  1 cup butter
  ½ cup whipping cream
  1 teaspoon Dijon-style mustard
  1 small dried hot red chile, finely
      crushed
  ¼ teaspoon coarsely ground black
      pepper
  2 tablespoons chopped capers
  ¼ cup chopped parsley
  ½ cup chopped pimiento-stuffed
      olives
    Salt (optional)
    Thinly sliced French bread or
      crackers, for accompaniment

1. Place tuna in food processor. Cut butter in pieces and add to tuna with cream, mustard, chile, and pepper. Process until mixture is smooth.

2. Turn into a bowl and blend in capers, parsley, and ¼ cup of the olives. Taste, and add salt if needed. Spoon into a crock or terrine. Cover and refrigerate until mixture is firm and flavors are well blended (2 to 3 hours or overnight).

3. Remove from refrigerator about 30 minutes before serving. Garnish with remaining chopped olives and serve with thin slices of French bread or crackers.

Makes about 3 ½ cups.

MINESTRONE MILANESE

1 cup dried cannellini or Great Northern beans, rinsed and drained

2 tablespoons olive oil

2 ½ to 3 pounds beef shanks, sliced ¾ to 1 inch thick

2 large onions, slivered

2 large carrots, chopped

2 stalks celery, thinly sliced

2 cloves garlic, minced

½ cup chopped parsley

1 smoked ham hock (about ¾ lb)

1 large can (28 oz) tomatoes

2 tablespoons dried basil

8 cups water

1 medium turnip, peeled and diced

2 cups chopped chard leaves

½ cup shelled fresh or frozen peas

1 ½ cups hot cooked rice

2 cups shredded cabbage

Salt, to taste (optional)

Grated Parmesan cheese, for garnish

1. Place beans in a large bowl; add 1 teaspoon salt and 3 cups water. Cover and let stand for at least 8 hours; drain, discarding soaking liquid. Or, to shorten the soaking period, place beans in a 2- to 3-quart pan with 4 cups water *(no salt);* bring to a boil; then boil briskly, uncovered, for 2 minutes. Remove from heat, cover, and let stand for 1 hour. Drain, discarding soaking liquid.

2. In a 7- to 8-quart kettle, heat olive oil over medium heat. Add beef shanks and brown on all sides. As you turn shanks to brown last side, add onions; cook, stirring occasionally, until onions are limp.

3. Add carrots, celery, garlic, parsley, ham hock, tomatoes (coarsely chopped) along with their liquid, basil, drained soaked beans, and the 8 cups water. Bring to a boil, cover, reduce heat, and simmer until meats and beans are tender (3 ½ to 4 hours). Skim and discard surface fat if necessary.

4. Remove beef shanks and ham hock with a slotted spoon. When cool enough to handle, discard bones and skin. Return beef and ham in large chunks to soup. (At this point, soup may be covered and refrigerated until ready to reheat and serve; skim fat from surface before reheating.)

5. Add turnip to soup and boil gently, uncovered, for 10 minutes. Mix in chard and peas and cook for 3 minutes more. Blend in rice and cabbage and cook, stirring occasionally, just until cabbage is wilted and bright green (3 to 5 minutes). Taste, and add salt if needed.

6. Serve with Parmesan cheese to sprinkle over each serving.

Makes about 5 ½ quarts, 8 to 10 servings.

SPICED NUT COOKIES

2 ½ cups flour

1 ½ teaspoons baking powder

1 teaspoon ground cinnamon

½ teaspoon ground nutmeg

½ teaspoon each salt and ground allspice

½ cup butter, softened

1 cup sugar

1 teaspoon vanilla extract

3 eggs

1 cup each unblanched whole hazelnuts or almonds and coarsely chopped walnuts

⅓ cup pine nuts

Sugar, for sprinkling

1. Lightly grease a baking sheet or line with parchment paper. In a medium bowl stir flour, baking powder, cinnamon, nutmeg, salt, and allspice to blend well.

2. In a large bowl beat butter with the 1 cup sugar until well combined. Blend in vanilla. Separate 1 of the eggs, reserving the white.

3. To butter mixture add the egg yolk, then the remaining whole eggs, one at a time, beating after each addition until smooth.

4. Gradually add flour mixture to butter mixture, mixing until smooth and well blended. Divide dough in half and wrap each portion in plastic wrap; refrigerate until firm (about 1 hour). Meanwhile, mix hazelnuts, walnuts, and pine nuts.

5. Preheat oven to 350º F. On a lightly floured surface, roll out each portion of dough to an 8- by 12-inch rectangle. Sprinkle half of the nuts over each portion. Starting with a long side of each rectangle, roll dough to make a compact roll; pinch edge and ends to seal. Place, sealed side down, on a lightly greased baking sheet.

6. Beat the reserved egg white until slightly bubbly and brush generously over each roll. Sprinkle rolls lightly with sugar.

7. Bake until golden brown (35 to 40 minutes). Remove from oven and allow rolls to cool on baking sheet for about 5 minutes.

8. Transfer rolls to a board and, using a serrated knife, slice each loaf diagonally into ½-inch-thick slices. Lay slices flat on baking sheets and bake them again in 350º F oven until crisply toasted (15 to 20 minutes). Cool on racks.

Makes about 4 dozen cookies.

Rye or pumpernickel bread goes well with this Russian-style Fish Soup With Capers and Onions.

FISH SOUP WITH CAPERS AND ONIONS

Sometimes called by its Russian name, *solyanka*, this soup uses a fresh or thawed frozen whitefish, such as halibut, cod, or flounder, for the base. Serve with a dark bread, such as rye or pumpernickel.

    2 cups minced onion
    2 tablespoons unsalted butter or
          vegetable oil
    ⅔ cup minced celery
    ⅔ cup minced carrots
    2 large tomatoes, seeded and cut
          into thin strips (see page 56)
    1 cup dry white wine
 1½ pounds whitefish, bones
          removed
    1 cup peeled, seeded, and sliced
          cucumber
    4 cups water
    2 tablespoons capers, drained
    2 tablespoons minced sour gherkin
          pickles
    1 to 2 tablespoons lemon juice, to
          taste

    *Salt and freshly ground pepper, to
       taste
    Minced parsley, for garnish*

1. In a large pot over medium-high heat, sauté onion in butter until soft, but not browned. Add celery, carrots, tomatoes, and wine. Continue to cook for 5 minutes.

2. Add fish and cucumber. Cook 3 to 4 minutes, then add the water. Bring to a boil. Lower heat and simmer until fish flakes (about 15 minutes). Add capers, pickles, and lemon juice; season with salt and pepper. Serve garnished with minced parsley.

Makes 8 servings.

MARY'S BOURRIDE

This low-calorie version of a French fish soup has a variety of exquisite seasonings, such as saffron, orange peel, and fennel. The garlic mayonnaise, called *aioli*, traditionally served with bourride is omitted here to keep the calories low.

 2 teaspoons olive oil
 ½ large onion, sliced
 1 medium carrot, sliced into rounds
 1 large leek, cleaned and sliced into rounds
 2 ripe tomatoes, cored and coarsely chopped
 6 cups Fish Stock (see page 27) or water
 ½ cup dry vermouth or dry white wine
 1 bay leaf
 ¼ teaspoon dried thyme
 1 clove garlic, halved
 ¼ teaspoon chopped orange peel
 2 pinches saffron
 ¼ teaspoon fennel seed
 1 ½ pounds fresh, firm-fleshed fish
    Salt, to taste
 6 to 8 slices French bread

1. In a large stockpot over medium-high heat, heat oil; add onion and sauté until onion is very soft. Add carrot, leek, and tomatoes, and sauté 5 minutes, stirring frequently.

2. Add stock, vermouth, bay leaf, thyme, garlic, orange peel, saffron, and fennel seed. Bring to a boil. Simmer until vegetables are tender (about 10 minutes).

Saffron, orange peel, and fennel lend exquisite flavor and aroma to Mary's Bourride, one of several versions of a famous French fish soup.

3. Wash fish and pat dry; remove all bones and cut fish into 3-inch chunks. Add fish to stockpot and cook just until fish flakes.

4. Season to taste with salt and serve hot over sliced bread in large soup bowls.

Makes 8 servings.

DILLED LAMB AND BARLEY SOUP

Lamb and dill are not traditionally paired, but you'll be pleased with the result in this very substantial lamb soup. If you prefer fresh dill, use three times the amount suggested for dried dill. Note that you can prepare the soup most of the way a day ahead.

⅔ cup pearl barley
2 tablespoons butter
4 lamb shanks (about 3 lbs)
2 onions, finely chopped
2 cloves garlic, minced
2 stalks celery, thinly sliced
2 carrots, sliced about ⅛ inch thick
6 cups water
¼ cup chopped parsley
2 teaspoons salt
1 bay leaf
⅛ teaspoon white pepper
1 teaspoon dill
Sour cream, for garnish

1. Soak barley in water to cover. Meanwhile, heat butter over medium heat in a large, deep pot or Dutch oven. Brown lamb shanks in butter on all sides. Mix in onions, garlic, celery, and carrots, then add the 6 cups water, parsley, salt, bay leaf, pepper, and dill. Bring to a boil, cover, and simmer slowly until lamb is very tender (2 ½ to 3 hours).

2. Remove lamb shanks from soup. Take meat off bones; discard bones, fat, and skin. Return meat in chunks to soup. Discard bay leaf. (At this point, you may chill soup and let barley stand overnight, then skim off fat from soup.)

3. Drain soaked barley and add it to the soup. Bring soup to a boil again; cook, covered, until barley is tender (45 minutes to 1 hour). Season with additional salt, if desired. Spoon sour cream over each serving.

Makes 6 servings.

EASY EGGPLANT SOUP

For short-notice meals, it's a good idea to have a few quick-cooking soups in your culinary repertoire. This vegetable-beef soup is ready to serve in less than an hour.

1 tablespoon each butter and olive oil
1 pound ground beef, crumbled
1 large onion, chopped
1 large clove garlic, minced
1 medium eggplant (about 1 ½ lbs), unpeeled, cut in ¾-inch cubes
2 medium carrots, shredded
1 green pepper, seeded and cut in 2-inch-long strips
1 can (28 oz) tomatoes, coarsely chopped, liquid reserved
1 teaspoon each salt, sugar, and dried basil
½ teaspoon ground nutmeg
¼ teaspoon freshly ground pepper
2 cans (13 ¾ oz each) regular-strength beef broth or 3 ½ cups homemade beef stock
½ cup chopped parsley
Salt, to taste
Grated Parmesan cheese, for garnish

1. In a large pot or Dutch oven over medium heat, heat butter and oil and brown beef and onion. Add garlic, eggplant, carrots, and green pepper. Cook, stirring occasionally, until eggplant browns lightly.

2. Stir in tomatoes and their liquid, salt, sugar, basil, nutmeg, pepper, and broth. Bring to a boil over medium-high heat, reduce heat to low, cover, and simmer until the eggplant is very tender (45 to 50 minutes).

3. Stir in parsley. Season with salt. Pass grated cheese at the table for garnish.

Makes 4 to 6 servings.

GREEK MEATBALL AND ZUCCHINI SOUP

Exceptionally simple and quick to assemble, this soup gets its character from ground lamb meatballs, accented with fresh lemon. It is especially tasty when made with homemade chicken stock. Serve with a loaf of braided egg bread.

1 ½ tablespoons olive oil or vegetable oil
1 large onion, finely chopped
½ teaspoon dried oregano
2 cans (13 ¾ oz each) chicken stock or 3 ½ to 4 cups homemade chicken stock
2 tablespoons long-grain rice
2 medium zucchini (about ¾ lb), thinly sliced
Salt, to taste
Lemon wedges, for accompaniment

Lamb Meatballs

1 egg
1 teaspoon salt
1 clove garlic, minced
Dash freshly ground pepper
¼ cup soft bread crumbs
1 pound ground lamb

1. In a large pot or Dutch oven over medium heat, heat oil and brown meatballs on all sides. Add onion, oregano, stock, and rice. Bring to a boil over medium-high heat, cover, reduce heat, and simmer until rice is tender (about 25 minutes).

2. Add zucchini and cook, uncovered, until just tender (4 to 6 minutes). Season with salt and serve with lemon wedges.

Makes 4 servings.

Lamb Meatballs In a medium bowl, beat egg. Mix in salt, garlic, pepper, and bread crumbs. Lightly mix in lamb. Shape into ¾-inch meatballs.

CHILI BEAN SOUP

If your family likes chili, this pork-studded red bean soup is sure to please. Accompany it with a green salad and tortilla chips for a hearty, Mexican-accented meal. For a hotter, more authentic Mexican soup, replace the chili powder with 3 fresh or dried chopped *ancho* chiles. The soup requires 4 to 5 hours' cooking time but very little preparation, and the cooking can be done in stages.

>   1 pound dried red beans, rinsed
>   and drained
>   7 cups water
>   1 tablespoon vegetable oil
>   2 pounds country-style spareribs
>   1 green bell pepper, seeded and
>   chopped
>   2 medium onions, sliced
>   2 cloves garlic, minced
>   2 teaspoons salt
>   2 tablespoons chili powder
>   ½ teaspoon ground cumin
>   1 can (8 oz) tomato sauce
>   1 cup shredded Monterey jack
>   cheese, for garnish

1. Place beans in a large bowl; add 4 cups of the water and let stand overnight. (Or bring beans and 4 cups water to a boil in a 4-quart kettle, boil briskly for 2 minutes, then remove from heat and let stand, covered, for 1 hour.)

2. In a large, deep pot or Dutch oven, heat oil over medium heat. Brown spareribs well in oil on all sides. Add green pepper, onions, and garlic; brown lightly. Add remaining 3 cups water, bring to a boil, reduce heat, cover, and simmer until meat is tender (1 ½ to 2 hours).

3. Remove spareribs from pot. Slice meat from bones and return to the cooking liquid in chunks; discard bones and fat. (At this point, you may refrigerate the stock overnight, then skim off fat and reheat.)

4. Add soaked beans and their liquid, salt, chili powder, and cumin; bring to a boil over medium-high heat. Cover, reduce heat to low, and simmer until beans are almost tender (about 1 ½ hours). Mix in tomato sauce. Cook until beans are very tender (about 1 hour longer). Serve sprinkled with jack cheese.

Makes 6 to 8 servings.

Lamb, zucchini, and fresh lemon combine to make this Greek Meatball and Zucchini Soup a delicious meal for four.

Aromatic basil and garlic are the main ingredients in the topping for Soup au Pistou, a Provençal vegetable soup.

SOUP AU PISTOU
(Vegetable soup with basil purée)

Stir a spoonful of pistou–a purée of basil, garlic, and cheese–into a thick vegetable soup to make one of the best-loved dishes of the Provençal kitchen. Note that the white beans need to soak overnight.

½ cup small dried white beans

12 cups chicken stock

1 onion, cut in ½-inch dice

1 leek (white part only), sliced ½-inch thick

1 stalk celery, cut in ½-inch dice

½ large potato, peeled and cut in ½-inch dice

2 carrots, cut in ½-inch dice

1 cup tomato, peeled, seeded, and coarsely chopped (see page 56)

¼ cup green beans, cut in 1-inch lengths

2 small zucchini, cut in ½-inch dice

½ cup elbow macaroni

1 cup grated Gruyère cheese, for garnish

Pistou

2 tablespoons minced garlic

¼ cup olive oil

1 cup fresh basil leaves

½ cup grated Gruyère cheese

1. Put white beans in a bowl and cover by 1 inch with cold water. Let soak overnight. Drain.

2. In a large pot over medium heat, bring stock to a boil. Add white beans, reduce heat to low, and simmer for 35 minutes. Add onion, leek, celery, potato, and carrots. Simmer 20 minutes. Add tomato, green beans, zucchini, and macaroni, and simmer until all vegetables are tender (about 20 minutes more). Serve in warm bowls; garnish each serving with 2 teaspoons pistou. Pass extra pistou and Gruyère at the table.

Makes 6 servings.

Pistou   Place all pistou ingredients in a blender or food processor and blend until smooth.

Makes about ½ cup.

SUBSTANTIAL SALADS

Full-meal salads often depend on leftovers as their base. The best ones are so creative in the way they recycle yesterday's grilled chicken or roast beef that the dish seems new in every way, like Lamb and White Bean Salad (see page 54), Mango Chutney Chicken Salad (see page 58), and Thai Noodle Salad with Chicken (see page 58). The recipes in this section are quick to put together for a light lunch or supper. Pair one of these salads with a soup from Chapter 3 to make a more filling meal.

CRACKED WHEAT SALAD WITH SCALLOPS AND GREEN BEANS

Cooked cracked wheat tossed with scallops and a rainbow of summer vegetables makes a light but satisfying main-course salad.

> 2 pounds bay scallops or sea scallops
> 1½ pounds fresh green beans
>   Salt, to taste
> 2 cups cracked wheat
> 2 red bell peppers
> 2 large tomatoes, seeded and diced (see page 56)
> ½ cup finely diced green cabbage
> 2 medium zucchini, cut in ¼-inch dice
> 6 green onions, minced
> 2 heads butter lettuce

Herb Vinaigrette

> 1 small hot chile pepper, seeded and minced
> 1½ cups minced Italian parsley
> 1 cup minced fresh mint
> ½ cup minced cilantro
> 5 tablespoons apple cider vinegar
> ¾ cup olive oil
>   Salt and freshly ground pepper, to taste

1. If using sea scallops, trim away any tough muscle. Steam bay or sea scallops over, not in, a large pot of boiling salted water until they taste done (bay scallops take only 1 minute or less; sea scallops 3 to 5 minutes). Cut sea scallops into quarters; leave bay scallops whole. Moisten with 2 tablespoons of the Herb Vinaigrette; cover and refrigerate.

The cooking style of the area of Nice in France, known for its olive oil, anchovies, and olives, lends an Italian accent to Rice Salad Niçoise.

2. Trim green bean tips. Cook in a large pot of boiling salted water until crisp-tender (5 to 7 minutes). Drain and plunge into a bowl of ice water to stop the cooking. When beans are completely cool, drain again. Cut into ½-inch pieces.

3. In a medium saucepan over high heat, bring 3 cups salted water to a boil. Add wheat, cover, and remove from heat; let stand 30 minutes.

4. Roast peppers according to directions on Roasting Bell Peppers and Chiles. (See page 67). Peel and dice.

5. In a large bowl combine peppers, tomatoes, cabbage, zucchini, green onions, cracked wheat, green beans, and scallops. Add remaining Herb Vinaigrette; toss with a fork to blend. Cover and refrigerate at least 2 hours or up to 12 hours.

6. Remove salad from refrigerator 30 minutes before serving. Wash and dry hearts of butter lettuce. Arrange lettuce leaves on a large serving platter. Spoon cracked wheat mixture onto center of platter.

Serves 8.

Herb Vinaigrette   In a bowl combine chile, parsley, mint, cilantro, and vinegar. Whisk to blend; let stand 5 minutes. Gradually whisk in olive oil. Season with salt and pepper.

Makes about 1¾ cups.

RICE SALAD NIÇOISE

The colorful ingredients of the popular salad from the Nice area of France enliven this refreshing main-dish rice salad. Note that the mixture needs to refrigerate for several hours to marry the flavors.

> 2 cups water
> 1 teaspoon olive oil
> 1 teaspoon salt
> 1 cup long-grain rice
> 1 jar (6 oz) marinated artichoke hearts
> 1 can (2 oz) flat anchovy filets, drained
> 1 green pepper, seeded and chopped
> 1 stalk celery, finely chopped
> 4 green onions, thinly sliced
> ¼ cup Niçoise olives or slivered ripe olives
> ½ cup chopped, peeled cucumber
> 1 small tomato, seeded and chopped
> 1 can (6 ½ oz) chunk light tuna, drained and flaked
> 2 hard-cooked eggs, sliced
>   Butter or Boston lettuce leaves
>   Tomato wedges, for garnish

Garlic Vinaigrette

> 2 tablespoons red wine vinegar
> 1½ teaspoons lemon juice
> 2 teaspoons Dijon-style mustard
> 1 clove garlic, minced
> ¼ teaspoon salt
>   Dash coarsely ground pepper
> 2 tablespoons olive oil
> ⅓ cup vegetable oil
> 1 tablespoon chopped parsley

1. In a medium saucepan, combine the water, oil, and salt; bring to a boil. Gradually add rice. Cover, reduce heat, and simmer until rice is just tender (20 to 25 minutes). Lightly mix in artichoke hearts (with their marinade). Transfer to a large bowl, cover, and refrigerate until cool.

2. Reserve about 5 anchovy fillets for garnish. Chop remaining anchovies and add to rice with pepper, celery, onions, olives, cucumber, tomato, tuna, and eggs. Add Garlic Vinaigrette and mix lightly. Cover and refrigerate at least 2 hours to blend flavors.

3. Serve in a bowl lined with lettuce. Garnish with tomato wedges and reserved anchovies.

Serves 6 to 8.

Garlic Vinaigrette   In a medium bowl, mix vinegar, lemon juice, mustard, garlic, salt, and pepper. Using a whisk or fork, gradually blend in oils, mixing until well blended and slightly thickened. Stir in parsley.

Makes ½ cup.

LAMB AND WHITE BEAN SALAD

Lamb and white beans are a classic spring combination, as good in a cold salad as in a stew. Prepare the beans at least a day ahead to allow them to develop flavor. This is the perfect use for leftover leg of lamb.

> 1½ pounds cooked leg of lamb, slivered
> 1½ cups dried cannellini beans or Great Northern beans
> 2 ounces minced prosciutto (Italian ham)
> ¼ cup olive oil
> 2 tablespoons minced garlic
> 2 tablespoons minced fresh sage
> 3 cups peeled, seeded, and diced tomatoes (see page 56)
>   Salt and freshly ground pepper, to taste
> 1 mild white onion, sliced paper-thin
> 1 cup mixed young lettuces, washed and dried

Thyme Vinaigrette

> ⅓ cup red wine vinegar
> 1 shallot, minced
> 1 tablespoon minced fresh thyme
> 1 cup olive oil
>   Salt and freshly ground pepper, to taste

1. Put sliced lamb in a bowl and add ½ cup Thyme Vinaigrette. Toss well to coat; cover and refrigerate overnight.

2. Cover beans with water and soak from 2 to 12 hours. Drain and cover with fresh cold water. Add prosciutto and bring to a boil over high heat. Reduce heat to maintain a simmer and cook until beans are tender but not mushy (about 1 ½ hours). Drain and cool. Beans may be cooked up to 2 days in advance, covered, and refrigerated.

3. In a large pot over low heat, heat olive oil. Add garlic and sage and cook until

Lamb and White Bean Salad, a classic spring dish, is complemented by the choicest and freshest of young lettuces.

fragrant. Add beans and tomatoes. Bring to a simmer and cook 15 minutes. Season with salt and pepper. If desired, beans may be cooled and refrigerated overnight.

4. Marinate onion slices 10 minutes in just enough Thyme Vinaigrette to coat them. Bring lamb and beans to room temperature. If beans appear somewhat dry, moisten with Thyme Vinaigrette. Taste and reseason, if necessary.

5. To serve, line a large serving platter with lettuces. Arrange beans and lamb atop lettuces. Garnish with marinated onion slices.

Serves 8.

Thyme Vinaigrette In a medium bowl, whisk together vinegar, shallot, and thyme. Add olive oil in a slow, steady stream, whisking constantly. Season with salt and pepper.

THAI BEEF SALAD

This dish is found on the menu of almost every Thai restaurant in the United States. Sometimes the beef is stir-fried in a minimum of oil and the salad is served while the beef is still warm. Sometimes it's served cold, using thinly sliced rare roast beef.

2 *tablespoons minced garlic*
3 *tablespoons minced fresh hot chiles (serrano or jalapeño)*
½ *teaspoon firmly packed dark brown sugar*
¼ *cup lime juice*
1 *tablespoon finely chopped unsalted roasted peanuts*
  Salt (optional)
12 *medium leaves of romaine or iceberg lettuce*
1 *medium red onion, diced fine*
4 *green onions, chopped*
1 *tablespoon peanut or corn oil (optional)*
1 *pound very lean steak (flank or round), trimmed of fat and gristle, very thinly sliced (⅛ by ¼ by 1 in.), or rare roast beef, sliced in thin strips*
1 *tablespoon freshly ground pepper, or to taste*
¼ *cup chopped cilantro, for garnish Mint leaves, for garnish (optional)*

1. Mix garlic, chiles, brown sugar, lime juice, peanuts, and salt (if desired) and reserve.

2. Arrange lettuce leaves on a flat serving platter. Top with diced red and green onions.

3. If using raw beef, heat a wok or large, heavy skillet over high heat for 30 seconds. Add peanut oil and heat until fragrant. Add raw beef and, stirring and flipping constantly, fry until browned all over. With a slotted spoon or spatula, remove beef from pan.

4. Scatter stir-fried beef or roast beef over lettuce and grind over it a very generous quantity of black pepper. Pour sauce over beef, sprinkle evenly with coriander, and garnish (if desired) with mint leaves.

Serves 4 as an appetizer or 2 or 3 as a light supper.

Thai Beef Salad does triple service as a delicious appetizer, a perfect start to a light dinner, or even a main course for a hot summer evening.

STEP BY STEP

PEELING, SEEDING, AND CHOPPING TOMATOES

1. Use a paring knife to core the tomatoes.

2. Turn tomatoes over and slit the skin in an X-shaped cut.

3. Put the tomatoes in a pan containing enough boiling water to cover them and boil for 15 seconds. Remove them with a slotted spoon and put them in a bowl of cold water. Leave for a few seconds.

4. Remove them from the cold water and use a paring knife to pull off the skins.

5. Halve the tomatoes horizontally with a chopping knife. Hold each half over a bowl, cut side down, and squeeze to remove the seeds.

6. Chop the tomatoes into small pieces.

POACHED SAUSAGE AND WARM POTATO SALAD

Typically served as a first course in French bistros, particularly around Lyon where it is a regional specialty, this combination is hearty enough to make a light luncheon dish. Any European-style link sausage is suitable: Consider French *boudin noir* or *cervelas,* Italian *cotechino,* German bratwurst, or Polish kielbasa. If the sausage is fresh (not cooked or smoked), it must be slowly poached until it is cooked throughout. Cooking time will vary depending on the size of the links; cut into one to test for doneness. Precooked or smoked sausages need only be heated through. The cooking time specified in the following recipe is for fresh 4-ounce links.

> 1 ½ *pounds red potatoes of similar*
> *size*
> ¼ *cup Dijon-style mustard*
> 6 *green onions, minced*
> *Basic Vinaigrette (see page 36)*
> ⅓ *cup minced parsley*
> ½ *cup dry white wine*
> 2 *cups water*
> 1 ½ *pounds sausage (in 4-oz links)*

1. In a large saucepan, cover potatoes with salted water. Bring to a boil over high heat. Reduce heat to maintain a simmer and cook until potatoes are tender when pierced with a knife (20 to 25 minutes). Drain. When potatoes are just cool enough to handle, slice them about ¼ inch thick and place in a bowl. Add mustard and toss gently to mix. Add green onions and vinaigrette. Toss gently but well with your hands. Add ¼ cup of the parsley.

2. In a large skillet over high heat, bring wine and 2 cups water to a boil. Add sausages and cover. Reduce heat to maintain a simmer and cook until sausages are firm and hot throughout (about 15 minutes).

3. Transfer potato salad to a warm platter. Surround with poached sausages. Garnish with the remaining parsley. Serve immediately.

Serves 6.

BON BON CHICKEN SALAD

In this chilled salad, a bed of bean thread noodles is studded with julienned cucumber. The flavor of the toasted sesame paste, a butter made from roasted sesame seed, is tantalizing. Bean thread noodles and the other Asian ingredients called for in this recipe are available at Asian markets and well-stocked supermarkets.

> 2 *whole chicken breasts*
> 2 *green onions, bruised*
> 1 *piece (1 in.) fresh ginger, bruised*
> 2 *teaspoons Asian sesame oil*
> 3 *quarts water*
> 2 *ounces bean thread noodles,*
> *soaked in warm water 20*
> *minutes, then drained*
> 1 *English cucumber, peeled, cut in*
> 1 ½*-inch-long julienne strips*
> 1 *tablespoon sesame seed, prefer-*
> *ably black, toasted, for*
> *garnish*

Toasted Sesame Paste Dressing

> 3 *tablespoons Chinese sesame paste*
> 1 *teaspoon finely minced fresh*
> *ginger*
> 2 *cloves garlic, finely minced*
> 1 *tablespoon peanut oil*
> 3 *tablespoons soy sauce*
> 2 *tablespoons wine vinegar*
> 1 *tablespoon sugar*
> 1 *teaspoon Asian sesame oil*
> 1 *teaspoon Asian hot chile oil, or to*
> *taste*
> 3 *tablespoons reserved chicken*
> *juices or water, or as needed*

1. *To steam chicken:* Fill a 14-inch wok or large Dutch oven partway with boiling water. Place chicken, green onions, and ginger in a heat-resistant bowl; set bowl on steaming rack, tray, or trivet set in wok or Dutch oven with at least 1 inch clearance between bowl and water and sides of pan. Cover and steam over medium-high heat 30 minutes (check water level frequently and replenish with boiling water when necessary). Let cool. Remove chicken, reserving juices for Toasted Sesame Paste Dressing. Tear meat into matchstick shreds, discarding skin and bones. In a medium bowl, toss chicken with sesame oil; refrigerate.

2. In a large saucepan over high heat, bring the water to a boil. Add bean thread noodles, reduce heat to medium, and simmer until noodles are plump (5 minutes). Pour into a colander, rinse with cold water, and drain. Cut into 2-inch lengths, place in a medium bowl, cover with cold water, and refrigerate until chilled (about 1 hour). Drain well.

3. On a serving platter, arrange drained bean thread noodles. Layer with cucumber, then reserved chicken. Top with Toasted Sesame Paste Dressing and garnish with sesame seed. Serve chilled.

Serves 8 as a first course salad or 4 as a main course.

Toasted Sesame Paste Dressing
Place sesame paste in a heat-resistant bowl; place ginger and garlic on top. In a small saucepan over high heat, heat peanut oil until almost smoking; pour

over paste and stir thoroughly. Add soy sauce, vinegar, sugar, sesame oil, and hot chile oil; mix well. Add chicken juices until mixture is consistency of thin cream. Chill. Before serving, check consistency of dressing. If too thick, add more chicken juices to thin. Adjust seasoning if necessary.

Makes about 1 cup.

Bon Bon Chicken Salad, a substantial entrée or a complete light meal, is dressed with a unique sesame paste dressing. Pouring hot peanut oil over the garlic, ginger, and sesame paste is a subtle but crucial step that the Chinese say "opens the flavor."

MANGO CHUTNEY CHICKEN SALAD

Use leftover chicken or simmer boneless chicken breasts, covered with water, until tender (25 to 35 minutes). Note that the chicken must marinate from 2 to 24 hours. Accompany with biscuits, cookies, and fresh fruit.

1 cup mayonnaise
1 cup sour cream
½ cup mango chutney
¼ cup minced cilantro
¼ cup minced green onion
1 teaspoon salt
6 cups diced, cooked boneless
    chicken breast
1 cup toasted pecans, for garnish

1. In a large bowl, combine mayonnaise, sour cream, chutney, cilantro, green onion, and salt.

2. Toss with chicken and let marinate for 2 to 24 hours. Sprinkle with pecans before serving.

Serves 8.

THAI NOODLES WITH CHICKEN

For a spicier salad, increase the amount of hot-pepper flakes. Asian sesame oil, made from toasted sesame seeds, contributes a characteristic flavor to the salad. Sesame oil and the Chinese dried egg noodles are available at Asian markets and well-stocked supermarkets.

1 pound Chinese dried egg noodles
    or linguine
4 cooked chicken breast halves
    Cilantro sprigs, mint leaves, and
    chopped peanuts, for garnish

Sesame-Soy Dressing

¾ cup soy sauce
¾ cup chicken stock or water
½ cup coarsely chopped peanuts
¼ cup smooth peanut butter
¼ cup firmly packed brown sugar
¼ cup white wine vinegar
¼ cup Asian sesame oil
2 tablespoons vegetable oil
1 ½ cups minced fresh mint
½ cup minced cilantro
2 cloves garlic, minced
2 cups shredded carrots
4 green onions, minced
1 teaspoon hot-pepper flakes

1. In a large saucepan, bring 4 quarts water to a boil. Add noodles, stir to separate, and reduce heat to medium. Cook noodles until tender but still firm (about 18 minutes). Remove from heat and drain.

2. While noodles are cooking, prepare the dressing. Toss warm noodles with dressing to coat thoroughly.

3. Tear each chicken breast half into 8 or 10 medium-sized pieces; add to noodles. Stir to coat chicken with dressing and to mix with noodles. Garnish with cilantro sprigs, mint leaves, and chopped pecans, and serve.

Serves 8.

Sesame-Soy Dressing In a large bowl, thoroughly combine all ingredients.

Makes about 2 ¾ cups.

PASTA FOR SUPPER

To many Americans, the heart of Italian cooking is pasta in all its forms. In Italy, the Italian meal follows a pattern that rarely varies. After an antipasto, usually an assortment of cured meats, pickled or marinated vegetables, or marinated shellfish, comes the *primo piatto,* "the first course," which is often pasta in some form. The meat course follows. American eating patterns are not as proscribed: Pasta has become a favorite main dish in this country, in part because it is so versatile and easy to prepare and also because pasta, when paired with the right sauces and accompaniments, can be part of a healthy diet. Each of the following pasta recipes will make a delicious weeknight meal or casual company dinner.

SPAGHETTI WITH CHUNKY TOMATO SAUCE

Cooks in northern Italy often enrich sauces with butter. They add vegetables and herbs for depth, then simmer the sauce slowly to marry the flavors. Use this basic northern-style tomato sauce alone tossed with spaghetti or your favorite pasta or as a building block for dozens of other dishes. If you can't get sweet, vine-ripened tomatoes, use the best available canned variety.

2 teaspoons olive oil
4 teaspoons butter
1 large carrot, peeled and diced
2 ribs celery, diced
1 onion, diced
2 tablespoons minced garlic
1 teaspoon flour
3 pounds ripe tomatoes, peeled,
    seeded, and chopped (see
    page 56), or one 28-ounce
    can plum tomatoes, whirled
    briefly in a blender or food
    processor
1 tablespoon tomato paste
    Pinch sugar
¼ cup fresh chopped basil or 1
    teaspoon dried basil
4 sprigs fresh parsley
2 sprigs fresh oregano

1 bay leaf
   Salt and freshly ground pepper, to
      taste
1 pound spaghetti
   Grated Parmesan cheese, for
      accompaniment

1. Heat oil and butter in a large, heavy saucepan over medium heat. When butter foams, add carrot, celery, onion, and garlic, and stew gently for 10 minutes. Stir in flour and continue cooking 5 minutes. Add tomatoes, tomato paste, sugar, basil, parsley, oregano, and bay leaf. Simmer, partly covered, for 1 hour.

2. Remove bay leaf and herb stems. Pass sauce through a food mill or process briefly in a food processor if you prefer a smoother texture. Adjust seasoning to taste with salt and pepper.

3. Bring a large pot of salted water to a boil over high heat. Cook spaghetti until just tender (about 8 minutes). Drain thoroughly. Top with tomato sauce and grated Parmesan cheese.

Serves 8.

The foundation for this Spaghetti With Chunky Tomato Sauce and countless other Italian dishes is a slowly simmered northern-style tomato sauce.

MENU

BRITTANY BRUNCH

For 8

Buckwheat Crêpes
Mixed Vegetable Crêpes
Breakfast Link Crêpes
Egg, Ham, and Cheese Crêpes
Honey-Pear–Butter Crêpes
Prune-and-Almond-Filled Crêpes
Preserve-Filled Crêpes
Apple, Raisin, and Walnut Crêpes
Sparkling Apple Cider

Hot-from-the-skillet Buckwheat Crêpes are spread with smooth honey-pear butter or wrapped around sizzling breakfast links, just two of the sweet and savory fixings for this festive do-it-yourself brunch. Toast the day with sparkling apple cider, a Breton specialty and the classic partner to Buckwheat Crêpes. Part of the fun of a crêpe party is turning everyone into a chef. Encourage each guest to take a turn at the crêpe pans. With two chefs and two or three pans working at once, the crêpes can be made almost as fast as they are eaten.

BUCKWHEAT CRÊPES

To serve eight guests generously, make the recipe twice. The first time, use all the optional ingredients to make a sweet batter suitable for sweet fillings. The second time, omit all the optional ingredients to make a savory batter suitable for savory fillings. Leftover batter can be frozen for up to six months. Crêpes can be frozen for up to six months, if well wrapped.

   ¾ *cup buckwheat flour*
   ¾ *cup plus 2 tablespoons*
         unbleached flour
   2 *tablespoons dark brown sugar*
         (optional)
   ¼ *teaspoon salt*
   ¼ *teaspoon ground cinnamon*
         (optional)

   Pinch ground nutmeg (optional)
   3 *eggs*
   2 *cups milk*
   ⅔ *cup half-and-half*
   ¼ *cup minced golden raisins*
         (optional)
   Melted Clarified Butter (see Note)

1. In a blender or food processor, place flours, sugar (if used), salt, cinnamon (if used), and nutmeg (if used). Pulse to blend.

2. Add eggs and process to blend. With machine running, add milk and half-and-half. Add raisins (if used) and blend. Transfer to a clean bowl, cover, and let rest at room temperature for 30 minutes. Or, refrigerate batter for up to 2 days; bring to room temperature before using.

3. If necessary, add water to batter to make it pourable. Heat a 6- to 7-inch crêpe pan or skillet over moderately high heat. Lightly brush pan with the clarified butter. When butter sizzles, add 3 tablespoons batter and swirl to coat pan. Cook until crêpe is browned on the bottom. Turn and brown briefly (about 5

seconds) on second side. Transfer crêpe to a plate and repeat with remaining batter.

Makes about thirty 6- to 7-inch crêpes.

Note To make clarified butter, melt 1 cup butter in a small heavy pan over low heat. Skim off froth and carefully pour clear butter from pan, leaving the milky residue behind. Discard residue.

MIXED VEGETABLE CRÊPES

This quick vegetable sauté offers a welcome contrast to the sweet crêpe fillings.

   2 *tablespoons butter*
   6 *tablespoons minced shallot*
   3 *cups coarsely grated zucchini*
   ¾ *cup coarsely grated carrot*
   ½ *cup toasted pine nuts*
   ¼ *cup balsamic vinegar*
    Salt and freshly ground pepper,
        to taste
   8 *savory Buckwheat Crêpes (see*
        page 60)
    Melted butter, for garnish

1. In a large skillet over moderate heat, melt butter. Add shallot and sauté 1 minute. Add zucchini and carrot and sauté until wilted (about 3 minutes). Add pine nuts and vinegar and cook 30 seconds. Add salt and pepper. Vegetables may be sautéed up to 1 day in advance and refrigerated; undercook vegetables slightly to allow for reheating. Reheat quickly over high heat before using.

2. To serve, spoon one eighth of filling down the center of each crêpe and roll. Brush rolled crêpes with a little melted butter, for garnish.

Makes 8 filled crêpes.

BREAKFAST LINK CRÊPES

You can substitute any type of link sausage for the breakfast links, but large sausages should be sliced after cooking.

> 8 breakfast link sausages (about 1 lb)
> 8 savory Buckwheat Crêpes (see page 60)
> Honey-Pear Butter (see page 61), optional

Prick sausages with a fork. In a lightly oiled skillet over moderate heat, brown sausages. Drain on paper towels. Spread warm crêpes with Honey-Pear Butter, if used. Wrap a hot sausage in each crêpe and serve immediately.

Makes 8 filled crêpes.

EGG, HAM, AND CHEESE CRÊPES

Almost every *crêperie* and street crêpe vendor in France sells a version of these fried-egg crêpes.

> Melted clarified butter (see Note, page 60)
> 2 cups savory Buckwheat Crêpes batter (see page 60)
> 8 eggs
> 4 ounces each shredded Danish ham and shredded Monterey jack or mozzarella cheese

1. Heat a 9- or 10-inch crêpe pan or skillet over moderately high heat. Brush generously with melted butter. When butter sizzles, add ¼ cup of Buckwheat Crêpes batter and swirl to coat pan.

2. Into center of batter gently break one egg, keeping yolk whole. Cook just until white is set; yolk should remain runny. Top with ½ ounce ham and ½ ounce cheese. Gently fold sides of crêpe in over cheese. Remove crêpe to a warm plate

with a spatula. Continue with remaining crêpe batter and eggs.

Makes 8 filled crêpes.

HONEY-PEAR BUTTER CRÊPES

The butter can be made up to two days in advance and refrigerated. If mixture separates, return to food processor and process briefly to reblend.

> 8 sweet Buckwheat Crêpes (see page 60)

Honey-Pear Butter

> 1 cup very ripe pear, peeled, cored, and cubed
> 1 cup butter, softened
> ¼ cup honey

Spread about 1 ½ tablespoons Honey-Pear Butter evenly over surface of hot crêpes; fold crêpes in quarters and serve immediately.

Makes 8 filled crêpes.

Honey-Pear Butter   Place pear in a food processor or blender and blend until puréed. Add butter and honey and process until completely smooth.

Makes about 2 ¼ cups.

PRUNE-AND-ALMOND-FILLED CRÊPES

The filling can be made up to one week in advance and refrigerated in an airtight container; bring to room temperature before using.

> 1 ½ cups pitted prunes
> ½ cup water
> 3 tablespoons light brown sugar
> 2 tablespoons lemon juice
> ½ teaspoon ground cinnamon
> 2 tablespoons sliced toasted almonds
> 8 sweet Buckwheat Crêpes (see page 60)

1. In a medium saucepan place prunes and the water. Bring to a simmer over moderate heat, reduce heat to maintain a simmer, and cook until prunes are very soft (about 10 minutes). Purée prunes in a food processor or blender; mixture will be very thick.

2. Transfer prune purée to a medium bowl and stir in sugar, lemon juice,

cinnamon, and almonds. Spread about 2 tablespoons filling on each warm crêpe; fold in quarters; serve .

Makes 8 filled crêpes.

PRESERVE-FILLED CRÊPES

Use homemade or best-quality store-bought preserves of any variety.

> 1 cup fruit preserves or marmalade
> 8 sweet Buckwheat Crêpes (see page 60)
> Melted butter, for garnish

Spread 2 tablespoons preserves evenly over the surface of each hot crêpe. Fold in quarters, brush with butter, and serve.

Makes 8 filled crêpes.

APPLE, RAISIN, AND WALNUT CRÊPES

This filling should be made no more than two hours in advance to keep the apples crisp.

> ¼ cup raisins
> 1 ½ tablespoons apple brandy
> 1 ½ cups coarsely grated green apple
> ½ teaspoon cinnamon
> ¼ cup chopped toasted walnuts
> 1 teaspoon grated lemon peel
> 2 tablespoons honey
> 1 tablespoon lemon juice
> 8 sweet Buckwheat Crêpes (see page 60)
> Melted butter, for garnish
> Cinnamon Sugar (see Note), for garnish

1. In a small bowl combine raisins and brandy and let stand 30 minutes. In a medium bowl combine raisin mixture, apple, cinnamon, and walnuts and stir to blend. Stir in lemon peel, honey, and lemon juice.

2. To serve, spoon about ¼ cup filling down the center of each hot crêpe and roll into a cylinder. Brush with melted butter and sprinkle with Cinnamon Sugar.

Makes 8 filled crêpes.

Note   To make Cinnamon Sugar, in a small bowl stir together ¼ teaspoon cinnamon and 2 tablespoons sugar.

LINGUINE WITH WINTER PESTO

Pesto, a popular sauce for pasta, is usually made with fresh basil leaves, pine nuts, and Parmesan cheese (see Pesto Sauce, page 115). In the winter, when fresh basil is scarce, try dried basil—which is hard to distinguish when the basil is mixed with other ingredients. This dish has fewer calories than the original version and also features parsley and spinach, which provide plenty of vitamin A.

  1 pound linguine
  ½ cup minced spinach leaves
  ½ cup chopped parsley
  1 tablespoon dried basil
  1 tablespoon minced garlic
  ¼ cup coarsely chopped walnuts
  3 tablespoons olive oil
  ¼ cup grated Parmesan cheese

1. Bring a large pot of salted water to a boil over high heat; cook linguine until just tender (8 minutes).

2. While noodles are cooking, combine spinach, parsley, basil, garlic, walnuts, oil, and Parmesan in a blender or food processor until a thick paste is formed.

3. Drain noodles and toss with pesto while still warm. Serve at once.

Serves 4.

PASTA WITH WALNUT-GARLIC SAUCE

A traditional favorite in southern France, this pasta dish is surprisingly simple and unusually delicious. The roasted garlic gives the sauce a sweet flavor that complements the walnuts. Decorate the top with minced fresh basil leaves and red bell pepper. It's a rich dish, so serve it with a simple green salad and crusty French bread.

  2 large heads garlic
  ⅓ cup olive oil
  ⅔ cup walnuts
  ¼ cup boiling water
  1 teaspoon salt
  ¼ teaspoon cayenne pepper
  6 cups cooked linguine or egg noodles
  1 teaspoon chopped parsley
  2 tablespoons minced fresh basil, for garnish

  2 tablespoons minced red bell pepper, for garnish

1. Preheat oven to 300° F. Slice tops of garlic heads to expose cloves. Brush lightly with 1 teaspoon olive oil. Place on ungreased baking sheet and roast for 20 minutes. Let cool slightly, then squeeze heads to extract roasted cloves.

2. Place garlic into a blender or food processor. Add walnuts, remaining oil, the water, salt, and cayenne. Blend until smooth.

3. Toss sauce with hot pasta, then add parsley. Garnish with basil and red bell pepper.

Serves 6.

PASTA WITH GARLIC, OLIVE OIL, FRESH TOMATOES, AND BASIL

This colorful pasta dish is very simple to prepare because the sauce does not require cooking. Good-quality olive oil, preferably extra virgin oil, is important for the taste of this dish. If fresh basil is not available, substitute 2 teaspoons dried basil and 2 tablespoons chopped fresh parsley. Note that the tomato sauce must sit at room temperature for 1 to 2 hours before serving.

  1 pound fettucine
  1 cup plus 6 tablespoons good-quality olive oil
  Salt and freshly ground pepper, to taste
  2 pounds ripe tomatoes, peeled, seeded, and chopped (see page 56)
  Salt and freshly ground pepper, to taste
  4 cloves garlic, minced
  ¼ cup chopped fresh basil
  Grated Parmesan cheese, for accompaniment (optional)

1. Bring a large pot of salted water to a boil over high heat; cook fettucine until just tender (8 minutes). Drain pasta and transfer to a large bowl; add 6 tablespoons of the olive oil and toss gently.

2. Mix tomatoes with salt, pepper, and garlic. Gradually stir in remaining 1 cup of olive oil. Stir in basil. Let sauce stand at room temperature for 1 or 2 hours. Taste and season with additional salt and

pepper, if needed. Pass grated Parmesan cheese (if used).

Serves 4.

VERMICELLI WITH EGGPLANT AND YELLOW PEPPERS

The Mediterranean flavor of this dish comes from the fresh basil, a taste of olive oil, Greek olives, and capers. The sautéed vegetables can be cooked up to 4 hours ahead of time and combined with the pasta just before serving.

  ¼ cup olive oil
  ¼ to ½ cup white wine
  2 cloves garlic, minced
  2 cups chopped tomato
  2 small Japanese-style eggplants, peeled and cubed
  2 yellow bell peppers, roasted, peeled, and seeded (see page 67)
  2 tablespoons pitted Greek olives
  2 tablespoons capers
  2 tablespoons chopped fresh basil
  6 cups cooked spaghetti or fettucine
  3 tablespoons grated Parmesan cheese
  Freshly ground pepper, to taste

1. In a skillet, heat olive oil and ¼ cup wine and sauté garlic for 1 minute at medium-high heat. Add tomato and eggplants and continue to cook, stirring frequently, for 10 minutes more. If the mixture dries out too fast, lower the heat, and add ¼ cup more wine.

2. Chop the peeled peppers coarsely and add to the sauté. Add olives, capers, and basil to sauté. Reheat spaghetti in heated water for 1 minute, then drain and toss with sauté. Season with Parmesan and pepper and serve immediately.

Serves 6.

VEGETABLE SPAGHETTI

The julienned carrots and zucchini mimic the shape of the spaghetti in this dish. Feel free to substitute your favorite pasta for the whole wheat version featured here. You can also substitute crookneck squash for yellow zucchini.

  ½ pound whole wheat spaghetti
  3 carrots
  3 green zucchini

3 yellow zucchini
1 tablespoon olive oil
1 tablespoon butter
2 cloves garlic, minced
1½ cups packed fresh basil, minced
¾ cup parsley, minced
½ cup fresh chives, minced
2 tablespoons fresh marjoram, minced
¾ teaspoon salt
½ cup grated Parmesan cheese

1. Bring a large pot of salted water to a boil over high heat; cook spaghetti until tender (about 12 minutes). Drain thoroughly. Peel carrots. Cut carrots and green and yellow zucchini into long, thin julienne strips (about ⅛ inch thick) to resemble spaghetti.

2. In a Dutch oven or large skillet, heat oil and butter over low heat. Add garlic and carrots. Sauté for 5 to 7 minutes. Add spaghetti, green and yellow zucchini, basil, parsley, chives, marjoram, and salt. Stir to combine and cook for 4 to 5 minutes. Remove from heat and place in a shallow serving bowl. Sprinkle with Parmesan cheese. Toss to combine. Serve immediately.

Serves 6 to 8.

PASTA SHELLS WITH PEAS AND CHICKEN

Try this colorful recipe in the summer-time, when fresh peas are ripe off the vine and bursting with flavor. This low-fat recipe can be made ahead of time and baked when ready to serve.

4 cups small pasta shells
2 cups slivered cooked chicken, skinned
2 teaspoons olive oil
½ cup shelled peas
1 tablespoon minced garlic
2 tablespoons chopped fresh basil
2 tablespoons chopped fresh thyme or 1 teaspoon dried thyme
3 tablespoons chopped parsley
¼ cup minced red bell pepper
¼ cup grated Parmesan cheese

1. In a large pot over high heat, bring 2 quarts of water to a boil and cook pasta shells until almost done (about 5 minutes). Drain and rinse under cold water, then set aside. Preheat oven to 400° F.

2. In a large skillet over medium-high heat, sauté chicken in olive oil for 2 minutes, then add peas, garlic, basil, thyme, parsley, and bell pepper. Cook 2 minutes more, then pour mixture into large

TIPS

. . . ON COOKING PASTA

☐ Both fresh and dried pasta require a large amount of boiling water, about 1 quart to every 2 cups of pasta you are cooking. Salting the water helps it boil faster and adds a little flavor to the pasta, but it is not essential if your diet precludes salt. Adding a small amount of oil to the boiling water helps the pasta strands stay separate.

☐ The trick to successful pasta is the cooking time, which differs considerably between fresh and packaged types. Once the water has boiled, cook dried fettucine and other wide noodles for 7 to 8 minutes, lasagne for 8 to 10 minutes, and fine pasta (such as angel hair) for 5 to 7 minutes, or until al dente. Fresh pasta cooks in only two minutes.

☐ If you're serving immediately, you can drain the freshly cooked pasta and toss it with the sauce or vegetables right away.

☐ If you're not serving for 10 minutes or more, it is advisable to rinse the pasta after cooking. (Pasta continues cooking even after it's out of the pot; unless it's rinsed, it can be surprisingly overcooked by the time you serve it.) Keep the pot of cooking water hot, remove pasta from water using tongs or pasta fork, and refresh it quickly under cold tap water. When it is time to serve, dip the pasta back into the heated water, drain again, and voilà: perfectly cooked pasta every time.

Olive oil, garlic, and fresh basil flavor this savory, low-fat dish of Pasta Shells with Peas and Chicken.

baking dish. Add pasta shells and toss well. Add Parmesan. Bake for 20 minutes. Serve hot.

Serves 4.

PASTA WITH FRESH TUNA

This brassy Sicilian sauce is not for delicate palates. Garlic, anchovies, capers, and olives enliven its fresh-tomato base; strips of tuna are tossed in at the last minute. This is a summer dish, to precede grilled fish or grilled shrimp.

> 4 cups fresh bread crumbs
> ½ cup minced parsley
> ¼ cup grated Romano cheese
> 8 ounces fresh tuna fillet, cut into strips approximately ¼ by ¼ by 2 ½ inches long
> Freshly ground pepper, to taste
> 3 tablespoons olive oil
> ⅓ cup minced onion
> 1 tablespoon minced garlic
> 3 anchovy fillets, minced
> 1 pound plum tomatoes, peeled, seeded, and chopped (see page 56)
> 1 tablespoon capers
> ¼ cup pitted green olives
> 1 pound elbow macaroni

1. Combine bread crumbs, parsley, and cheese in a small bowl. Set aside. Season tuna lightly with pepper.

2. Heat olive oil in a large skillet over medium heat. Add onion and garlic and sauté 3 minutes. Add anchovies and mash them with a wooden spoon until they "melt" into the garlic and onions. Add tomatoes. Cover partially and simmer 15 minutes. Raise heat to medium-high, add tuna, and toss quickly, cooking just until tuna is barely done. Stir in capers and olives, cook 30 seconds, cover, and remove from heat. Taste and adjust seasoning as necessary.

3. Cook pasta in a large pot of boiling water until just tender (8 to 10 minutes). Drain thoroughly and transfer to a warm serving bowl. Add half the bread-crumb mixture and toss well. Ladle the sauce over the top, then garnish with the remaining bread-crumb mixture.

Serves 4.

THE VERSATILE EGG

It used to be that when the cupboard was otherwise bare, you could always count on scrambled eggs for a quick meal, whether breakfast, lunch, or dinner. The lowly egg also achieved elegance in after-theater omelet suppers. These days not all of us eat as many eggs as we used to because of dietary concerns. But most of us still enjoy them, although perhaps only occasionally. Egg dishes make wonderful light meals, especially when blended with other pantry staples such as potatoes, cheese, peppers, and vegetables.

POTATO-BASIL FRITTATA

This simple pepper and potato omelet is based on the famous Spanish dish, *tortilla española.*

> 2 large boiling potatoes (about 1 lb)
> 1 small onion
> 1 red bell pepper
> 1 green bell pepper
> 1 bunch basil (15 to 20 large leaves)
> 1 tablespoon olive oil
> 5 eggs
> ¾ teaspoon salt
> ½ teaspoon freshly ground pepper
> 2 tablespoons grated Parmesan cheese (optional)

1. Preheat oven to 350° F. Oil a 9-inch-round, 2-inch-deep baking dish. Wash and quarter potatoes, and place in a small saucepan. Cover with water and bring to a boil. Reduce heat and simmer for 12 minutes. Remove potatoes from pan, cool, and slice into ¼-inch-thick rounds.

2. Peel onion, and slice into 1/4-inch-thick strips. Seed bell peppers and slice into ¼-inch-thick strips. Slice basil into thin strips.

3. Heat olive oil in a large sauté pan, and cook onion and peppers for 8 to 10 minutes over medium heat. Add potatoes and basil and cook 1 minute more.

4. Beat eggs with salt and pepper in a large bowl. Add onion-pepper-potato mixture. Mix well and pour into prepared pan. Sprinkle with cheese (if used), and

bake until top is dry and lightly golden (45 to 50 minutes).

Serves 4.

GREEN CHILE SOUFFLÉ

This quick soufflé is equally good as breakfast, brunch, or late-night supper. A 27-ounce can of whole green chiles can be used when fresh chiles are unavailable.

> 1 teaspoon butter
> 20 fresh Anaheim or California long green chiles
> 1 jalapeño chile
> 4 eggs
> ½ teaspoon salt
> ¼ cup flour
> 3 cups cooked brown rice
> 6 ounces Monterey jack cheese, grated

1. Preheat oven to 400° F. Butter a shallow, 1 ½-quart oval gratin dish.

2. Roast and peel Anaheim chiles (see page 67). Pat dry. Remove stem from jalapeño chile.

3. Separate egg yolks from egg whites. Reserve egg whites. Place yolks, 5 Anaheim chiles, jalapeño chile, salt, and flour in a blender or food processor. Process until smooth. Place egg whites in a 5-quart mixing bowl, and beat until soft peaks form. Stir one third of the egg whites into chile-egg mixture. Fold in remaining egg whites.

4. Place 5 Anaheim chiles in bottom of prepared dish. Cover with one third of the rice, one third of the cheese, and one third of the chile-egg mixture. Finish with the last 5 Anaheim chiles and the remaining rice, the cheese, and the chile-egg mixture.

5. Bake until top is golden brown (30 to 35 minutes). Serve immediately.

Serves 8.

JOE'S SPECIAL

San Francisco has had a number of restaurants named Joe's, all claiming to be the "original" Joe's and all featuring some variation of the following recipe. According to local legend, the dish was concocted when a hungry patron arrived at the end of a particularly busy night.

About all the cook had left was eggs, spinach, and hamburger (sausage in some versions of the story)... and Joe's Special was born.

1 ½ tablespoons olive oil
  1 pound ground beef, crumbled
  1 large onion, finely chopped
  1 clove garlic, minced
  ¼ pound mushrooms, sliced
  1 teaspoon salt
  ⅛ teaspoon each freshly ground
       pepper and dried oregano
     Pinch ground nutmeg
  2 cups coarsely chopped fresh
       spinach
  3 eggs
     Freshly grated Parmesan cheese

1. In a large skillet over high heat, heat olive oil and brown ground beef well.

2. Add onion, garlic, and mushrooms; reduce heat and continue cooking, stirring occasionally, until onion is soft. Stir in salt, pepper, oregano, nutmeg, and spinach; cook for about 5 minutes longer, stirring several times, until spinach is limp.

3. Reduce heat to low and break eggs over meat mixture; quickly stir just until eggs begin to set. Serve immediately, with cheese to sprinkle over each serving to taste.

Serves 3 to 4.

HANGTOWN FRY

Dating back to California Gold Rush Days, this classic Western oyster, bacon, and egg dish is a sort of frittata.

  6 slices bacon, cut in halves
  ¼ cup butter
  1 jar (10 oz) small oysters
  6 eggs
     Flour
  ⅓ cup fine dry bread crumbs
  1 tablespoon water
  ½ teaspoon salt
     Pinch white pepper
  1 tablespoon finely chopped parsley

1. In a medium nonstick frying pan, cook bacon until crisp and brown; remove bacon, drain, and keep warm. Discard bacon drippings. Add 3 tablespoons of the butter to pan, swirling until melted.

This version of Joe's Special features a mixture of ground beef, onion, mushrooms, and fresh spinach topped with Parmesan cheese.

Lightly cooked oysters in a bacon-topped frittata combine to create Hangtown Fry, a favorite from the Old West.

65

STEP BY STEP

HOW TO COOK AN OMELET

1. Coat a hot omelet pan with butter and add beaten eggs. Swirl pan with one hand while stirring eggs in a circular motion with a fork (tines of fork should be parallel to but not touching bottom of pan).

2. When omelet begins to set, rapidly push cooked egg toward center of pan, allowing uncooked egg to run underneath. The omelet is ready when it is firm on the bottom but still moist in the center. Total cooking time is about 30 seconds.

3. Tilt pan slightly away from you and fold bottom third of omelet (side closest to you) toward center.

4. Holding pan in one hand at a 45-degree angle and a warm serving plate in the other hand, also at a 45-degree angle, carefully slide top third of omelet onto plate.

5. Raise angle of pan even more to allow rest of omelet to roll over onto top third.

2. While bacon cooks, drain oysters and pat dry. Beat 1 of the eggs in a medium bowl. Coat oysters first with flour, then with egg, and finally with bread crumbs. Add oysters to melted butter in pan and cook over medium-low heat until brown on first side. Turn to brown second side.

3. As oysters brown, add to the egg in which oysters were dipped the remaining 5 eggs, water, salt, and white pepper. Beat until frothy and well combined (about 30 seconds). After turning oysters, sprinkle with parsley, and then pour beaten eggs into frying pan.

4. Pour egg mixture into pan and cook without stirring until about ¼ inch around the outer edge is set. With a wide spatula, lift some of the egg mixture from sides of pan, all the way around, tipping pan to let uncooked egg flow to pan bottom. When eggs are nearly set, cover pan with a large plate, invert eggs and oysters onto it, and add remaining 1 tablespoon butter to pan. Swirl until melted. Slide eggs back into pan and cook until bottom is lightly browned.

5. Cut in wedges and serve from pan, or invert onto warm serving plate and cut in wedges. Serve with bacon.

Serves 4.

BARBARA'S SOUTHWEST TORTA

If it is more convenient, prepare this colorful and simple *torta* ahead and warm in a 350° F oven for 20 minutes before serving.

     5 tablespoons butter, melted
     7 flour tortillas (10-in. diameter)
     1 pound ground sausage
     1 onion, diced
     1 red bell pepper, diced
     1 jalapeño chile, diced
     1 teaspoon chili powder
  1 ¼ teaspoons salt
     ¼ teaspoon dried oregano
     1 tablespoon toasted cumin seed
     1 can (15 oz) cooked black beans
     ¾ cup (6 oz) grated Monterey jack
          cheese
     8 eggs, beaten
     ¼ teaspoon freshly ground pepper
     3 green onions, diced

STEP BY STEP

ROASTING BELL PEPPERS AND CHILES

To remove the papery outer skin of bell peppers and chiles, first blister the skin thoroughly, then let the vegetables steam until cool in a tightly closed bag. Peeled bell peppers are delicious in salads, pasta dishes, and sandwiches; peeled whole chiles can be seeded and stuffed, minced, or puréed for use in such dishes as salsas, soups, and stews.

1. Char peppers over an open gas flame or charcoal fire or under a broiler. Turn often until blackened on all sides. Transfer peppers to a paper or plastic bag; close and let steam until cool (15 to 20 minutes).

2. Peel peppers; halve; remove stem and seeds. Lay halves flat and use dull side of a small knife to scrape away any bits of black skin and stray seeds.

1. Preheat oven to 350° F. Line a 9-inch springform pan with aluminum foil. Brush foil with 1 tablespoon melted butter. Place 5 tortillas around perimeter of foil-lined pan. Place 1 tortilla in center of pan to cover bottom entirely. Brush tortillas with melted butter.

2. In a large skillet over medium heat, sauté sausage until browned and crumbly (about 10 minutes). Add onion, bell pepper, chile, chili powder, ¼ teaspoon salt, oregano, and cumin seed, and cook until onion is tender (about 10 minutes).

3. Place sausage mixture in tortilla-lined baking dish; reserve cooking pan. Cover sausage with beans and Monterey jack.

4. In reserved skillet over medium heat, add remaining 2 tablespoons butter and scramble eggs. Stir in remaining salt, pepper, and green onions, undercooking eggs slightly. Press eggs over beans and cheese. Place remaining tortilla over eggs and brush with remaining butter. Place in oven and bake 25 minutes. Cool 5 minutes before serving. To unmold, loosen edge with a knife; remove pan sides. Loosen pan bottom, then remove. Peel away foil. Cut torta into 8 wedges and serve.

Serves 8.

Fresh vegetables and pasta are combined in a light cheese sauce to create Baked Macaroni Primavera, an elegantly simple springtime main course.

THE MAIN COURSE

A main course is the heart of the menu. But while it may need more time to put together than other courses, it shouldn't be so demanding that the cook never leaves the kitchen. That's the rationale behind the recipes in this chapter: poultry, fish, meat, and vegetable main courses with star quality but without prima-donna preparation. You'll even find directions for a traditional Thanksgiving dinner with turkey, stuffing, and all the trimmings that can be organized in a day (see page 76).

POULTRY

For universal acceptability, economy, and ease of preparation, nothing beats poultry as a main-course choice. Even turkey, once available mostly during one season, is now a year-round bird in response to consumer demand. What makes poultry even more appealing is that we can buy it in so many forms: whole, halves, parts, ground, with bone, or without. Boneless chicken breast halves are very popular because they are so convenient and quick-cooking. Three recipes in this section use them: Cheese-Crusted Chicken (see page 70), Chicken Breasts With Green Peppercorn Sauce (see page 70), and Chicken Italienne (see page 71). Cut-up turkey is another convenience food now readily available at meat counters today. Curried Turkey Breast (see page 73) is a flavorful turkey-breast roast, while Grilled Turkey Fillets With Cilantro Butter and Salsa (see page 74) features boneless turkey fillets that pick up special flavor from the grill.

CHEESE-CRUSTED CHICKEN

The flavor secret of this chicken sauté is in its coating of flour, bread crumbs, and Swiss cheese. It is a perfect picnic dish because it is as good cold as it is hot. Have a spatula nearby while the breasts are browning—as the cheese coating melts, it may stick to the pan.

---

4 boneless chicken breast halves, skinned
1 1/4 cups flour
1/2 teaspoon salt
1/8 teaspoon each ground nutmeg and pepper
1 egg, lightly beaten
2/3 cup grated Swiss, Gruyère, or Emmenthaler cheese
1/2 cup dry bread crumbs
1/4 cup butter
1 lemon, cut in wedges, for garnish

1. Pound breasts lightly to flatten to a uniform 1/4 inch thick; set aside.

2. Sift together flour, salt, nutmeg, and pepper; set aside. Have beaten egg in a pie pan. Mix together cheese and bread crumbs; set aside.

3. Coat breast halves with seasoned flour, shaking off excess. Dip in egg, then in cheese-crumb mixture, coating well.

4. In a large, heavy-bottomed skillet over medium heat, melt butter. Add chicken and sauté until golden brown on both sides (about 5 minutes per side). Drain on paper towels. Serve with lemon wedges.

Serves 4.

CHICKEN BREASTS WITH GREEN PEPPERCORN SAUCE

Unripe (green) peppercorns, sold in most gourmet stores, have a slightly less acidic taste than white or black pepper. They are used whole in this recipe, enhanced by a sweet wine and cream sauce.

4 boneless chicken breast halves, skinned
1 teaspoon vegetable oil
1/4 cup dry sherry
2 tablespoons minced onion
1/4 cup white wine
1/2 cup half-and-half
1 tablespoon green peppercorns
1/4 teaspoon dried tarragon

1. Preheat oven to 400° F. In a large skillet over medium-high heat, sauté chicken breasts in oil and sherry until lightly browned on both sides. Transfer to a baking dish; bake 15 minutes.

2. While chicken is baking, in the same skillet over medium heat, sauté onion in pan drippings until soft. Add wine, half-and-half, peppercorns, and tarragon. Heat until sauce coats the back of a spoon. Serve over baked chicken.

Serves 4.

A sherry sauté provides a healthful way to achieve the rich taste of classic French cooking in this recipe for Chicken Breasts With Green Peppercorn Sauce.

CHICKEN ITALIENNE

This do-ahead dish–pretty pinwheels of chicken, prosciutto, and cheese–is perfect buffet food. Serve warm with a rice pilaf or cold with a pasta salad.

> 8 boneless chicken breast halves, skinned
> 1 teaspoon salt
> ½ teaspoon freshly ground pepper
> ½ cup Pesto Sauce (see page 115)
> 8 slices prosciutto (Italian ham)
> ½ pound provolone cheese, cut into 8 pieces
> 2 eggs, beaten
> 1½ cups toasted bread crumbs
> ½ cup butter, melted

1. Pound chicken breasts lightly to flatten to a uniform ¼ inch thick. Season with salt and pepper.

2. Spread each chicken breast with 1 tablespoon Pesto Sauce. Place a strip of prosciutto on each pesto-covered breast. Place 1 piece provolone at narrow end of breast.

3. Roll up each breast to form a cylinder, enclosing the cheese. Roll cylinder in egg, then bread crumbs. Chill 30 to 60 minutes.

4. Preheat oven to 350° F. Place cold chicken breast rolls on an ungreased baking sheet. Pour melted butter over rolls and bake for 1 hour. Remove from baking sheet and slice each roll diagonally into 3 pieces, to show spiral of prosciutto, cheese, and chicken.

Serves 8.

HONEY-GLAZED BAKED CHICKEN QUARTERS

Put the chicken in the oven for its initial baking right after you come home from work. The sweet-and-sour glaze is quickly prepared and a special family or company dinner can be on the table in a little over an hour.

> ⅓ cup flour
> 1 teaspoon garlic salt
>   Dash freshly ground pepper
> 1 chicken (3 to 3 ½ lbs), quartered
> 6 tablespoons butter
> ¼ cup honey

> 3 tablespoons lemon juice
> 2 tablespoons soy sauce
>   Dash ground ginger

1. Preheat oven to 350° F. Mix flour, garlic salt, and pepper, then coat chicken quarters thoroughly. Put 2 tablespoons of the butter in a shallow baking dish just large enough to hold the chicken in a single layer; put dish in oven to melt butter while oven preheats. Arrange chicken, skin side down, in melted butter. Bake, uncovered, 30 minutes.

2. Meanwhile, melt remaining 4 tablespoons butter with honey, lemon juice, soy sauce, and ginger. After 30 minutes remove chicken from oven, turn skin side up, and cover with butter mixture. Continue baking, brushing occasionally with butter-honey sauce, until chicken is tender and richly browned (30 to 40 minutes more). Serve immediately.

Serves 4.

This recipe for Honey-Glazed Baked Chicken Quarters features a sweet-and-sour glaze of honey, lemon juice, soy sauce, and ginger.

STEP BY STEP

HOW TO SAUTÉ AND DEGLAZE

The following sequence shows how to sauté Turkey Piccata (opposite page) and make a simple deglazing sauce from the pan juices and the browned, crusty bits that form on the bottom of the pan.

1. *Place a large, heavy skillet or sauté pan over medium-high heat. Coat with butter and oil. Place floured turkey cutlets in butter-oil mixture. Leave some space between pieces of food (¼ to ½ inch) so that food will brown and not steam.*

2. *Cook cutlets in butter-oil mixture until lightly browned on first side. With a spatula, turn cutlet and cook second side until lightly browned. Thicker pieces of turkey cutlet will require a longer cooking time. Remove cutlets to a serving plate and cover loosely with aluminum foil to keep warm while the sauce is made.*

3. *To prepare a pan sauce, add lemon juice to natural juices left in pan from sautéing turkey.*

4. *Stir and scrape bottom of pan to loosen any flavorful browned bits of turkey or flour coating stuck to the pan. Cook briefly to blend flavors.*

5. *For a more refined sauce, strain through a fine-mesh wire sieve. Season with salt and pepper to taste. Stir in parsley and capers. Pour sauce over turkey cutlets and serve immediately.*

BROCCOLI-CHICKEN POT PIE

Deep-dish pie goes elegant with a topping of puff pastry. Cut out decorative shapes from pastry scraps and fasten to pastry lid with egg wash.

>   1 pound broccoli, cut into florets
>   4 tablespoons butter
>   1 onion, diced
>   2 cloves garlic, minced
>   4 tablespoons flour
>   2 cups chicken stock or milk
>   1 1/2 teaspoons salt
>   1/2 teaspoon freshly ground pepper
>   1 1/2 teaspoons dried thyme
>   1/8 teaspoon ground nutmeg
>   1 jar (4 oz) roasted red peppers, drained and diced
>   3 cooked chicken breast halves, skinned and shredded
>   1 sheet prepared puff pastry (thawed if frozen)
>   Egg wash (1 egg yolk and 1 tablespoon water, beaten together), for glazing

1. In a large saucepan, bring 4 quarts water to a boil. Blanch broccoli florets in boiling water until bright green (3 minutes). Drain in a colander and drop into ice water to stop cooking and set color. Pat dry and reserve.

2. In another large saucepan over medium heat, melt butter. Sauté onion and garlic until onion is translucent but not browned (3 to 4 minutes). Whisk in flour and cook until mixture thickens and starts to turn golden brown (about 2 minutes). Whisk in stock and cook, stirring constantly, until thickened (about 3 minutes). Season with salt, pepper, thyme, and nutmeg. Stir in reserved broccoli, roasted peppers, and shredded chicken.

3. Preheat oven to 400° F. Butter a shallow 2-quart baking dish. Fill with broccoli-chicken filling. Roll out puff pastry sheet slightly larger than baking dish. Brush edge of underside of pastry with egg wash; set over filling and press pastry edge all around to adhere to baking dish. Brush top of pastry with egg wash. Bake until pastry has puffed slightly and is golden brown (30 to 35 minutes). Serve immediately.

Serves 4 to 6.

MUSTARD MADNESS

This recipe is designed for a vertical roaster—an upright, stainless steel frame used to roast chicken and smaller birds. The vertical roaster cooks poultry faster than conventional methods because the metal frame is an excellent heat conductor. The bird cooks from inside as well as outside, sealing in the natural juices.

After cooking, large game hens can be halved to make four servings: With a sharp knife or poultry shears, begin to cut at the breastbone and continue along this line all the way around the bird.

>   2 Cornish game hens (1 to 1 1/2 lbs each)
>   Salt, to taste
>   Dijon-style mustard, to taste

1. Preheat oven to 450° F. Wash and dry game hens. Salt inside and out.

2. Set vertical roasters in a roasting pan containing 1/4 inch of water. Lower game hens onto roasters. Fasten wings to body of each bird. Paint each game hen with plenty of mustard.

3. Set pan on middle rack of oven and roast for 30 minutes. When birds are done, remove from oven and allow to rest 15 to 30 minutes on frames. Remove from frames to serve.

4. Serve accompanied with additional mustard.

Serves 2 to 4.

TURKEY CHILI BURRITOS

This chili, made with small chunks of turkey, is seasoned perfectly and wrapped in warm flour tortillas. Serve this fast and easy entrée with salsa and chopped cilantro.

>   1 cup minced onion
>   1 teaspoon vegetable oil
>   1/2 cup chicken stock
>   1 tablespoon minced garlic
>   4 cups diced skinless turkey meat
>   1/2 cup diced celery
>   1/2 cup chopped carrot
>   1/4 cup minced parsley
>   1 cup diced tomatoes
>   1 cup water
>   1/2 teaspoon ground cloves
>   2 tablespoons chili powder, or to taste
>   1/2 teaspoon hot-pepper sauce
>   4 ounces canned green chiles, chopped
>   Salt and freshly ground pepper, to taste
>   12 flour tortillas
>   1/2 cup grated Cheddar cheese
>   Chopped cilantro, for garnish
>   South-of-the-Border Salsa (see page 114), for accompaniment

1. In a Dutch oven over medium-high heat, sauté onion in oil and stock until soft. Add garlic, turkey, celery, carrot, parsley, and tomatoes and sauté, stirring frequently, for 10 minutes.

2. Add the water, cloves, chili powder, hot-pepper sauce, and green chiles. Lower heat, cover, and cook for 25 minutes. Taste for seasoning and add salt and pepper, if needed.

3. Wrap tortillas in aluminum foil and warm in a 325° F oven 10 minutes.

4. To serve, spoon approximately 1/3 cup chili into each tortilla, cover with grated cheese, sprinkle with cilantro, top with salsa, and roll.

Serves 6.

TURKEY PICCATA

Turkey cutlets (turkey breast sliced about 1/4 inch thick) are substituted for the more traditional and expensive veal in this recipe. If you wish to use veal scallops, which are much thinner, reduce the cooking time by half.

>   6 tablespoons flour
>   1/2 teaspoon salt
>   1/2 teaspoon ground white pepper
>   4 boneless turkey cutlets (about 1 1/2 lb total), sliced 1/4 inch thick
>   2 tablespoons butter
>   2 tablespoons olive oil
>   Juice of 1 lemon
>   Salt and ground white pepper, to taste
>   3 tablespoons minced parsley
>   2 tablespoons capers, drained

1. Sift together flour, salt, and pepper. Dredge turkey cutlets in flour mixture.

2. In a large skillet over medium heat, swirl butter and oil. Sauté cutlets in butter-oil mixture until lightly browned (4 minutes). Turn and cook second side until lightly browned (about 3 minutes). Thicker pieces of turkey cutlet will need to cook a bit longer.

3. Remove cutlets to a serving plate and cover loosely with aluminum foil. Add lemon juice to pan to deglaze, stirring to loosen any flavorful browned bits in pan. Season with salt and pepper. Stir in parsley and capers and pour sauce over cutlets.

Serves 6.

CURRIED TURKEY BREAST

Skin the turkey breasts, then let the meat marinate for several hours in the spice mixture. It will roast to a juicy turn.

> *2 large turkey breasts, skinned*
> *½ teaspoon each ground coriander, paprika, and cumin*
> *¼ teaspoon each ground turmeric, cayenne pepper, and cinnamon*
> *2 tablespoons grated fresh ginger*
> *1 tablespoon olive oil*
> *2 tablespoons lemon juice*
> *½ cup nonfat plain yogurt*
> *Minced green onions, for garnish*

1. Place turkey breasts in a large baking pan. In a small bowl, combine coriander, paprika, cumin, turmeric, cayenne, cinnamon, fresh ginger, olive oil, lemon juice, and yogurt. Spread over top of turkey breasts. Cover pan with plastic wrap and refrigerate for 2 hours.

2. Preheat oven to 350° F. Bake turkey, uncovered, for 40 minutes, basting occasionally with pan juices. To serve, slice turkey, drizzle with pan juices, and garnish with green onions.

Serves 4.

GRILLED TURKEY FILLETS WITH CILANTRO BUTTER AND SALSA

The mild flavor of turkey is a perfect foil for Mexican seasonings like fresh cilantro and spicy salsa. Prepare the salsa ahead so the flavors will blend.

> *4 turkey fillets, halved lengthwise*
> *Cilantro Butter (see page 75)*
> *South-of-the-Border Salsa (see page 114), for accompaniment*

1. Prepare a charcoal fire; lay turkey fillets diagonally across grill bars. When fillets are seared, lift them and set back on grill along opposite diagonal. When diamond pattern appears on the surface, turn fillets over and sear diamond pattern onto other side.

2. Grill 5 inches from heat, brushing both sides of fillets with Cilantro Butter, about 8 minutes.

3. Serve dotted with remaining Cilantro Butter and accompanied with salsa.

Serves 6 to 8.

FISH

The current culinary emphasis on meals that are light, nutritious, fresh, and easy to prepare makes fish an obvious main-course choice. Fish takes less time to cook than just about any other type of food, making it perfect for quick family meals or for easy, elegant entertaining. Because of improved transportation, refrigeration, and freezing methods, a wide choice of species is now available across the country. Any of the recipes in this section make special company meals. Try Cornmeal-Crusted Orange Roughy (see page 79), a very simple skillet preparation that produces juicy fish fillets with a crunchy, crusty coating; or Scallops en Papillote (see page 80), cooked and served with aromatic fennel, tomatoes, and herbs in foil packages; or Teriyaki Shrimp (see page 80), an easy Asian stir-fry that needs only rice to complete the meal.

FISH IN MOROCCAN CHARMOULA SAUCE

For more flavor, let the fish marinate in the sauce for 30 minutes before baking; baste with the sauce as the fish cooks.

> *3 pounds firm fish fillets*
> *4 potatoes, roasted and sliced*
> *2 green peppers, sliced and sautéed briefly*
> *2 tomatoes, sliced*
> *Salt and freshly ground pepper, to taste*
> *1 lemon*

Charmoula Sauce

> *½ cup chopped cilantro*
> *½ cup chopped parsley*
> *5 cloves garlic, finely chopped*
> *5 tablespoons lemon juice*
> *1 ½ teaspoons salt*
> *1 teaspoon paprika*
> *⅓ teaspoon ground cumin*
> *Cayenne pepper, to taste*
> *½ cup or more olive oil*

1. Preheat oven to 425° F. Prepare Charmoula Sauce. In a 9- by 13-inch baking pan, lay roasted potato slices, sautéed green peppers, and sliced tomatoes. Arrange fish fillets on top of the vegetables. Season with salt and pepper and top with Charmoula Sauce. Add a squeeze of lemon.

2. Bake until fish is done (10 to 15 minutes, depending on size of fish).

Serves 6 to 8.

Charmoula Sauce Combine cilantro, parsley, garlic, lemon juice, salt, paprika, cumin, and cayenne. Add enough olive oil to make a thick sauce.

BAKED SALMON PROVENÇALE

In this hearty dish from Provence, salmon steaks are sautéed in a savory sauce of tomatoes, herbs, and olives, then baked briefly until done. Serve with rice and a fresh vegetable.

> *4 salmon steaks (¾ in. thick)*
> *1 teaspoon unsalted butter*
> *1 teaspoon olive oil*
> *1 gram (2 teaspoons) saffron threads*
> *1 tablespoon minced garlic*

½ teaspoon dried tarragon
¼ teaspoon dried thyme
Pinch of dried sage
2 bay leaves, crushed
1 cup coarsely chopped plum tomatoes
8 to 10 Greek olives, pitted and chopped
1¼ cups white wine
1 cup fish stock or bottled clam juice
1 teaspoon salt

1. Preheat oven to 400° F. In a large, deep, ovenproof skillet or stovetop casserole over medium-high heat, sauté salmon briefly (about 1 minute) on each side in butter and oil. Remove to a platter. Add saffron, garlic, tarragon, thyme, sage, bay leaves, tomatoes, olives, wine, stock, and salt to skillet. Bring to a boil, lower heat and simmer for 10 minutes, uncovered.

2. Add salmon steaks. Remove pan from heat and place in oven. Bake until salmon is lightly pink and done to taste (10 minutes).

3. To serve, place salmon steaks on platter and spoon sauce over them.

Serves 4.

GRILLED SWORDFISH WITH CILANTRO BUTTER

The beauty of grilling is rarely more evident than when cooking impeccably fresh swordfish over hot, smoky, mesquite charcoal. Be sure to buy fillets of uniform thickness so they will cook evenly.

4 center-cut fillets fresh swordfish (8 oz each)
2 tablespoons olive oil

Cilantro Butter

1 bunch cilantro
½ cup unsalted butter
Juice of 1 lemon
Salt and freshly ground pepper, to taste

1. Prepare a charcoal fire. Swordfish is especially good cooked over mesquite charcoal, although other types of fuel are fine.

2. Lightly coat fillets with olive oil. When fire is ready, place fish on oiled grill and cook until just firm to the touch (about 4 minutes per side for thick fillets, less for thinner fillets; don't overcook). Serve immediately with Cilantro Butter.

Cilantro Butter Wash cilantro thoroughly and remove thick stems. Combine with butter in food processor or blender with metal blade and mix for several seconds until light and fluffy. Blend in lemon juice. Season with salt and pepper.

Makes ⅔ cup.

The flavors of Provence–tomatoes, Italian herbs, and olives–highlight Baked Salmon Provençale.

Sumptuous Grilled Swordfish With Cilantro Butter exemplifies the simple beauty of perfectly grilled foods.

MENU

SPEEDY THANKSGIVING FEAST

For 12 to 16

Rapid Roast Turkey With Cream Gravy
Cranberry and Corn Bread Stuffing
Old-fashioned Mashed Potatoes
Steamed Broccoli With Toasted
*   Hazelnuts*
Fresh Fruit Salad
Sweet Potato and Cinnamon Muffins
Chris's Pumpkin Pecan Pie
Zinfandel and Sparkling Apple Cider

Holiday dinners are always easier when preparation is shared by many willing hands. Once in a while, though, either because of an emergency or a last-minute change, you may find that you are responsible for the entire meal. Make the best of it, and ensure success by simplifying as much of the meal as possible and by being well organized (see Get Ready, Get Set, Relax, page 2). The only appetizers you need are olives, carrot sticks, celery, and Creole Pecans (see page 10).

RAPID ROAST TURKEY WITH CREAM GRAVY

Removing the backbone of the turkey and pressing bird as flat as possible in the pan reduces roasting time by half. Purchase a fresh turkey to avoid thawing time.

> *1 turkey (16 lb)*
> *½ cup butter, melted*
> *2 cloves garlic, minced*

Cream Gravy

> *Turkey backbone, wing tips, and*
> *   giblets*
> *1 onion, quartered*
> *1 carrot, coarsely chopped*
> *1 bay leaf*
> *1 sprig parsley*

> *1 teaspoon dried thyme*
> *6 tablespoons butter*
> *6 tablespoons flour*
> *2 cups whipping cream*
> *2 teaspoons salt*
> *½ teaspoon ground white pepper*
> *¼ teaspoon ground nutmeg*

1. Preheat oven to 400° F. Place turkey, breast side down, on a cutting surface. Using poultry shears or sturdy kitchen scissors, remove backbone from turkey by cutting along each side of backbone. Cut off wing tips. Reserve backbone, wing tips, and giblets for Cream Gravy.

2. Place turkey in roasting pan. Push legs down slightly so that they are flat in pan. Stir butter and garlic together in a small bowl; pour over turkey.

3. Roast turkey 15 minutes; reduce heat to 375° F and roast until 170° F on an instant-read thermometer and exterior of bird is a rich dark brown and juices run clear when joint is moved (about 2 hours and 20 minutes). After first hour baste turkey with pan juices from roasting pan. While turkey is roasting begin gravy.

4. Place roast turkey on carving board. Loosely cover with aluminum foil and let rest for 15 to 20 minutes before carving to maintain moisture of turkey and make it easier to carve. Strain pan juices into turkey broth (see next page).

5. Carve turkey and serve piping hot with Cream Gravy.

Serves 16 to 20.

Cream Gravy In a large saucepan place backbone, wing tips, and giblets, onion, carrot, bay leaf, parsley, and thyme, and cover with water. Bring to a boil, reduce heat, and simmer for 30 minutes. Remove from heat and strain turkey broth into a mixing bowl. Discard turkey pieces. Stir in strained pan juices from roasted turkey. In a large saucepan over medium heat, melt butter. Whisk in flour, mixing until well combined and cooked (about 2 minutes). Add reserved turkey broth mixture and whisk until smooth. Cook over medium heat until reduced slightly (10 minutes). Whisk in whipping cream and cook another 10 minutes. Season with salt, pepper, and nutmeg.

Makes about 6 cups.

CRANBERRY AND CORN BREAD STUFFING

Cranberries, walnuts, and corn bread mingle to make a superb stuffing for turkey, pork roast, and roast chicken. This stuffing is particularly appropriate for Thanksgiving. Corn and cranberries are native American foods that were part of the Indian diet when the Pilgrims arrived in the New World. If desired, add 8 ounces chopped fresh oysters to the stuffing mixture.

> 4 *tablespoons butter*
> 1 *carrot, minced*
> 1 *stalk celery, minced*
> 1 *medium onion, minced*
> ¼ *cup minced parsley*
> 3 *tablespoons dried whole sage leaves*
> 2 *teaspoons salt*
> 1 *teaspoon freshly ground pepper*
> 1 *cup cranberries*
> 1 *cup toasted walnuts*
> 3 *cups hot turkey broth, chicken stock, or water*

Quick Corn Bread

> 4 *tablespoons butter, plus butter for greasing pan*

> 1 *cup milk*
> 2 *eggs*
> 1 *cup flour*
> 1½ *teaspoons baking powder*
> 2 *teaspoons salt*
> 1½ *teaspoons sugar*
> 1 *cup cornmeal*

1. Prepare corn bread; let cool. In a large skillet over medium heat, melt butter; add carrot, celery, and onion and sauté until softened and cooked thoroughly (10 minutes).

2. Cut corn bread in 1-inch cubes. In a large bowl toss corn bread cubes with cooked carrot, celery, onion, parsley, sage, salt, and pepper. Add cranberries and walnuts. Mix in turkey broth.

3. Preheat oven to 350° F (or turn heat down to 350° F while turkey rests). Place stuffing in a 3-quart casserole and cover loosely with aluminum foil. Bake until hot (about 30 minutes).

Makes 10 cups stuffing, 12 to 16 servings.

Quick Corn Bread Preheat oven to 400° F. Butter an 8-inch square baking pan. In a small bowl combine the 4 tablespoons butter, milk, and eggs. In a medium bowl, sift together flour, baking powder, salt, and sugar; stir in cornmeal and make a well in center. Gradually stir milk mixture into dry ingredients until just combined and slightly lumpy. Do not overmix or corn bread will be tough. Place mixture in prepare pan; bake until top is golden brown (about 35 minutes).

Serves 8.

OLD-FASHIONED MASHED POTATOES

These wonderfully simple potatoes are easily assembled, but can also be prepared a week or two ahead of the big day if you have the time; store in freezer and reheat at serving time. If used from refrigerator or if defrosting first, warm potatoes in a 350° F oven for 30 minutes. Frozen potatoes need to bake at 350° F for about 1¼ hours. If you don't have two ovens, you may want to defrost the casserole in the refrigerator to shorten the

baking time or partially bake it before the turkey goes into the oven, rewarming casserole at serving time. Serve with Cream Gravy (see page 77).

> 10 *potatoes, peeled and cut in 1-inch cubes*
>   6 *cloves garlic, peeled*
>   8 *tablespoons butter*
> ⅔ *cup milk or whipping cream*
>   3 *ounces cream cheese, at room temperature*
>   2 *eggs*
> ½ *cup (about 2 small bunches) minced chives*
> 1½ *tablespoons salt*
> ½ *teaspoon ground white pepper*

1. In a large saucepan cover potato cubes and garlic with water. Bring to a boil over medium heat, reduce heat to low, then simmer until tender and easily pierced with a sharp knife (30 minutes).

2. When potatoes are cooked, drain water. Press potatoes and garlic through a potato ricer or mash in their cooking pan. Stir in butter, milk, cream cheese, eggs, chives, salt, and pepper. Serve immediately or store in an ovenproof casserole.

Serves 12 to 16.

SWEET POTATO AND CINNAMON MUFFINS

Scrub 1 medium-large sweet potato, cut into 2-inch-long pieces, place in a small saucepan, and cover with water. Cook about 25 minutes before puréeing in a food processor. Remove purée and cream the butter and sugar.

> ½ *cup butter, softened*
> 1½ *cups firmly packed brown sugar*
>   1 *cup sweet potato purée*
>   1 *egg*
> 1¾ *cups flour*
> ½ *teaspoon each salt, ground nutmeg, and ground ginger*
>   1 *teaspoon baking soda*
>   2 *teaspoons ground cinnamon*
> ⅛ *teaspoon ground cloves*
> ⅓ *cup water*

1. Preheat oven to 375° F. Butter and flour muffin pan or line with muffin papers. With an electric mixer, cream the ½ cup butter and sugar until light and fluffy; stir in sweet potato purée and egg.

2. Sift together flour, salt, nutmeg, ginger, baking soda, cinnamon, and cloves. Stir half the dry ingredients into creamed mixture; stir in water, then remaining dry ingredients.

3. Using an ice cream scoop, fill muffin cups two thirds full of batter; bake until dry on top and a skewer inserted in center comes out clean (18 to 20 minutes). Serve warm.

Makes 1 dozen muffins.

CHRIS'S PUMPKIN PECAN PIE

Partially baked tart shells and pie crusts keep in the freezer, well wrapped, for several months. Making the easy filling and doing the final baking before serving give the pie a fresher flavor, although you can bake the pie a day or two ahead and refrigerate it. Then, while enjoying the rest of the dinner, heat the pie in a 350° F oven for 15 to 20 minutes.

    2 cups firmly packed brown sugar
    4 tablespoons butter, softened
  1 ⅓ cup pecan halves
    6 eggs
    4 egg yolks
    2 cups pumpkin purée
    2 tablespoons flour
    ½ teaspoon ground cloves
    ½ teaspoon ground cinnamon
    1 teaspoon salt
    4 cups whipping cream
    ¾ cup confectioners' sugar, for
        garnish

Tart Pastry

  1 ½ cups flour
    1 teaspoon sugar
    ½ teaspoon salt
    ½ cup unsalted butter, chilled and
        cut into ½-inch cubes
    1 egg
    2 tablespoons cold water

1. Prepare 2 unbaked tart shells. Preheat oven to 400° F. Line unbaked shells with aluminum foil and fill with dried beans or metal pie weights. Bake 12 minutes; remove foil and beans. Set shells aside to cool completely. Mix ⅔ cup brown sugar and butter. Spread half of mixture in bottom of each of the cooled tart shells. Dot each shell with half the pecans and bake 10 minutes; set aside.

2. While pastry bakes, mix eggs, egg yolks, pumpkin purée, flour, remaining brown sugar, cloves, cinnamon, salt, and 2 cups whipping cream.

3. Reduce oven to 325° F. Place an equal amount of filling in each pastry shell; bake until a knife inserted into pie is dry when removed (about 45 minutes). Cool.

4. Beat remaining cream with confectioners' sugar and pipe onto pies at serving time.

Makes two 8-inch pies, serves 12 to 16.

Tart Pastry

1. Place flour, sugar, and salt in a medium mixing bowl or in work bowl of food processor. Cut butter into flour using a pastry blender or 2 knives, or with quick on-and-off bursts if using food processor. Beat together egg and the water. When flour mixture resembles coarse crumbs, stir in egg-water mixture; mix only until dough begins to hold together.

2. Divide dough in half and press each half into an 8-inch tart pan. Refrigerate for 1 hour or wrap carefully and freeze for up to 1 month. Use as directed in recipe.

Makes one 11-inch tart shell, two 8-inch tart shells, or fourteen 3-inch miniature tart shells.

FISHERMAN'S WHARF CIOPPINO

This is a gloriously sloppy dish to eat. With pieces of cracked crab in their shells, there's nothing to do but wade in with both hands–with lots of paper napkins at the ready. Provide shellfish or nut crackers in case the crab needs more cracking.

    ¼ cup olive oil
    1 large onion, finely chopped
    1 red or green bell pepper, seeded
        and chopped
    3 cloves garlic, minced
    ½ cup finely chopped parsley
    1 teaspoon dried basil
    ½ teaspoon dried oregano
    1 large can (28 oz) Italian plum
        tomatoes, coarsely chopped
    1 can (6 oz) tomato paste
    2 cups dry white wine
    1 teaspoon salt
    ¼ teaspoon coarsely ground pepper
    ¾ to 1 pound rock cod fillets, cut in
        1-inch squares
    2 medium Dungeness crabs
        (about 1 ½ lbs each), cooked,
        cleaned, and cracked
    1 pound shrimp, shelled and
        deveined
   12 fresh clams in shells, scrubbed

1. In a deep, heavy, large kettle or Dutch oven, heat olive oil over medium heat. Add onion and bell pepper. Cook, stirring often, until onion is soft but not browned. Mix in garlic, parsley, basil, and oregano. Stir in tomatoes and their liquid, tomato paste, wine, salt, and pepper.

2. Bring to a boil, cover, reduce heat, and simmer for 1 hour. Uncover and boil gently, stirring occasionally, over medium-low heat until sauce is fairly thick (30 to 35 minutes).

3. Add, in order given, rock cod, crabs, shrimp, and clams. Cover and cook until crab meat is heated through, the shrimp are pink, and the clams are open (20 to 25 minutes). Discard any clams that do not open. Taste; add salt if needed.

4. Serve in large, shallow bowls that have been warmed.

Serves 6.

CORNMEAL-CRUSTED ORANGE ROUGHY

Orange roughy is a New Zealand fish that is now readily available in U.S. fish markets. Other firm-fleshed fish, such as sole, can be substituted. The fish can be coated up to 8 hours ahead of cooking time and stored in the refrigerator. Toast almonds on a baking sheet in a 350° F oven 6 to 8 minutes. If you make this recipe often, toast and chop the almonds when you have spare time and freeze until needed.

> *¹⁄₄ cup cornmeal*
> *¹⁄₂ cup finely chopped toasted almonds*
> *¹⁄₂ teaspoon each salt and dried thyme*
> *¹⁄₄ teaspoon freshly ground pepper*
> *6 fillets (about ¹⁄₄ lb each) orange roughy*
> *3 tablespoons unsalted butter*
> *Lemon wedges and parsley sprigs, for garnish*

Rémoulade Sauce

> *¹⁄₂ cup minced small dill pickles*
> *1 tablespoon capers*
> *2 cloves garlic, finely minced*
> *¹⁄₃ cup finely minced parsley*
> *2 green onions, minced*
> *2 tablespoons tomato paste*
> *1 ¹⁄₂ cups mayonnaise*

1. In a shallow bowl or pie plate, stir together cornmeal, almonds, salt, thyme, and pepper. Coat fillets in cornmeal mixture.

2. In a large skillet over medium heat melt butter. Sauté fillets on one side until golden brown (about 6 minutes). Turn and cook second side until done (about 4 minutes). Serve with lemon wedges, parsley sprigs, and Rémoulade Sauce.

Serves 6.

Rémoulade Sauce   In a small bowl, stir pickles, lemon juice, capers, garlic, parsley, green onions, and tomato paste into mayonnaise.

Makes about 2 cups.

You won't waste even a morsel of Fisherman's Wharf Cioppino, a glorious blend of cod fillets, Dungeness crab, shrimp, and clams, if you use the clam shells as spoons and the tips of the crab claws as picks.

TERIYAKI SHRIMP

You can also use this sauce as a marinade for boneless chicken breasts; marinate the chicken for 30 minutes to several hours before broiling or grilling. There is enough marinade for four chicken breast halves. It is also delicious as a marinade for fresh tuna steaks. Serve with rice to absorb the delicious sauce. Toast sesame seed in a dry skillet over medium heat until lightly browned, 3 to 5 minutes.

    1 tablespoon grated fresh ginger
    2 cloves garlic, minced
    2 green onions, chopped
    1/4 cup soy sauce
    2 tablespoons honey
    1 tablespoon rice wine vinegar or
        apple cider vinegar
    1/2 tablespoon Asian sesame oil
    1 pound (about 24) shrimp,
        shelled and deveined
    1 tablespoon vegetable oil
    1/2 teaspoon cornstarch
    1 tablespoon water
    2 tablespoons sesame seed, toasted,
        for garnish
        Steamed rice, for accom-
            paniment

1. In a large bowl, stir together ginger, garlic, onions, soy sauce, honey, vinegar, and sesame oil. Reserve half of this marinade in another bowl. Place shrimp in first bowl and toss with marinade. Marinate 30 minutes to 4 hours in refrigerator.

2. In a wok or large skillet over medium-high heat, warm vegetable oil. Sauté shrimp on one side until bright pink (2 to 3 minutes). Toss and cook second side until done (about 2 minutes). Remove to a dish and reserve.

3. Combine cornstarch and the water in a small bowl. Pour reserved marinade into skillet, bring to a boil over medium-high heat, and stir in cornstarch mixture. Stir until sauce thickens (about 1 minute). Add shrimp, stirring to coat with sauce.

4. To serve, place shrimp on a serving dish, sprinkle with toasted sesame seed, and accompany with steamed rice.

Serves 4.

SCALLOPS EN PAPILLOTE

Not only is this recipe delicious and quick to prepare, but the technique of steaming in foil packages is equally successful with cubes of other firm-fleshed fish such as salmon, sea bass, halibut, and turbot. Mint, fennel seed, or thyme would be a fine substitute when basil is out of season. The packages can be prepared ahead and stored in the refrigerator for up to 24 hours. Bake about 7 minutes longer when baking chilled fish.

    8 shallots, minced
    3 large tomatoes, diced
    1 large bulb fennel, thinly sliced
    4 tablespoons olive oil
    1 teaspoon salt
    1/2 teaspoon freshly ground pepper
    1 cup plus 4 tablespoons unsalted
        butter
    2 pounds scallops
    1/2 cup minced fresh basil
        Grated peel of 1 lemon

1. Preheat oven to 400° F. In a large skillet over medium heat, sauté shallots, tomatoes, and fennel in oil until most of the liquid has evaporated (about 2 minutes). Add salt and pepper and continue cooking until liquid is absorbed (about 3 minutes); set aside to cool.

2. Cut 8 squares of aluminum foil, about 10 inches by 10 inches each; smear each with 2 tablespoons butter. Place an equal amount of tomato-fennel mixture in center of each foil square. Place 1/4 pound (about 3/4 cup) scallops on tomato-fennel mixture. Cut any very large scallops so they will cook evenly. Place 1 tablespoon basil on each mound of scallops, top with 1 1/2 teaspoons butter, and 1/2 teaspoon lemon peel. Seal foil packages securely. Refrigerate if not baking immediately.

3. Place packages on a baking sheet and bake until packages puff (12 to 14 minutes, depending on size of scallops). To serve, place a package on each dinner plate and open at the table so the aroma can be enjoyed.

Serves 8.

Rice is the basis for versatile Jambalaya One-Pot Meal. Be sure to try the paella-style variation of this recipe, or invent one of your own.

JAMBALAYA ONE-POT MEAL

Although there are a number of ingredients to prepare, this New Orleans-style dish needs no attention while it cooks.

  2 tablespoons olive oil
  2 cloves garlic, minced
  ½ cup chopped onion
  1 stalk celery, sliced
  1 medium green bell pepper,
      seeded and cut into strips
  1 cup long-grain white rice
  1 can (16 oz) stewed tomatoes
  1 cup water
  ⅛ teaspoon hot-pepper sauce
      (optional)
  ½ cup chopped cooked ham
      (optional)
  8 thin slices chorizo or other spicy
      hard sausage
  1 teaspoon dried thyme or oregano
  1 teaspoon salt
     Freshly ground pepper, to taste

  1 pound medium shrimp, shelled
      and deveined
     Lemon slices and minced
      parsley, for garnish

1. In a large skillet or paella pan, heat oil over medium heat. Add garlic, onion, celery, and green pepper and sauté just until softened (about 3 minutes).

2. Add rice, tomatoes and their juice, the water, hot-pepper sauce, ham (if used), chorizo, thyme, salt, and pepper. Bring to a boil, cover, reduce heat, and simmer 15 minutes.

3. Quickly add shrimp, cover, and cook 5 minutes longer, or until rice is tender and shrimp have turned pink.

4. Toss with a fork. Garnish with lemon and parsley.

Serves 4.

Paella One-Pot Meal   In a large skillet or paella pan, heat 2 tablespoons olive oil. Add 2 cloves garlic, minced; ½ cup chopped onion; and 2 hot or mild chorizos, broken into pieces, casings removed; sauté 3 to 5 minutes. Add 1 cup long grain white rice; 2 cups chicken stock; 1 whole boned chicken breast, cut in strips or bite-sized pieces; ⅛ teaspoon saffron *or* ¼ teaspoon ground turmeric; 1 teaspoon salt. Season with pepper to taste. Bring to a boil, cover, reduce heat, and simmer 15 minutes. Then add 10 ounces frozen petite peas *or* 1 can (16 oz) artichoke hearts, drained, and 1 pound medium raw shrimp, shelled and deveined. Cover and cook 5 minutes longer.

NOTE

FASHION A MARRIAGE OF FOOD AND HERBS

Over the centuries certain combinations of herbs and foods have become traditional because they work so well together. The following are complementary pairings. Refer to them for ideas or for substitutions if you run out of a needed herb during cooking. Also try new combinations, making notes on your favorites. The most flavorful and economical way to cook with herbs is to grow them yourself, but this isn't always practical. Store purchased dried herbs in a dry cupboard away from heat and light. Rotate your inventory of dried herbs every three months since herbs lose potency after a while.

Since herbs intensify in flavor when they are dried, if substituting fresh herbs for dried herbs, use three times the suggested amount. The exception is rosemary, which is the same, fresh or dried. Fresh herbs are often added to dishes at the last minute so they keep their intensity of flavor. Dried herbs, which need heat and moisture to yield their flavor, can be added earlier in the cooking. To release oils, crush dried herbs before adding to food.

Meat, Fish, and Eggs

Beef   Basil, bay, marjoram, oregano, parsley

Chicken   Basil, bay, chervil, chives, dill, marjoram, mint, oregano, parsley, rosemary, sage, tarragon, thyme

Eggs   Basil, bay, chervil, chives, dill, marjoram, mint, oregano, parsley, tarragon, thyme

Fish   Basil, bay, chervil, chives, dill, marjoram, mint, oregano, parsley, tarragon, thyme

Lamb   Basil, bay, marjoram, mint, oregano, parsley, rosemary, sage, thyme

Pork   Basil, bay, chives, marjoram, oregano, parsley, rosemary, sage, thyme

Veal   Basil, bay, chervil, chives, dill, marjoram, oregano, parsley, sage, tarragon, thyme

Fruits and Vegetables

Corn   Basil, chervil, chives, cilantro, dill, mint, parsley, rosemary, sage, tarragon, thyme

Cruciferous vegetables (broccoli, Brussels sprouts, cauliflower, cabbage)   Chives, cilantro, dill, marjoram, mint, oregano, parsley, sage

Fruits   Basil, bay, chervil, chives, dill, marjoram, mint, oregano, parsley, rosemary, sage, tarragon, thyme

Gourds (chayote, cucumber, summer and winter squash)   Chervil, chives, cilantro, dill, marjoram, mint, oregano, parsley, tarragon, thyme

Leafy green vegetables (chard, kale, spinach)   Chives, dill, marjoram, oregano, parsley, thyme

Legumes (green beans, jícama, shell beans)   Basil, bay, chervil, chives, cilantro, dill, marjoram, mint, oregano, parsley, rosemary, sage, tarragon, thyme

Lettuces   Basil, chervil, chives, cilantro, dill, marjoram, mint, oregano, parsley, rosemary, tarragon, thyme

Mushrooms   Basil, bay, chervil, chives, dill, marjoram, oregano, parsley, tarragon, thyme

Onion family (garlic, leek, onion, shallot)   Basil, bay, chervil, chives, cilantro, dill, marjoram, oregano, parsley, rosemary, sage, tarragon, thyme

Root and bulb vegetables (beet, carrot, celery, fennel)   Chervil, chives, dill, mint, parsley, rosemary, sage, tarragon, thyme

Tomato family (eggplant, pepper, potato, tomato)   Basil, bay, chervil, chives, cilantro, dill, marjoram, mint, oregano, parsley, rosemary, tarragon, thyme

MEAT

Although we all are aware of the virtues of fish, poultry, pasta, and vegetables, America has long been a nation of meat eaters. In light of recent nutritional guidelines, we may be eating less meat than in the past or choosing the cut and the cooking method more carefully, but meat is still definitely on the menu. A flavorful roast like Beef Tenderloin Roll (see page 83) has cachet as the center-piece of a celebratory dinner. Easy Beef Fajitas (see page 83) reflects our passion for southwestern flavors. Lamb Chops with Pepper-Tomato Salsa (see page 93), Grilled Veal Chops with Chive Cream (see page 95), and Creole Skewers with Mustard Butter (see page 97) satisfy a yen for meat along with a yearning for anything grilled.

EASY BEEF FAJITAS

A Tex-Mex favorite, *fajitas* are made by combining strips of beef or chicken fried in a skillet with sautéed onions, mushrooms, and chiles, and rolling the mixture into warm flour tortillas. This recipe uses lean sirloin steak strips, sautéed quickly in a serrano chile sauce and garnished with nonfat yogurt and slices of avocado.

1 cup sliced onions
1 cup sliced mushrooms
1 teaspoon vegetable oil
⅓ cup dry sherry
1 pound sirloin tips, fat trimmed
2 serrano or jalapeño chiles, seeded and minced
½ teaspoon ground cumin
¼ teaspoon ground coriander
1 teaspoon minced cilantro
4 large flour tortillas
½ cup South-of-the-Border Salsa (see page 114)
½ avocado, thinly sliced
1 cup plain nonfat yogurt

1. In a large skillet over medium-high heat, sauté onions and mushrooms in oil and sherry for 10 minutes. Cut steak into 1 ½-inch strips and add to skillet, cooking for 2 minutes more. Add chiles, cumin, coriander, and cilantro, and cook 3 more minutes, stirring frequently.

2. Wrap tortillas in aluminum foil and warm in a 325° F oven for 10 minutes. Arrange bowls of salsa, sliced avocado, and yogurt on a tray. Wrap warmed tortillas in a clean cloth napkin. Serve meat filling out of skillet or in prewarmed serving dish. Invite guests to assemble their own fajitas.

Serves 4.

BEEF TENDERLOIN ROLL

Bake the Baked Potato Sticks alongside this tenderloin of beef. The tenderloin can be served hot from the oven or prepared early in the day and served at room temperature.

1 beef tenderloin (3½ lb), trimmed of fat
4 strips bacon, diced
1 bunch spinach, washed and dried
2 tablespoons Dijon-style mustard
2 tablespoons brandy
2 tablespoons olive oil
Baked Potato Sticks (see page 111), or Potato Gratin (see page 111), for accompaniment

1. To make a flat ¾-inch-thick piece of beef, butterfly tenderloin by cutting, from top to bottom, through center to within ¾ inch of bottom; open like a book and press to flatten. Cut horizontally, starting at the center of each half, to within ¾ inch of each side. Open and flatten tenderloin slightly with a meat pounder or side of a meat cleaver or Chinese cleaver so that whole piece is about the same thickness.

2. In a large skillet over medium heat, sauté diced bacon until golden brown. When fat is rendered and bacon is crisp, add spinach and cook until wilted (about 6 minutes). Place spinach-bacon mixture over tenderloin. Roll up tenderloin, jelly-roll fashion. Tie with kitchen twine in 4 places to fasten tightly.

3. In a small bowl mix together mustard and brandy. Rub over tenderloin. At this point, meat can be refrigerated for about 8 hours, if desired; bring meat to room temperature 1 hour before cooking.

You can roast this Beef Tenderloin Roll ahead of time and serve it at room temperature; it's equally delicious served hot from the oven.

4. Preheat oven to 425° F. Return skillet to medium heat, add olive oil, and place tenderloin, seam side down, in skillet; brown on all sides (5 minutes per side). Place tenderloin in oven; roast until medium-rare (about 40 minutes, or until internal temperature is 125° F on an instant-read thermometer). Let tenderloin rest 12 to 15 minutes, loosely covered with aluminum foil, before slicing. Slice into 6 pieces across the grain of the meat, and serve immediately with Baked Potato Sticks.

Serves 6.

GROUND BEEF ROULADE PIZZAIOLA

This simple roulade is half the work of pizza but has the same spicy flavors. It can be doubled or tripled for big parties and stored in the freezer until needed. To cook frozen roulade, add an extra 30 minutes to the baking time.

> 1½ *pounds ground beef*
> 1½ *pounds ground pork*
>   1 *onion, minced*
>   4 *cloves garlic, minced*
>   1 *green bell pepper, diced*
>   1 *egg*
>   2 *tablespoons tomato paste*
>   1 *tablespoon dried oregano*
>   1 *tablespoon dried basil*
> 1½ *teaspoons salt*
>   ½ *pound mozzarella cheese, thinly sliced*
>   ¼ *pound salami, thinly sliced*
>   3 *tablespoons grated Parmesan cheese*
>   *Fresh Tomato Sauce (see page 115), for accompaniment*

1. Preheat oven to 350° F. In a large bowl, combine beef, pork, onion, garlic, bell pepper, egg, tomato paste, oregano, basil, and salt.

Oven-baked Korean Bulgoki combines inexpensive beef short ribs and an Asian-style marinade.

2. Cut a piece of aluminum foil about 16 inches long. Pat ground meat mixture onto aluminum foil, covering foil (mixture will be about ¼ to ½ inch thick). Place mozzarella on meat mixture to cover. Next, place salami over cheese, also to cover. Roll up ground meat mixture jelly-roll fashion, peeling mixture from foil as it is rolled.

3. Press ends together to seal in filling. Place ground meat roll on a baking sheet with sides and sprinkle with Parmesan. Bake until browned (35 minutes). Let rest 5 minutes before cutting. To serve, slice about ¾ inch thick. Accompany with Fresh Tomato Sauce.

Serves 10 to 12.

KOREAN BULGOKI

Salty, spicy, grilled Korean short ribs have attained worldwide popularity in recent years. This version is oven baked.

> ¾ *cup soy sauce*
>   1 *cup rice wine (such as sake or Shaoxing) or dry sherry*
>   1 *teaspoon dark sesame oil*
>   2 *or 3 small jalapeño or serrano chiles to taste, stems trimmed, thinly sliced*
>   1 *teaspoon freshly ground pepper*
>   5 *green onions (including crisp green tops), trimmed and thinly sliced*
>   1 *tablespoon minced garlic*
>   *Thumb-sized piece of fresh ginger, peeled and finely minced*
>   4 *pounds meaty, thickly cut short ribs*
>   ¼ *cup sesame seed*
>   2 *tablespoons minced cilantro*
>   *Steamed rice, for accompaniment*

1. Mix soy sauce, wine, oil, chiles, black pepper, green onions, garlic, and ginger in large roasting pan. Add ribs, turning them several times in liquid. Cover pan with foil or plastic wrap and let ribs marinate 3 hours at room temperature or overnight in the refrigerator, turning several times to coat meat thoroughly.

2. Preheat oven to 375° F. Remove and reserve ribs and pour marinade into bowl. Return ribs to pan, bone side down, leaving some space between them. Bake until tender (40 minutes to 1 hour, depending on thickness), brushing with reserved marinade every 10 minutes.

3. At the final basting, sprinkle ribs with sesame seed. When done, remove from oven, sprinkle with cilantro, and serve immediately with steamed rice.

Serves 3 or 4.

PROVENÇAL BEEF STEW

Garlic, thyme, and orange peel mark this as the Provençal version of beef stew. Buttered noodles are the traditional accompaniment. Note that the meat needs to marinate at least 12 hours. The stew may be made up to 2 days in advance and refrigerated.

> 2 pounds beef chuck
> 1 1/3 cups white wine vinegar
> 1/4 cup olive oil
> 1/2 teaspoon each salt and freshly
>   ground pepper
> 1 bay leaf
> 2 cloves garlic, peeled and crushed
>   with flat side of knife
> 1 teaspoon minced fresh thyme or
>   1/2 teaspoon dried thyme
> 2 narrow strips orange peel
> 2 cups dry red wine
> 2 tablespoons minced parsley, for
>   garnish
>   Buttered noodles, for accom-
>   paniment

1. Trim meat of excess fat and cut into 2-inch cubes. In a large bowl, whisk together vinegar, 2 tablespoons of the oil, salt, pepper, bay leaf, garlic, thyme, and orange peel. Add meat, cover bowl with plastic wrap, and refrigerate for 12 to 18 hours. Drain meat, reserving marinade. Pat meat dry with paper towels.

2. In a Dutch oven or large skillet with lid heat remaining 2 tablespoons olive oil over moderately high heat. Brown meat well on all sides. Add wine and reserved marinade. Bring to a simmer and cook, uncovered, for 3 minutes. Reduce heat to maintain a bare simmer. Cover and cook until meat is meltingly tender (about 3 hours). For best flavor, allow stew to cool to room temperature, then refrigerate, covered, overnight. Reheat gently to serve. Ladle stew into warm soup bowls, over buttered noodles, if desired, and garnish each serving with parsley.

Serves 6.

TIPS

. . . ON GRILLING

Getting the best from your outdoor grill involves practice, patience, and proper equipment. To aid your results:

☐ Allow 30 to 45 minutes for coals to burn down; when ready, they should be covered with a light ash. Cooking over flaming coals only burns the outside of the food, leaving the inside raw.

☐ Your hand is the best judge of when a fire is ready. If you can hold your hand over the fire at grill level for only 2 seconds, the fire is very hot; for 3 to 4 seconds, the fire is medium-hot; for any longer, the fire is not hot enough.

☐ Try to arrange the coals so that there are areas of the grill with no heat under them. That way, finished food can keep warm while the remainder of the meal cooks.

☐ Brush the grill lightly with oil before you put it over the fire to prevent food from sticking. Always keep the grill clean.

☐ To judge how many coals you need, first estimate the size of the cooking surface that the food requires. Spread the coals in a single layer to cover an area about 1 inch larger than you have estimated. Add about half again as much charcoal, and you should have enough for 1 hour of heat. Usually 30 to 40 briquettes are enough to cook food for four people.

☐ Use indirect heat when cooking foods that are in an oil-based marinade or foods that contain a lot of fat. Set an aluminum pan or some heavy-duty aluminum foil underneath the grill, beneath the items being cooked, to catch drippings that would otherwise cause flare-ups. Arrange the hot coals on either side of the pan.

☐ To make a fire for slow cooking, use about 25 briquettes on each side of the drip pan. Plan on adding 8 to 10 briquettes to each side for every hour of additional cooking time. For slow cooking, it is helpful to have a second grill so you can keep a mound of hot coals ready to stoke the main fire.

☐ To maintain optimal flavor and prevent accidents, do not squirt starter fluid onto the fire or add briquettes impregnated with starter fluid to coals already cooking.

☐ Briquettes? Mesquite charcoal? Hardwoods? Wood chips? To choose the right fuel, consider the special features of each: Briquettes are inexpensive, widely available, easy to use, and burn evenly and consistently; but they do not impart the appealing flavor of hardwoods or burn as hot. Mesquite charcoal burns very hot, cooking foods quickly and sealing in juices. It also imparts a more subtle, smoky flavor to foods than do hickory, oak, or fruit woods, making mesquite preferable for fish and delicate-flavored foods. Leftover pieces of mesquite can be reused, which can't be said for briquettes.

Hardwoods such as oak, hickory, and apple provide a flavorful smoky comple-ment to food; the disadvantages are scarcity, price, and–most significant–the inability to burn as hot as mesquite. Hardwoods also take a long time to burn down to coals, and then don't burn very long. To provide maximum smoke, hardwood chips or chunks can be soaked in cold water for 30 minutes. To combine the best of all worlds, try using mesquite charcoal as your fuel source and presoaked hardwood chunks as your smoke source.

Hardwood chips and sawdust can be used to impart a smoky flavor to foods cooked over gas or charcoal briquettes.

MENU

ALL-AMERICAN BEEF AND SPIRITS

For 6

Autumn Broccoli Salad
Three-Pepper Beef
Five-Day Beans
Frozen Whiskey Pudding
Zinfandel

A juicy steak, a green salad, and a rich and creamy dessert have special appeal with the arrival of cool autumn weather. Here, the typical steak dinner takes an imaginative turn in a meal that includes flank steak crusted with mixed peppercorns, a fresh broccoli salad, and a whiskey-spiked custard nestled in homemade chocolate cups.

AUTUMN BROCCOLI SALAD

Mustard, garlic, and Parmesan cheese flavor the dressing for this simple salad. Serve the dish family style with a basket of warm crusty bread.

 1 *teaspoon mustard*
 2 *tablespoons red wine vinegar*
 2 *teaspoons lemon juice*
 ½ *cup garlic oil (see Note) or olive oil*
 ½ *cup grated Parmesan cheese*
   Salt and freshly ground pepper, to taste
 2 *pounds broccoli*
 1 *pint cherry tomatoes, halved*
 ⅓ *cup minced green onion*

1. In a small bowl whisk together mustard, vinegar, and lemon juice. Add garlic oil gradually, whisking constantly. Whisk in ¼ cup of the Parmesan. Season with salt and pepper. Cover and set aside for at least 1 hour or up to 1 day.

2. Trim broccoli and cut into florets (reserve stalks for soup, if desired). Bring a large pot of salted water to a boil over

high heat; add florets and cook until tender-crisp. Drain and immediately plunge into ice water. When cool, drain again and pat dry. Broccoli may be cooked up to 6 hours ahead, cooled, and stored in a plastic bag in the refrigerator.

3. Transfer broccoli to a large bowl along with tomatoes. Add dressing to vegetables and toss to coat well. Add green onion and remaining ¼ cup Parmesan and toss to blend. Taste and adjust seasoning. Transfer to a serving platter.

Serves 6.

Note To make garlic oil, add 6 whole peeled garlic cloves to 1 pint extra virgin olive oil. Marinate at least 1 week before using. Oil will keep indefinitely if covered and refrigerated.

Variation Cauliflower may be substituted for all or part of the broccoli.

THREE-PEPPER BEEF

Lean flank steak is marinated in papaya juice to tenderize it, then seasoned with a trio of crushed peppercorns. The thin steak, which some butchers label *London Broil,* cooks quickly on a grill or under a broiler; for best flavor, serve it rare or medium-rare.

 2½ *pounds flank steak*
 1 *cup papaya juice*
 1½ *tablespoons each green, black, and white peppercorns, coarsely cracked*
 6 *tablespoons olive oil*
 ¼ *cup lemon juice*
   Salt, to taste

1. With a small sharp knife, make ½-inch-long slits in the flank steak in several places. Put steak in a glass baking dish and pour papaya juice over; cover and refrigerate for 2 to 4 hours. Remove steak from marinade and pat dry.

2. Combine peppercorns. Press them into both sides of flank steak; put flank steak in a clean baking dish, cover, and refrigerate for 2 hours. Bring to room temperature before cooking.

3. Prepare a medium-hot charcoal fire or preheat broiler. In a small bowl whisk together olive oil and lemon juice. Salt steak lightly on both sides. Grill or broil to desired doneness, turning once and basting once with half of the oil mixture. Transfer steak to wooden cutting board; brush with remaining oil mixture. Let stand 5 minutes to settle juices, then slice on the diagonal across the grain into wide, flat slices.

Serves 6.

FIVE-DAY BEANS

For busy cooks, it's nice to have a repertoire of dishes that can be assembled a little at a time over several days. The preparation of these beans can be stretched over five days, although it doesn't need to be. If you prefer, you can do step 1 on one day, steps 2 and 3 the next day, and step 4 the day of the party. Refrigerating the beans for at least one day improves their flavor.

> *1⅓ cups Great Northern beans or lima beans*
> *1 bay leaf*
> *1 teaspoon dried thyme*
> *½ teaspoon salt, plus salt to taste*
> *2 tablespoons butter*
> *¾ cup minced green onion*
> *½ cup grated carrot*
> *½ cup minced celery*
> *2 tablespoons minced fresh sage*
> *Freshly ground pepper, to taste*
> *½ cup whipping cream*
> *¼ cup seasoned bread crumbs*

1. On Day 1 cover beans with cold water and let stand 24 hours.

2. On Day 2 drain beans. Place in a medium saucepan, add bay leaf, thyme, ½ teaspoon of the salt, and water to cover. Over high heat bring to a boil, reduce heat to maintain a simmer, and cook until tender (about 1 hour). Drain beans, reserving 1 cup liquid. Transfer beans to a bowl, add reserved liquid, cover, and refrigerate.

3. On Day 3 in a large skillet over moderate heat, melt butter. Add onion, carrot, and celery and sauté 3 minutes. Add sage and cook 1 minute. Stir in beans with their liquid and simmer 5 minutes. Remove from heat, cool, cover, and refrigerate 2 days.

4. On Day 5 preheat oven to 400° F. Butter an 11- by 13-inch baking dish. Season beans with salt and pepper, then transfer to baking dish. Drizzle cream over dish and dot with bread crumbs. Bake until hot and lightly browned (15 to 20 minutes). Serve from the baking dish, if desired.

Serves 6.

FROZEN WHISKEY PUDDING

Molded chocolate cups hold a smooth frozen custard spiked with Irish whiskey. You will need 6 paper muffin cups and a pastry brush.

> *6 ounces bittersweet chocolate*
> *1½ cups each milk and whipping cream*
> *½ teaspoon salt*
> *6 egg yolks*
> *¾ cup sugar*
> *2 tablespoons Irish whiskey*

1. In a double boiler over barely simmering water, melt chocolate. Brush 6 paper muffin cups with melted chocolate and place in freezer 5 minutes. Repeat 5 times, forming 6 thin layers of chocolate on each cup. (Repeated layerings gives cups strength.) Put muffin cups on tray in freezer until frozen (1 to 3 hours), then remove and carefully place in an airtight container and return to freezer. They may be made up to 1 week ahead.

2. In a medium saucepan over moderate heat, bring milk, cream, and salt to a simmer. With an electric mixer at medium-high speed, beat yolks 3 minutes. Add sugar gradually, beating until mixture is pale and thick (5 to 7 minutes). Remove bowl from mixer and whisk in ¾ cup of the hot-milk mixture by hand. Pour resulting mixture into the saucepan and cook over moderately low heat, stirring constantly with a wooden spoon, until mixture reaches 180° F on an instant-read thermometer. Do not allow custard to boil.

3. Strain custard through a fine sieve into a bowl set over ice. Stir occasionally until completely cold. Stir in whiskey.

4. Remove coated muffin cups from freezer. Peel off paper. Spoon in custard mixture. Return cups to freezer for at least 2 hours or up to 1 day. If custard seems very firm, remove cups from freezer 5 minutes before serving.

Serves 6.

CHIHUAHUA CHILAQUILES

Chilaquiles (pronounced chee-la-*kee*-less) beautifully utilize leftover roast beef, pork, turkey, or chicken. It's also worth a trip to the market to purchase fresh meat for this dish. Buy approximately 4 pounds beef chuck roast and simmer, covered with beef stock or water, until tender and falling apart (about 4 hours).

> *2 onions, diced*
> *4 cloves garlic, sliced*
> *2 tablespoons vegetable oil*
> *6 dried New Mexico chiles, diced*
> *1 or 2 jalapeño chiles, sliced*
> *7 cups beef stock*
> *6 to 8 cups leftover shredded beef chuck roast*
> *1 package (10 oz) frozen corn kernels*
> *1 can (15 oz) plum tomatoes, drained and diced*
> *1 tablespoon each toasted cumin seed and salt*
> *¼ teaspoon freshly ground pepper*
> *½ teaspoon hot-pepper flakes*
> *6 corn tortillas, cut into thin strips*
> *1 cup sour cream, for garnish*
> *¼ cup sliced green onions, for garnish*
> *6 sprigs cilantro, for garnish*
> *Marinated Onions (see page 114), for garnish (optional)*

1. In a large saucepan over medium heat, sauté onion and garlic in oil until softened and translucent (4 to 5 minutes). Add chiles, stock, beef, corn, tomatoes, cumin, salt, black pepper, and hot-pepper flakes. Reduce heat to low and simmer, uncovered, for 45 minutes.

2. While chilaquiles simmer, heat oven to 350° F. Toast tortilla strips on a baking sheet in the oven until dried out and lightly browned (12 to 15 minutes); reserve.

Canned tomatoes and tortillas from the pantry transform meat leftovers into hearty Chihuahua Chilaquiles.

3. Serve chilaquiles in a shallow soup bowl, topped with toasted tortilla strips, sour cream, green onions, and cilantro sprigs. Serve Marinated Onions (if used), on the side.

Serves 6.

BEEF WITH ASPARAGUS

When asparagus is in season, virtually every Chinese restaurant features this simple but delicious stir-fry. Shaoxing wine is a medium-brown Chinese rice wine. Look for it at Asian markets or substitute a dry, full-bodied Spanish sherry.

> *2 teaspoons minced fresh ginger*
> *2 tablespoons Shaoxing wine or dry sherry*
> *3 tablespoons dark soy sauce or 2 parts light and 1 part black soy sauce*
> *½ teaspoon sesame oil*
> *½ pound lean beef, sliced into stir-frying strips*
> *1½ teaspoons cornstarch*
> *2 to 3 tablespoons vegetable oil*
> *1 pound asparagus, cut diagonally into 2-inch pieces*

1. In a medium bowl, combine ginger, wine, soy sauce, and sesame oil. Toss the beef strips in mixture and marinate 30 minutes to several hours.

2. Drain beef well and reserve marinade. Combine marinade with enough water to make ⅓ cup. Dissolve cornstarch in this mixture.

3. Heat wok or large skillet over high heat, and add 1 tablespoon of the oil. Add beef to pan; stir-fry until meat loses its raw color (about 1 minute). Remove meat from pan.

4. Add remaining oil to wok. Add asparagus and stir-fry over medium heat until just heated through. Return beef to pan; add reserved marinade. Increase heat to high and cook until sauce thickens. Serve immediately.

Serves 4 to 6 (with other dishes).

Beef with Broccoli   When asparagus is not in season, substitute sliced broccoli. Blanch broccoli briefly in boiling water before using.

The key to preserving flavor and texture in this recipe for Beef With Asparagus is stir-frying.

Rich Beef with Asparagus For a richer sauce, reduce soy sauce in marinade to 1 tablespoon dark soy sauce; add 2 tablespoons oyster sauce to pan in step 4.

MEDITERRANEAN LEG OF LAMB

Lamb is wonderful when marinated, then roasted in the oven. It is also delicious grilled. Leftover lamb can be made into sandwiches or used in salads (see Lamb and White Bean Salad, page 54).

> 4 cloves garlic, minced
> 2 teaspoons minced fresh or dried rosemary
> 1 cup olive oil
> ½ cup red wine vinegar
> 1 teaspoon salt
> ½ teaspoon freshly ground pepper
> 1 leg of lamb (about 3 ½ lb), butterflied

1. In a large glass, ceramic, or stainless steel bowl, whisk together garlic, rosemary, oil, vinegar, salt, and pepper. Place lamb in marinade, turning to coat thoroughly. Marinate 2 to 24 hours.

2. *To roast in oven:* Preheat oven to 425° F. Drain marinade from lamb and discard marinade. Place lamb in a 9- by 12-inch roasting pan. Roast in oven until medium-rare (about 45 minutes, or until internal temperature is 135° F on an instant-read thermometer). Let lamb rest 15 minutes before serving. Carve across grain into ½-inch-thick slices. *To grill:* Prepare a charcoal fire; brush grill rack with vegetable oil. Drain marinade from lamb and reserve. Place lamb on rack and grill 10 minutes, baste with marinade, turn and grill 10 minutes, baste again, and turn and cook 10 minutes more. Repeat until internal temperature is 135° F (about 15 minutes more). Rest and carve lamb as for roasting.

Serves 6.

Mediterranean Lamb Chops
Marinate 4 lamb sirloin steaks (about ¾ pound each) in one half of the marinade; sauté steaks in 4 tablespoons olive oil, 3 minutes on each side.

MENU

TEXAS CHILI FEED AND FIXIN'S

For 12

Soft Tacos With Beans and Salsa
All-Beef Texas Chili
Pickled Relish Platter
Soft Lemon Pudding Cake
Cold Beer and Iced Tea

You don't have to be a Texan to cook a mean bowl of red or greet guests with a "Howdy, y'all!" Even without the greeting, transplanted Texans will feel right at home in the presence of chili, pinto beans, and pickles. Country music and cold beer are the other authentic essentials. This menu is especially easy on the cook, because everything can be made ahead.

SOFT TACOS WITH BEANS AND SALSA

Soft fat beans and salsa spooned into a warm tortilla make a quick and delicious accompaniment for the chili. For a variation, spoon some chili into the tacos, too.

> 1½ *pounds dried pinto beans*
> ¼ *cup corn oil*
> 2 *cups chopped green onion*
> 1 *cup chopped yellow onion*
> 1 *tablespoon minced garlic*
> 2 *teaspoons each ground cumin*
> *and dried oregano*
> *Salt, to taste*
> 24 *corn tortillas*
> *South-of-the-Border Salsa*
> *(double recipe; see page 114)*

1. Soak beans overnight in cold water to cover. Drain and place beans in large pot. In a large skillet over moderately low heat, warm oil. Add onions and garlic and sauté until fragrant (about 3 minutes). Add to beans. Add cumin and

oregano and enough cold water to cover. Over high heat bring to a simmer, then reduce heat to maintain a simmer. Cook until beans are just tender (about 1½ hours). Season with salt. Cool, cover, and refrigerate for up to 2 days, if desired.

2. *To steam tortillas:* Wrap tortillas in a damp tea towel and heat over simmering water. *To fry tortillas:* Fry on both sides on a griddle or in a lightly oiled skillet, then stack and wrap in napkins.

3. To serve, reheat beans; taste and reseason if necessary. Place a scoop of hot beans on each tortilla and top with 2 tablespoons salsa. Either roll tortillas or serve open-faced with the chili on the side. Or, serve beans and tortillas family style, allowing guests to make their own soft tacos.

Serves 12.

ALL-BEEF TEXAS CHILI

No Texan worth his or her ten-gallon hat would put beans in chili. This one's all beef, calling on beer and freshly ground cumin to give it distinction. *Masa harina*, the finely ground corn used for corn tortillas, is often used to thicken soups or chili. It is available in Latin markets and some supermarkets.

> 1/3 cup (approximately) corn oil
> 6 pounds beef chuck, cut into 1/2-inch cubes
> 4 cups minced onion
> 1/3 cup minced garlic
> 3 cups (approximately) beef broth
> 3 cups flat beer
> 1 1/2 cups water
> 1/4 cup high-quality chili powder, or more, to taste
> 3 cans (2 lbs each) tomatoes, drained and chopped
> 1/3 cup tomato paste
> 1 1/2 tablespoons minced fresh oregano
> 3 tablespoons cumin seed
> Salt, to taste
> Cayenne pepper, to taste
> Masa harina or cornmeal, if needed

1. In a large heavy skillet over moderately high heat, warm 3 tablespoons of the oil. Brown beef in batches, adding more oil as necessary and transferring meat with a slotted spoon to a large stockpot when well browned. Do not crowd skillet.

2. Reduce heat to moderately low. Add onion and garlic and sauté until softened (about 10 minutes). Add to stockpot along with broth, beer, the water, chili powder, tomato, tomato paste, and oregano.

3. In a small skillet over low heat, toast cumin seed until fragrant; do not allow to burn. Grind in an electric minichopper or with a mortar and pestle. Add to stockpot.

4. Over high heat bring mixture to a simmer. Add salt, cayenne, and more chili powder to taste. Reduce heat to maintain a simmer and cook, partially covered, until beef is tender (about 1 1/2 hours). Check occasionally and add more broth if mixture seems dry. If chili is too thin when meat is tender, stir in up to 2 tablespoons masa harina. Cook an additional 5 minutes to thicken. Serve chili hot.

Serves 12.

PICKLED RELISH PLATTER

This quick sweet relish is ready to eat in one day, although the flavor continues to improve for at least one week. Mushrooms, yellow squash, or Jerusalem artichoke could substitute for any vegetable listed.

> 2 pounds zucchini, sliced thin
> 1 1/2 cups onion, sliced 1/4 inch thick
> 2 cups carrot, cut into 1/4- by 1/4- by 3-inch strips
> 3 cups celery, cut into 1/4- by 1/4- by 3-inch strips
> 12 radishes
> 2 tablespoons salt
> 3 cups white vinegar
> 1 1/2 cups sugar
> 1 tablespoon each celery seed and fennel seed
> 2 tablespoons ground mustard
> 3 dried red-hot pepper pods

1. In a large bowl combine zucchini, onion, carrot, celery, radishes, and salt. Cover with cold water and let stand 45 minutes. Drain thoroughly.

2. In a large pot combine vinegar, sugar, celery seed, fennel seed, mustard, and pepper pods. Bring to a simmer. Remove from heat and pour over vegetables. Let cool, then refrigerate at least 1 day. To serve, lift vegetables out of their brine with a slotted spoon. Transfer to relish trays or bowls. Vegetables may be stored, in their brine, and refrigerated, for up to 1 month.

Serves 12.

SOFT LEMON PUDDING CAKE

Not quite a pudding and not quite a cake, this luscious dessert is a little of both. It's soft on the bottom and firm on top, with a lively lemon kick.

> 1/2 cup finely ground almonds or walnuts
> 4 eggs, separated
> 1 1/3 cups buttermilk
> 1/2 cup lemon juice
> 2 teaspoons vanilla extract
> 1/2 cup flour
> 1 1/2 cups sugar
> 1/2 teaspoon each salt and baking powder
> 1 tablespoon grated lemon peel, plus 1 teaspoon grated lemon peel, for accompaniment (optional)
> 1/4 teaspoon cream of tartar
> 2 cups whipping cream, lightly whipped but not sweetened, for accompaniment (optional)

1. Preheat oven to 375º F. Lightly butter two 4-cup soufflé dishes or baking dishes. Dust sides and bottoms with nuts.

2. In a medium bowl whisk together egg yolks, buttermilk, lemon juice, and vanilla. Sift together flour, sugar, salt, and baking powder. Add to egg yolk mixture, along with 1 tablespoon lemon peel. Beat egg whites with cream of tartar until stiff but not dry. Fold into egg yolk mixture. Pour batter into prepared dishes and place dishes in a large roasting pan. Place pan in oven. Add boiling water to pan to come halfway up sides of baking dishes. Bake 20 minutes, then reduce heat to 350º F and bake until well browned and firm to the touch (20 to 25 minutes longer).

3. Serve at room temperature or chilled. Fold 1 teaspoon lemon peel into whipped cream (if used) and serve alongside.

Serves 12.

SPICY LAMB MEATBALLS WITH MINT-CHILE SAUCE

Prepare packaged quick couscous or steamed rice to serve with these meatballs. Drizzle both the skewered lamb and the accompanying couscous or rice with Mint-Chile Sauce.

Sixteen 8-inch bamboo skewers
2 pounds ground lamb
1 onion, minced
2 cloves garlic, minced
6 tablespoons minced parsley
½ jalapeño chile, minced
¼ cup dried bread crumbs
2 eggs
1 teaspoon salt
½ teaspoon freshly ground pepper
½ cup cornmeal
Couscous or steamed rice, for accompaniment

A spicy sauce, served separately, is the perfect accompaniment to lamb. Serve Lamb Chops With Pepper-Tomato Salsa with potatoes or crusty French or Italian bread.

Mint-Chile Sauce

1 cup plain yogurt
1 cup fresh mint or ¼ cup dried mint
½ cup minced cilantro
½ jalapeño chile, minced
1 teaspoon salt
¼ teaspoon freshly ground pepper

1. Soak skewers in water 15 minutes. In a large bowl, thoroughly mix together ground lamb, onion, garlic, parsley, minced chile, bread crumbs, eggs, salt, and pepper.

2. Preheat broiler. Wrap ⅓ cup lamb mixture around each bamboo skewer to form a meatball about 3 inches long by 1 ½ inches in diameter. Place cornmeal on a plate and roll skewered meatball in cornmeal to coat completely.

3. Brush broiler pan with a thin film of oil. Place meatball skewers on broiler pan and broil 3 inches from heat until lightly browned on one side (about 3 minutes). Turn and broil second side until lightly browned (about 2 minutes).

4. To serve, place couscous on individual dinner plates, top with 2 meatballs on skewers, and drizzle with Mint-Chile Sauce.

Serves 8.

Mint-Chile Sauce In a small bowl stir together all ingredients. Let sit 30 minutes for flavors to meld.

Makes about 2 cups.

LAMB CHOPS WITH PEPPER-TOMATO SALSA

Grilled lamb chops are rich enough to be served without accompaniment, but for a special treat, serve them with a spicy sauce, such as this one.

   3 tablespoons vegetable oil
   1 large onion, chopped
   2 red bell peppers, finely chopped
   2 cloves garlic, chopped
   1 jalapeño chile, seeds and ribs discarded and chopped finely
1 1/2 pounds ripe tomatoes, peeled, seeded, and chopped (see page 56)
   Salt and freshly ground pepper, to taste
   8 rib lamb chops (1 1/2 in. thick)

1. In a deep skillet over low heat, heat 2 tablespoons of the oil. Add onion; cook, stirring often, until soft but not browned (about 5 minutes). Add bell peppers, garlic, and jalapeño chile; cook, stirring often, until peppers soften (about 5 minutes).

2. Add tomatoes and a pinch of salt; raise heat to medium. Cook, uncovered, stirring often, until mixture is thick (about 30 minutes). Taste and add more salt, if needed. The sauce can be refrigerated, covered, for about 4 days, or frozen.

3. Prepare a charcoal fire or preheat broiler with rack about 3 inches from heat source.

4. Trim excess fat from chops, brush both sides with the remaining tablespoon of oil, and sprinkle them with salt and pepper. Put chops on hot grill or on broiler pan; grill or broil until done (about 6 minutes per side for medium-rare). To check for doneness, press meat with your finger; rare lamb does not resist; medium-rare lamb resists slightly; well-done lamb is firm.

5. Meanwhile, reheat sauce in a saucepan over medium heat. Transfer chops to platter. Serve sauce separately.

Serves 4.

WINTER LAMB RAGOÛT

In the spring, add small green beans, asparagus, new peas, tiny potatoes, or green onions for a bright variation.

   6 tablespoons olive oil
   3 pounds lamb stew meat, cut in 2-inch cubes
   4 medium yellow onions, diced
   2 cloves garlic, sliced
   2 tablespoons tomato paste
   1/4 cup minced parsley
   2 teaspoons salt
   1 teaspoon freshly ground pepper
1 1/2 teaspoons dried thyme
   2 bay leaves
   1 pound small turnips, peeled and quartered
   1 pound carrots, peeled
  12 ounces pearl onions, peeled

1. In a large Dutch oven over medium heat, add 2 tablespoons olive oil and toss half the lamb cubes in oil; brown lamb on all sides (5 to 7 minutes). Remove to a bowl or platter and reserve.

2. Add 2 more tablespoons oil and remaining lamb cubes, browning while stirring constantly (5 to 7 minutes). Push meat to one side and add remaining oil, yellow onions, and garlic. Return reserved lamb cubes to pan and cook until onions are translucent (4 to 5 minutes).

3. Add tomato paste, parsley, salt, pepper, thyme, bay leaves, turnips, and water to cover. Reduce heat to simmer, cover, and cook 1 hour. Cut carrots into 2-inch lengths.

4. After 1 hour add carrots and pearl onions to ragoût. Cook 1 hour and 10 minutes more. Serve hot.

Serves 8.

Winter Lamb Ragoût is substantial cold-weather fare. The addition of new peas, asparagus, new potatoes, or green onions makes a delightful springtime variation.

Morocco is the inspiration for Lamb Shanks With Honey and Spices. Brown rice complements the exotic flavor of this dish.

LAMB SHANKS WITH HONEY AND SPICES

Inspired by the exotically flavored stews of Morocco, these lamb shanks are good accompanied by brown rice and a lettuce and tomato salad.

> 1 tablespoon each butter and olive oil
>
> 2 medium onions, thinly sliced
>
> 1 clove garlic, minced
>
> 1 teaspoon salt
>
> ½ teaspoon each ground turmeric and ginger
>
> ¼ teaspoon each ground allspice and coriander
>
> ¾ cup water
>
> ¼ cup honey
>
> 2 cinnamon sticks
>
> 4 to 5 pounds lamb shanks, cracked
>
> 1 lemon, thinly sliced
>
> Brown rice, for accompaniment

1. Preheat oven to 350° F. In a large skillet heat together butter and oil. Sauté onions until limp but not browned. Add garlic, salt, turmeric, ginger, allspice, and coriander and stir to coat onions; simmer about 2 minutes. Mix in water, honey, and cinnamon sticks; bring to a boil, then remove from heat.

2. Arrange lamb shanks in a deep ovenproof casserole just large enough to hold them in a single layer. Pour on onion mixture. Arrange lemon slices over lamb. Cover and bake until lamb is very tender (about 2 hours).

3. Remove lamb and lemons to a serving dish and keep warm. Skim fat from cooking liquid; boil liquid to reduce and thicken it slightly. Pour over lamb and serve with brown rice.

Serves 4 to 6.

GRILLED VEAL CHOPS WITH CHIVE CREAM

Small veal rib chops each consist of just a few tender bites. Serve 2 or 3 rib chops to each guest for an ample portion. The sauce adds an elegant finale, although the veal chops are also delicious served plain, simply grilled or broiled.

 2 tablespoons lemon juice
 2 tablespoons vegetable oil
 1 teaspoon salt
 ½ teaspoon ground white pepper
 3 shallots, minced
 2½ pounds small veal rib chops
   (about 12)

Chive Cream

 1½ cups whipping cream
 1½ tablespoons lemon juice
 ¼ teaspoon salt
 ⅛ teaspoon ground white pepper
 ¼ cup minced fresh chives

1. In a shallow pan, stir together lemon juice, oil, salt, pepper, and shallots. Place veal chops in pan, coat with marinade on both sides, and let rest for 15 to 30 minutes.

2. Prepare a charcoal fire or preheat broiler. Place veal chops on grill or under broiler, about 4 inches from heat, and cook until browned on one side (about 4 minutes). Turn and cook second side until lightly browned and slightly firm (but not rigid) when pressed with a metal spatula (about 3 minutes). Serve veal chops immediately, drizzled with Chive Cream.

Serves 4 to 6.

Chive Cream   In a small saucepan over medium heat, place cream and lemon juice. Simmer until reduced by about one third; keep warm over low heat. Just before serving, season with salt and pepper, then stir chives into warm cream sauce.

Makes 1 cup.

VEAL AND APPLE SCALOPPINE

This recipe calls for tender scallops of veal. Ask the butcher to prepare thin slices, then pound them between sheets of waxed paper until you can almost see through them. When cooked, they will be butter-soft and easy to cut with a fork. The slightly caramelized sauce of tart apples and applejack is a good foil for the savory veal slices. Serve with steamed green beans and wild rice.

 1 pound veal scallops, thinly sliced
 2 green apples
 1 tablespoon vegetable oil
 ½ cup applejack or apple brandy
 ½ cup half-and-half

1. Preheat oven to 350° F. Pound slices of veal between sheets of waxed paper until very thin and tender. Peel, core, and slice apples.

2. Lightly oil a medium-sized baking dish or casserole with some of the vegetable oil. Spread apple slices over bottom of dish. Bake for 20 minutes, uncovered.

3. In a large skillet over medium-high heat, heat remaining oil and lightly brown each piece of veal on both sides. Place veal slices on top of apples in baking dish.

4. Pour applejack into skillet to deglaze pan, allowing brandy to heat; scrape pan as it cooks. Add cream and cook over medium heat for 5 minutes. Pour sauce over veal and apples. Bake veal until bubbling (about 20 minutes). Serve at once.

Serves 4.

Fork-tender Veal and Apple Scaloppine makes a satisfying, low-calorie main course.

A delightful springtime dish is Veal Stew With Fresh Peas, accompanied by new potatoes browned in butter.

VEAL STEW WITH FRESH PEAS

Tender veal chunks and bright green peas go well with butter-browned new potatoes. To complete the menu add a leafy green salad, French bread, and a dry white wine. For dessert, fresh fruit would be ideal.

> 2 pounds cubed boneless veal shoulder
> Salt, ground white pepper, and paprika, to taste
> 2 tablespoons butter
> 1 tablespoon vegetable oil
> 1 small onion, finely chopped
> 1 medium tomato, peeled, seeded, and chopped (see page 56)
> 1 large carrot, cut in 1/4-inch slices
> 1/8 teaspoon dried tarragon
> 3/4 cup dry white wine
> 1/2 cup shelled fresh peas or thawed frozen peas
> Chopped parsley, for garnish

1. Sprinkle veal with salt, white pepper, and paprika. In a large skillet, heat butter with oil over medium heat and brown veal lightly on all sides. Add onion, tomato, carrot, tarragon, and wine. Bring to a boil, cover, reduce heat, and simmer until veal is very tender (about 1 1/2 hours).

2. Mix in peas and cook, uncovered, 5 to 8 minutes longer, until they are just tender. Salt to taste. Sprinkle with parsley and serve.

Serves 6.

TERIYAKI PORK TENDERLOIN

Let the tenderloin sit in the roasting pan in its marinade for up to 48 hours. Then simply roast in the oven, slice, and serve. This same marinade also enhances shrimp, chicken, scallops, or beef.

> 1 tablespoon grated fresh ginger
> 2 cloves garlic, minced
> 2 green onions, chopped
> 1/4 cup soy sauce
> 2 tablespoons honey
> 1 tablespoon rice-wine vinegar or apple cider vinegar
> 1/2 tablespoon Asian sesame oil
> 1 tablespoon vegetable oil
> 1 teaspoon cornstarch
> 1 tablespoon water
> 2 pork tenderloins (1 lb each)
> 2 tablespoons toasted sesame seed

1. Stir together ginger, garlic, green onions, soy sauce, honey, rice-wine vinegar, oils, cornstarch, and the water. Whisk until smooth.

2. Trim any fat from pork tenderloins and place pork in a shallow roasting pan. Pour marinade over pork and marinate 1 hour to 2 days in the refrigerator. From time to time, turn pork tenderloins to be sure they marinate evenly.

3. About 1 hour before serving, preheat oven to 350° F. Drain off marinade and sprinkle pork with toasted sesame seed. Cook until medium (40 to 45 minutes; about 140° F on an instant-read thermometer).

4. To serve, slice pork thinly across grain of meat.

Serves 8.

CREOLE SKEWERS WITH MUSTARD BUTTER

Use this simple skewer as an hors d'oeuvre or main course. For a main course, serve four or five skewers per person. The spicy mustard butter is also excellent on grilled fish, chicken, or meat. It freezes well, so you can keep some on hand for last-minute inspirations or drop-in guests. Andouille is a smoked Cajun sausage, available in specialty delis and butcher shops.

>   25   bamboo skewers
>   1   red bell pepper, cut into 1-inch
>   chunks
>   1   red onion, cut into 1-inch
>   chunks
>   1   pound Andouille sausage, cut
>   into 1/2-inch-thick rounds
>   1   green bell pepper, cut into 1-inch
>   chunks
>   1   pound large shrimp with tails,
>   peeled, and deveined

Mustard Butter

>   1   cup unsalted butter
>   2   tablespoons minced garlic
>   3   tablespoons Creole mustard or
>   other coarse-grained mustard
>   2   teaspoons Worcestershire sauce
>   1   teaspoon hot-pepper sauce
>   1/3 cup lemon juice
>   Salt and freshly ground pepper,
>   to taste

1. Soak skewers in water 15 minutes. Skewer ingredients in the following order: red pepper, onion, sausage (push skewer through casing side of sausage so the cut edge is parallel with the skewer), onion, green pepper, shrimp (push skewer through the length of the shrimp), red pepper, onion, sausage, onion, and green pepper.

2. Prepare a charcoal fire. When fire is ready, brush chunks of skewered food generously with Mustard Butter, place on oiled grill over heat, and cook 2 to 3 minutes per side. Serve with remaining Mustard Butter.

Serves 5 to 6 as a main course.

Mustard Butter   In a small saucepan, melt butter. Add garlic and whisk in mustard, Worcestershire, hot-pepper sauce, and lemon juice. Season with salt and pepper. Butter can be used at this point or chilled and remelted later.

Makes 2 cups.

This succulent grilled main dish doubles as an hors d'oeuvre, making Creole Skewers With Mustard Butter a fine dish for entertaining.

Menu

AUTUMN FAMILY SUPPER

For 8

Allium Bisque (see page 28)
*Walnut Bread (purchased or
    homemade)*
Curried Vegetable Stew
Cinnamon Brown Rice
Apple and Cheddar Cheese Crumble
Cranberry Juice

CURRIED VEGETABLE STEW

In India traditional curry powder is a personal, specially made blend rather than the ready-mixed spice available in this country. This recipe is a mix of complex flavors that can be adjusted to taste. Four tablespoons of packaged curry powder may be substituted for the variety of spices.

    3 zucchini
    2 Japanese eggplant
    1 red bell pepper
    1 pound cauliflower
    1 pound broccoli
    2 carrots, peeled
    1 teaspoon coriander seed
    2 tablespoons vegetable oil
    1 tablespoon butter
    2 onions, diced
    2 cloves garlic, minced
    *1 ½ tablespoons minced fresh
        ginger*
    ½ teaspoon cayenne pepper
    2 teaspoons ground cumin
    1 teaspoon ground turmeric
    ½ teaspoon salt
    2 cups chicken stock
        Cilantro sprigs, for garnish

1. Cut zucchini into 2-inch pieces. Slice eggplant into ½-inch-thick disks. Cut bell pepper into 2-inch cubes. Cut florets from cauliflower and broccoli and cut stems into ½-inch-thick disks. Cut carrots into 1-inch-thick pieces. Crack open coriander seed.

2. Heat oil and butter together in a large, shallow skillet. Add onion, garlic, and ginger, and cook together over medium heat for about 10 minutes. When onions are translucent, add coriander, cayenne, cumin, turmeric, and salt. Stir to mix well and cook for 5 minutes. Add chicken stock, mixing thoroughly.

3. Add eggplant and carrots. Cover and cook for 15 minutes. Add broccoli, cauliflower, and red bell pepper. Stir to mix well. Cover and cook for 5 minutes. Add zucchini and cook uncovered for 5 minutes. Garnish with sprigs of cilantro.

Serves 8.

CINNAMON BROWN RICE

Almonds, which provide texture in this rice dish, are high in carbohydrates, protein, and calcium.

    1 cup brown rice
    2 ½ cups water
    ¼ teaspoon salt
    ½ cup dried currants
    ½ cup toasted slivered almonds
    1 ½ teaspoons ground cinnamon

1. Wash rice under running water to remove starch, dust, stones, or broken grains. Place brown rice, the water, and salt in a medium saucepan over medium heat.

2. Bring to a boil, reduce temperature to medium-low, and cover pan. Cook until grains are tender and separated (35 to 40 minutes). All the liquid will be absorbed. Let pan rest, covered, 10 minutes. Just before serving, stir in currants, almonds, and cinnamon. Serve immediately, or

keep warm in the pan on the stove for up to 20 minutes.

Makes 6 servings.

APPLE AND CHEDDAR CHEESE CRUMBLE

This is an old-fashioned apple dessert, best served warm from the oven. Tart pippin or Granny Smith apples best complement the sweet and pungent crumb topping. If using a sweeter apple, you may want to reduce the amount of sugar.

    5 large apples
    1 tablespoon ground cinnamon
    ½ cup firmly packed brown sugar
    ½ pound Cheddar cheese, grated
    ½ cup flour
    ½ cup rolled oats
    ½ cup granulated sugar
    *½ cup unsalted butter, cut into
        small pieces*

1. Preheat oven to 375° F. Grease a 10-inch square baking dish.

2. Peel and core apples. Cut each into 8 pieces. In a medium bowl, toss together apples, cinnamon, and brown sugar. Place in baking dish.

3. In a medium bowl, combine cheese, flour, oats, and granulated sugar. Cut unsalted butter into dry ingredients with your fingers, a pastry blender, or two knives. Combine until mixture holds together in large crumbs. Cover apples with crumb mixture. Bake until apples are tender and topping is slightly browned (35 minutes).

Serves 6.

VEGETABLE MAIN COURSES

Vegetable main dishes can be a pleasant change from menus based on meat. These dishes are not "vegetarian." They don't attempt to replace meat. Rather, they use pasta, beans, vegetables, and cheeses as the main ingredients. Lasagne With Three Cheeses (see page 99) and Eggplant, Parma Style (see page 100) are new versions of favorite vegetable casseroles. Black Bean Chile With Cilantro (see page 100) is a very substantial Latin American main course.

LASAGNE WITH THREE CHEESES

A perennial favorite, lasagne is always a crowd pleaser. This version features fresh tomatoes and spinach.

4 tablespoons olive oil
2 shallots, minced
1 bunch spinach, washed and shredded
¾ pound fresh lasagne noodles (4 noodles, about 5 in. by 10 in.) or 6 ounces dried lasagne noodles, cooked until almost tender and drained
3 pounds ricotta cheese
2 large tomatoes, sliced
1 pound mozzarella or provolone cheese, sliced
1 cup parsley, minced

Parmesan Sauce

4 tablespoons butter
5 tablespoons flour
2 cups milk
1 teaspoon salt
¼ teaspoon ground white pepper
⅛ teaspoon ground nutmeg
½ cup grated Parmesan cheese

1. Prepare Parmesan Sauce and reserve. Grease an 8- by 12-inch baking dish with 2 tablespoons of the olive oil. Preheat oven to 350° F. In a large skillet over low heat, heat remaining oil. Sauté shallots and spinach together until spinach is wilted (about 8 minutes).

2. Place ½ cup Parmesan Sauce in baking dish. Place one layer of lasagne noodles on sauce. For first layer: Spread 1 pound ricotta on noodles, cover with one half the tomato, then ½ cup Parmesan Sauce, and finally another layer of lasagne noodles. For second layer: Spread 1 pound ricotta cheese on noodles, cover with all of spinach mixture, one half of the mozzarella, another ½ cup Parmesan Sauce, and top with another layer of noodles. For the final layer: Spread on remaining ricotta, remaining tomato, remaining mozzarella, ½ cup Parmesan Sauce, and remaining noodles. Top with remaining Parmesan Sauce and sprinkle with parsley.

3. Bake until lightly browned on top and bubbly around edges (about 35 minutes). Cool 10 minutes before serving.

Serves 8.

Parmesan Sauce   In a medium saucepan over low heat, melt butter. Whisk in flour and cook until golden brown (4 to 5 minutes). Slowly add milk, whisking until smooth and slightly thickened. Add salt, pepper, nutmeg, and Parmesan.

Makes about 2 ½ cups.

Fresh tomatoes and spinach highlight this version of everybody's favorite pasta casserole. Lasagne With Three Cheeses is ideal for a family supper or party dish.

Simmering black beans with South American-style herbs, garlic, and sherry yields velvety Black Bean Chili With Cilantro, a low-calorie meal-in-a bowl.

BLACK BEAN CHILI WITH CILANTRO

A favorite dish at San Francisco's Greens restaurant, this southwestern chili has been influenced by South American cuisine. Black beans are blended with cilantro, grated onion, and cheese for a meal in one dish.

> *¹⁄₄ cup dry sherry*
> *1 tablespoon olive oil*
> *2 cups chopped onion*
> *¹⁄₂ cup chopped celery*
> *¹⁄₂ cup chopped carrot*
> *¹⁄₂ cup seeded and chopped red bell pepper*
> *4 cups cooked black beans (approximately 3¹⁄₂ cups uncooked)*
> *2 cups chicken stock*
> *2 tablespoons minced garlic*
> *1 cup chopped tomatoes*
> *2 teaspoons ground cumin*
> *4 teaspoons chili powder, or to taste*
> *¹⁄₂ teaspoon dried oregano*
> *¹⁄₄ cup chopped cilantro*
> *2 tablespoons honey*
> *2 tablespoons tomato paste*
> *Grated onion, grated Monterey jack cheese, and yogurt for garnish*

1. In a large, heavy pot, heat sherry and oil over medium heat and sauté onions until soft but not browned.

2. Add celery, carrot, and bell pepper and sauté 5 minutes, stirring frequently.

3. Add remaining ingredients, except garnishes, and bring to a boil. Lower heat and simmer for 45 minutes to 1 hour, covered. Chili should be thick, with all water absorbed. Garnish with grated onion, cheese, and a dollop of yogurt.

Serves 6 to 8.

EGGPLANT PARMA STYLE

An elegant eggplant Parmigiana is definitely not a contradiction in terms. When the eggplant is fried without breading and layered with a lively sauce, prosciutto (an Italian ham), and peppers, the result is a vibrant dish that's appropriate for company meals. It's equally tasty at room temperature and is thus well suited for buffets. The dish can be assembled a day in advance, then covered and refrigerated. Bring to room temperature before baking. For a more formal, dinner-party presentation, bake the dish in individual ramekins. Note that the eggplant must stand 2 hours.

> *2 large eggplants (about 1 to 1¹⁄₄ lb each)*
> *Salt*
> *1 cup light olive oil*
> *6 ounces prosciutto, sliced paper-thin*

1 large red onion, sliced paper-thin

⅓ cup grated Parmesan cheese, plus ¼ cup for garnish

1 teaspoon freshly ground pepper

1 ½ cups chunky Tomato Sauce (see page 115)

3 tablespoons minced parsley, for garnish

Roasted Red Peppers

2 red bell peppers, roasted, peeled, and sliced into ¼- inch strips (see page 67)

1 clove garlic, finely minced

2 tablespoons extra virgin olive oil

1 teaspoon minced fresh oregano or ¼ teaspoon dried oregano

Salt, to taste

1. Wash and dry eggplants; slice into rounds about ½ inch thick. Place rounds on baking sheets lined with paper towels. Sprinkle with salt and let stand 2 hours to draw out the bitter juices. Pat dry.

2. Preheat oven to 350° F. Using ¼ cup olive oil at a time, fry eggplant slices on both sides in a large skillet over moderately high heat. Blot them lightly on paper towels and set aside.

3. Using an 11- by 13-inch baking pan, make layers as follows: eggplant slices, then prosciutto, then onion, then a few red pepper strips, then a light dusting of Parmesan and a sprinkling of pepper, then one-third of the tomato sauce.

Repeat two times, ending with tomato sauce. Bake 35 minutes, or until bubbling hot throughout. Dust top with additonal Parmesan and parsley. Cool slightly before serving directly from the baking dish.

Serves 4 generously.

Roasted Red Peppers Place sliced peppers in a medium bowl; add minced garlic, olive oil, and oregano. Salt to taste. Toss to blend and let marinate at room temperature for 1 hour before using.

BAKED MACARONI PRIMAVERA

Primavera is a much-loved Italian springtime dish of pasta and vegetables. This low-calorie version combines whole-wheat macaroni with a medley of fresh vegetables sautéed in sherry and olive oil, then tossed with a light béchamel made from nonfat milk and a little Parmesan cheese.

8 ounces dried whole wheat, spinach, or artichoke macaroni

¼ cup dry sherry

1 teaspoon olive oil

⅓ cup chopped green onion (including green tops)

1 teaspoon minced garlic

1 red bell pepper, seeded and chopped

¼ teaspoon ground cumin

½ teaspoon dried oregano

1 tablespoon chopped fresh basil

½ cup asparagus, cut diagonally into 2-inch pieces

1 cup halved cherry tomatoes

½ cup whole snow peas, trimmed

Primavera Sauce

2 teaspoons butter

2 teaspoons flour

1 cup nonfat milk

⅓ cup grated Parmesan cheese

¼ teaspoon ground white pepper

1. Preheat oven to 400° F. In a large pot, heat water to boil. Add pasta and cook until just tender (about 8 minutes). Drain and rinse pasta under cold water. Place in a large bowl and set aside.

2. Lightly grease a large baking dish. In a skillet heat sherry and olive oil and sauté green onion, garlic, and bell pepper until pepper is soft but not mushy. Add cumin, oregano, basil, asparagus, cherry tomatoes, and snow peas, and sauté 2 minutes, stirring frequently.

3. Remove from heat and toss with pasta and Primavera Sauce. Spoon into baking dish. Bake until lightly browned and bubbling (about 25 minutes).

Serves 4 to 6.

Primavera Sauce In a saucepan heat butter and stir in flour. Cook 2 minutes, stirring, to eliminate floury taste, then slowly add milk, stirring with a whisk. If milk is added slowly enough, the sauce should thicken to a heavy cream consistency. Add cheese and pepper.

Eggplant Parma Style can be transformed into an elegant company entrée. Frying the eggplant without breading lightens the flavor and texture of this vibrant dish.

This Gratin of Summer Squash is equally delicious served hot from the oven or at room temperature.

VEGETABLES

AND SIDE DISHES

Whether as simple as a slice of fresh fruit on a sandwich plate or as seemingly elaborate as Olive and Asparagus Sauté (see page 107), side dishes are indispensable complements to any main course. But while they may look involved, they needn't be. Colorful vegetable stir-fries, for example, are ready in minutes. Easy potato, rice, and pasta accompaniments can often be prepared early in the day and finished at mealtime. Homemade salsas, chutneys, and other condiments add a personal touch. Stock your preserve pantry with recipes from this chapter (see page 3).

VEGETABLE ACCOMPANIMENTS

Food groups aside, a meal seems incomplete without a vegetable course. Vegetables add flavor, texture, and color to the plate. Keep in mind which vegetables are at their seasonal best when you are planning a menu, although some, like carrots, broccoli, onions, and spinach, are plentiful all year. Orange-Accented Carrots (see page 104); Stir-Fried Broccoli, Red Onion, and Red Pepper (see page 104); and Sautéed Vegetable Medley (see page 106) are good choices in any season.

ORANGE-ACCENTED CARROTS

Oranges and carrots are a classic and colorful combination. Orange juice, sherry, brandy, or vodka will taste equally delicious in place of orange-flavored liqueur.

>   4 large carrots, peeled and sliced
>   2 tablespoons butter
>   2 tablespoons orange-flavored
>   liqueur
>   2 tablespoons orange juice or water
>   1 tablespoon grated orange peel
>   1 teaspoon salt
>   ¼ teaspoon ground white pepper

1. In a medium saucepan, combine carrots, butter, liqueur, orange juice, orange peel, salt, and pepper.

2. Cover saucepan tightly and cook over medium-low heat until carrots are tender when pierced with a knife (about 15 minutes). Serve carrots immediately with sauce.

Serves 6.

Careful timing preserves the lovely color and texture of the vegetables in Stir-Fried Broccoli, Red Onion, and Red Pepper.

STIR-FRIED BROCCOLI, RED ONION, AND RED PEPPER

Blanching the broccoli will shorten the time it needs to stir-fry: Boil the broccoli florets for about 3 minutes. Remove to ice water to stop the cooking. Cooking time in step 1 is for unblanched broccoli.

>   3 tablespoons olive oil
>   1 tablespoon butter
>   1 head broccoli, cut into florets
>   ½ red onion, thinly sliced
>   1 red bell pepper, sliced
>   2 tablespoons fresh basil or
>   2 teaspoons dried basil
>   1 tablespoon fresh oregano or
>   1 teaspoon dried oregano

1. In a large skillet over medium-high heat, add oil and butter. Add broccoli and toss to coat with oil and butter. Cook until bright green and heated through (5 to 8 minutes).

2. Add onion slices; cook, tossing with broccoli, until onion is translucent (about 5 minutes). Add red pepper and continue cooking until pepper is soft but still holds its shape (2 minutes). Toss basil and oregano with broccoli, onion, and red pepper, and serve immediately.

Serves 6.

SPINACH IN SESAME DRESSING

Tahini is found in Middle Eastern markets or health-food stores; substitute peanut butter if it's unavailable. This is a quick-moving preparation. Be sure to have all ingredients measured, ready to toss with the spinach after it has sautéed.

>   5 tablespoons vegetable oil
>   3 bunches spinach, washed and
>   dried
>   ¼ cup tahini
>   1½ teaspoons Asian sesame oil
>   1 teaspoon salt
>   ½ teaspoon freshly ground pepper
>   ½ cup toasted sesame seed, for
>   garnish

1. In a deep sauté pan or Dutch oven over medium-high heat, add vegetable oil and stir in one third of the spinach; sauté until spinach begins to wilt (about 2 minutes). Add one third more spinach and cook by tossing with oil and hot spinach already in pan (about 2 minutes more). As second batch of spinach begins to wilt, add remaining spinach and sauté until wilted (2 to 3 minutes).

2. As soon as last addition of spinach has wilted and any moisture in the pan has evaporated, quickly stir in tahini, sesame oil, salt, and pepper. Toss to combine. Remove from pan to a serving dish and sprinkle with toasted sesame seed.

Serves 6.

ZESTY GREEN BEANS

Fresh green beans get a flavor boost from garlic and wine vinegar, and extra color from the addition of strips of sweet red bell pepper.

> 2 tablespoons butter or vegetable oil
> 1 clove garlic, minced
> 1 pound green beans, cut diagonally in 1-inch lengths
> Half a small red bell pepper, seeded and cut in ½-inch strips
> 5 tablespoons water
> 2 teaspoons wine vinegar

1. In a large skillet over medium-high heat, melt butter. Add garlic and sauté briefly. Add beans, pepper, and water. Cover and steam until tender-crisp (about 6 minutes).

2. Remove cover, add vinegar, and increase heat to high to evaporate most of the liquid (1 to 2 minutes).

Serves 4.

MINTED GREEN PEAS WITH LETTUCE

This is a classic French side dish that pairs well with light meats like veal or with any poultry dish. Try to use fresh mint, if possible.

> 2 tablespoons butter
> 1 package (10 oz) frozen peas
> 1 tablespoon chopped fresh mint or 1 teaspoon dried mint leaves
> 2 tablespoons minced parsley (optional)
> Salt and sugar, to taste
> Mint sprigs, for garnish

1. In a large skillet over medium heat, melt butter. Add peas (breaking up with a fork), cover, and cook until thawed (about 5 minutes).

2. Add lettuce, chopped mint, and parsley (if used) and cook, uncovered, until lettuce wilts. Toss occasionally. Season to taste and garnish with mint.

Serves 4.

Red bell pepper adds just the right touch of color to these flavorful Zesty Green Beans.

Minted Green Peas

The deliciously earthy flavors of potatoes, carrots, onions, and mushrooms are highlighted in Sauteed Vegetable Medley.

SAUTÉED VEGETABLE MEDLEY

Potatoes, carrots, onions, and mushrooms are not seasonal, so you can prepare this substantial side dish throughout the year. It seems particularly appropriate for fall and winter, when we begin to think of root vegetables and more hearty foods.

> ¾ *pound small new potatoes, quartered*
> 1 *large carrot, cut in sticks*
> 4 *small white onions, peeled and halved*
> 2 *tablespoons butter*
> ½ *pound (about 20 medium) mushrooms, halved*
> 1 *teaspoon dried basil*
> *Grated Parmesan, Romano, or Sapsago cheese, for garnish*

1. In a large saucepan over medium-high heat, cook potatoes in boiling, salted water 5 minutes. Add carrot and onions and cook 5 minutes more.

2. Meanwhile, melt butter in a large skillet; add mushrooms and sauté 1 minute. Drain boiled vegetables, add to skillet, and sauté briefly with mushrooms.

3. Add basil; toss vegetables to mix. Serve garnished with a sprinkling of cheese.

Serves 4.

VEGETABLE COMPOTE

Quickly cooked corn, red bell peppers, lima beans, and onions combine to make a colorful vegetable mosaic. Pair this compote with potato pancakes for a satisfying vegetarian supper.

> 2 *red bell peppers*
> 4 *ears corn (2 cups kernels) or 1 package (10 oz) frozen corn kernels*
> ½ *pound small green beans*
> 1 *tablespoon olive oil*
> 2 *onions, diced*
> 3 *cloves garlic, minced*
> 2 *cups cooked fresh lima beans or 1 can (17 oz) lima beans*
> ½ *cup water*
> ¼ *teaspoon cayenne pepper*
> 1 *teaspoon dried thyme*
> ½ *teaspoon dried oregano*
> 1 *teaspoon salt*
> ½ *teaspoon ground black pepper*

1. Cut red peppers into ½-inch-square pieces. Cut corn from cobs. Trim stem ends from beans and cut into 2-inch lengths.

2. Place oil in a large skillet over medium heat. Sauté onions and garlic for 7 to 8 minutes. Add red peppers, corn, and green beans, and cook 5 minutes. Add lima beans, the water, cayenne, thyme, oregano, salt, and pepper. Cook 10 minutes.

Serves 6.

OLIVE AND ASPARAGUS SAUTÉ

This simple sauté uses pungent Greek olives. The dish is equally good with carrots, eggplant, or zucchini.

> 1 *pound thin asparagus*
> 2 *cloves garlic, minced*
> 20 *Kalamata olives, pitted and halved*
> 2 *tablespoons olive oil*
> ½ *teaspoon salt*
> ¼ *teaspoon freshly ground pepper*
> ½ *cup water*

1. Trim tough stems from asparagus. In a large skillet over medium heat, sauté garlic and olives in oil about 5 minutes.

2. Add asparagus, salt, pepper, and the water. Cover and cook over medium heat until asparagus is tender (3 to 5 minutes).

Serves 6.

GRATIN OF SUMMER SQUASH

This quick gratin can be prepared ahead, held for baking, and served hot or it can be prepared and baked ahead and served at room temperature.

> 2 *tablespoons olive oil*
> 1 *small red onion*
> 3 *zucchini*
> 2 *plum tomatoes*
> 3 *cloves garlic, minced*
> ¼ *teaspoon each salt and freshly ground pepper*
> 1 *tablespoon fresh thyme, minced or 1 teaspoon dried thyme*
> 3 *ounces Gruyère cheese, grated*

1. Preheat oven to 350° F. Lightly oil an 8-inch round baking dish. Slice onion into rounds. Slice zucchini and tomatoes about ½ inch thick.

2. In a large skillet over medium heat, place 1 tablespoon of the oil, and sauté onion and garlic until translucent (5 to 8 minutes).

3. Place zucchini slices vertically along the edge of the baking dish (cut edge against side of dish). Place the tomato slices against the zucchini, then some of the sautéed onion-garlic mixture against the tomato slices so vegetables stand up around perimeter of baking dish. Repeat with zucchini, tomato, and onion-garlic mixture to form alternating rings. Place remaining vegetables in center. Sprinkle with salt, pepper, thyme, and cheese.

4. Bake for 25 minutes. Serve warm or at room temperature.

Serves 6.

Satisfying and colorful, this Vegetable Compote is a nutritious complement to potato pancakes.

MENU

SPRING SALMON DINNER

For 4

Chilled Soup of Mixed Peas
Roasted Salmon With Garlic Cream
Potato, Turnip, and Chard Sauté
Fresh Fruit Marinated in Wine (see
page 118)
California Sauvignon Blanc or White
French Côtes-du-Rhône

The appearance of the first spring salmon is a fine excuse for a party. To make it a full-fledged salute to the season, the menu weaves in a wealth of spring bounty, from sweet peas and new potatoes to ripe strawberries and other fresh fruit. The dinner is an easy one to host. Only the vegetable sauté needs last-minute attention. The salmon should be slipped into the oven after the soup course is cleared and the vegetables sautéed shortly thereafter.

CHILLED SOUP OF MIXED PEAS

This 10-minute soup is made with fresh English peas, then garnished with finely shredded sugar snap peas. The sugar snaps are entirely edible, including the pod, but they require stringing. When purchasing English peas, open a pod or two and sample; the peas inside should be small, firm, and sweet.

> *¼ pound sugar snap peas, strings*
> *   removed*
> *¼ cup butter*
> *2 shallots, minced*
> *2 pounds English peas, shelled*
> *2 cups chicken stock*
> *2 cups half-and-half*
> *½ cup crème fraîche (see Note) or*
> *   sour cream*
> *Lemon juice, to taste*
> *Salt and freshly ground pepper,*
> *   to taste*
> *¼ cup fresh basil leaves*

1. Blanch sugar snap peas 30 seconds in lightly salted boiling water; drain and plunge into ice water to stop the cooking. Julienne the peas and set aside for garnish.

2. In a medium saucepan melt butter over moderately low heat. Add shallots and sauté 1 minute. Add English peas, reduce heat to low, and cook until peas are slightly softened (about 5 minutes). Raise heat to high, add chicken stock, and bring to a simmer. Reduce heat to maintain a simmer and cook 2 minutes. Transfer soup to a blender or food processor and blend until smooth. Chill thoroughly.

3. Whisk together half-and-half and crème fraîche. Whisk into chilled soup. Season with lemon juice, salt, and pepper. Just before serving, shred basil finely with a knife. Ladle soup into chilled bowls. Garnish the top of each serving with julienned sugar snap peas and finely shredded basil.

Serves 4.

Note: Crème fraîche can be found in specialty stores and some well-stocked supermarkets.

ROASTED SALMON WITH GARLIC CREAM

Whole garlic cloves turn soft and mild when simmered or roasted slowly. Purée the soft cloves with butter and cream, spread it on the salmon, and bake until done to your liking. The dish couldn't be simpler or more aromatic. Note that the salmon should marinate for at least 30 minutes.

> *4 whole bulbs garlic*
> *3 tablespoons butter*
> *1 cup crème fraîche (see Note) or*
> *   sour cream*
> *1 teaspoon stone-ground mustard*
> *2 pounds fresh salmon fillets*

1. Remove papery outer shell from garlic, but leave bulbs intact and cloves unpeeled. Place bulbs in a saucepan just large enough to hold them. Add water to barely cover and bring to a simmer over high heat. Reduce heat to maintain a simmer and cook 40 minutes, adding

more water as necessary to keep heads barely covered. Remove from heat, cool, and peel. Cloves will be very soft and easy to peel. Place cloves in a food processor with butter and purée. Add crème fraîche and mustard and process until blended. Transfer to a bowl and set aside.

2. Cut salmon into 8-ounce fillets. Spread top surface of each fillet with some of the garlic purée. Cover with plastic wrap and refrigerate for at least 30 minutes or up to 1 day.

3. Preheat oven to 350° F. Place fillets on a lightly buttered baking sheet or in a buttered baking dish and roast until done to your liking (7 to 10 minutes). Serve immediately.

Serves 4.

Note: Crème fraîche can be found in specialty stores and some well-stocked supermarkets.

POTATO, TURNIP, AND CHARD SAUTÉ

For best flavor, choose small new potatoes, young turnips, and tender chard leaves with narrow ribs.

> *1 pound red new potatoes*
> *1 pound turnips, peeled*
> *1 pound chard*
> *4 tablespoons butter*
> *2 tablespoons minced shallots*
> *1 teaspoon minced garlic*
> *2 tablespoons olive oil*
> *1 teaspoon stone-ground mustard*
> *2 tablespoons crème fraîche (see*
> *   Note) or sour cream*
> *2 tablespoons lemon juice*
> *Salt and freshly ground pepper,*
> *   to taste*

1. Boil potatoes in lightly salted water until tender when pierced with a knife. Drain and set aside. Cut large potatoes in halves or quarters; leave small ones whole.

2. Boil turnips in lightly salted water until tender when pierced with a knife. Drain and set aside. Cut large turnips in halves or quarters; leave small ones whole.

3. Cut chard ribs away from leaves. Blanch leaves and ribs separately in lightly salted water, cooking just until tender (3 to 5 minutes). Drain and

plunge into ice water to stop the cooking. Drain again. Chop leaves coarsely; dice ribs.

4. In a small skillet over moderately low heat, melt 2 tablespoons butter. Add shallots and garlic and sauté until fragrant (2 to 3 minutes). Set mixture aside.

5. At serving time, in a large skillet warm remaining butter and olive oil over moderately high heat. Add softened shallot-garlic mixture and chard ribs and sauté quickly to heat through. Add potatoes and turnips and sauté quickly to heat through. Add chard leaves and cook 20 seconds. Stir in mustard and crème fraîche. Add lemon juice and season with salt and pepper.

Serves 4.

Note: Crème fraîche can be found in specialty stores and some well-stocked supermarkets.

FEATURE

HERB GARDENING

Spice up almost any meal with a touch of fresh herbs. Mince them over pizza; julienne them onto salads; slow-cook them into soups and stews. Most growing herbs prefer lots of sunlight—five to eight hours a day—and lots of water. Seeds can be started indoors in small pots and then transplanted outside or kept indoors on a sunny windowsill. Plants can also be started directly outdoors by scattering seeds over raked soil and covering them to about twice their depth. Label beds carefully. Keep soil moist as seeds grow. After two to four weeks, carefully thin the tiny seedlings, and transplant the extra seedlings elsewhere or use them in cooking. Herbs should be soaked rather than sprayed so that water reaches the roots. Fertilize only twice a year. Too much fertilizer creates lush foliage at the expense of flavor.

A BASIC HERB GARDEN

Basil   Rich flavor blends well with tomatoes; grow in full sun or partial shade; keep moist.

Chervil   Dried has little flavor, fresh is delicate and aromatic; grow in partial shade; keep slightly moist.

Chives   Use flowers as garnish; grow in full sun and moist soil.

Marjoram   Can be substituted anytime a recipe calls for oregano; grow in full sun and moist soil.

Mint   Easy to grow, likes partial shade and moisture; can easily overrun a garden so is best potted.

Nasturtium   Beautiful in garden or salad, leaves edible but peppery, flowers edible; prefers full sun and overrich soil.

Oregano   Hearty and tasty; grow in full sun and moist soil.

Parsley   Easy to grow in partial shade and moist soil.

Rosemary   Beautiful aromatic needles with edible flowers; use dried or fresh; grow in full sun and dry soil.

Tarragon   French tarragon is preferred; grow in partial shade.

Thyme   Extremely aromatic; grow in full sun.

HERB BUTTER

Mix available herbs for creative combinations. Mold in butter forms or ice-cube trays. Use on vegetables or as a spread for bread.

½ cup unsalted butter, softened
2 shallots, minced
3 tablespoons minced fresh herb
1 tablespoon white wine vinegar
¼ teaspoon salt
⅛ teaspoon ground white pepper

Place butter in a blender, food processor, or 2-cup mixing bowl. Add shallots, herb, vinegar, salt, and pepper. Mix well. Roll into a cylinder or place in mold. Wrap in foil for storage in the refrigerator for 1 week or the freezer for 2 months.

Makes ½ cup.

ROASTED ONIONS WITH BALSAMIC VINEGAR

Balsamic vinegar is a pungent, almost sweet, aged vinegar. It adds a special flavor to the roasted onions. Serve with pasta dishes and roasted meats and poultry.

    3 red onions
    1 clove garlic, minced
    ¼ cup balsamic vinegar
    ¼ cup olive oil
    ⅛ teaspoon salt
    ⅛ teaspoon freshly ground pepper

1. Leaving root end attached, slice onions in half lengthwise. Peel papery skin off onion. In a 9- by 12-inch baking pan, mix garlic with 2 tablespoons of the vinegar, oil, salt, and pepper to make a marinade. Add onions. Toss marinade with onions. Let sit for 1 hour.

2. Preheat oven to 350° F. Bake onions in marinade for 1 ¼ hours. Onions are done when a knife inserted into center meets no resistance. Remove from oven to a serving dish and sprinkle with remaining vinegar.

Serves 6.

GRILLED JAPANESE EGGPLANT

Japanese eggplant is ideal for grilling because it is thin and can be grilled whole, rather than cut into pieces. The outside skin browns beautifully while the sweet meat inside steams from the juices. Over a hot fire, Japanese eggplant usually takes about 5 minutes to cook. To broil, halve the eggplant lengthwise, brush cut sides with oil, and broil close to the heat for about 3 minutes.

    6 Japanese eggplant (about 2 lbs total)
    2 tablespoons olive oil
    1 teaspoon minced garlic
      Salt and freshly ground pepper, to taste

1. Wash eggplant and pat dry. Lightly coat with olive oil, garlic, salt, and pepper. Prepare a charcoal fire.

2. Place eggplant on grill over direct heat and cover with lid. Turn several times during cooking. Eggplant should be done in about 5 minutes.

Serves 4 to 6.

SAVORY SIDE DISHES

The best side dishes can either be prepared ahead and then simply heated to serve or are so quick to put together that they are ready in minutes. This section features delicious recipes of both kinds. Do-aheads include Potato Gratin (see page 111), Fontina Polenta (see page 112), Tomato-Rice Casserole (see page 112), and Borracho Beans (see page 113). Among the fast-to-the-table dishes are Baked Potato Sticks (see page 111), Couscous With Mushrooms (see page 113), and Pasta With Broccoli and Snow Peas (see page 114).

POTATO GRATIN

Early in the day, prepare potato gratin up to the point of baking. Store in refrigerator until ready to bake; add an extra 10 minutes to baking time if chilled. To keep potatoes from darkening while the dish is held, press plastic wrap on surface of gratin to submerge potatoes in liquid.

    2 ½ pounds (about 4 large) baking
          potatoes
    2 cups half-and-half
    1 cup milk
    2 cloves garlic, minced
    1 ½ teaspoons salt
    ½ teaspoon freshly ground pepper

1. Preheat oven to 350° F. Grease a 10- by 15-inch baking dish with butter. Peel potatoes; slice about ⅛ inch thick. In a medium bowl, whisk together half-and-half, milk, garlic, salt, and pepper.

2. Layer one third of sliced potatoes in buttered baking dish. Pour in one third of milk mixture. Place another third of potatoes into baking dish. Pour in another third of milk mixture. Finish with remaining potatoes and milk mixture. Bake until browned slightly on top and tender when pierced with a knife (about 1 hour). Serve immediately.

Serves 8 to 12.

BAKED POTATO STICKS

For an easy oven dinner, bake potatoes on the rack along with Mediterranean Leg of Lamb (see page 89) or Beef Tenderloin Roll (see page 89).

    6 medium baking potatoes
    9 tablespoons butter
    1 ½ teaspoons salt
    1 teaspoon freshly ground pepper

1. Preheat oven to 400° F. Scrub and quarter potatoes. Melt butter in a 9- by 12-inch ovenproof baking dish in oven.

2. Place potato quarters in dish and turn to coat with melted butter; arrange potatoes cut side down and sprinkle with salt and pepper. Bake until tender when pierced with a sharp knife (30 to 35 minutes).

Serves 6.

SWEET POTATO PANCAKES

Although wonderful when baked, vitamin-rich sweet potatoes are also tasty when sautéed with garlic and tarragon. For variety, shred apples and add to the sweet potatoes. The mixture can be prepared in advance and held in the refrigerator for several hours before cooking.

    2 medium sweet potatoes (about
          1 lb), peeled and shredded
    1 small onion, minced
    3 cloves garlic, minced
    2 teaspoons dried tarragon
    1 teaspoon salt
    ¼ teaspoon freshly ground pepper
    2 tablespoons dried bread crumbs
    2 eggs, lightly beaten
    1 tablespoon butter
    2 tablespoons vegetable oil

1. Place shredded sweet potatoes in a medium bowl. Stir in onion, garlic, tarragon, salt, pepper, bread crumbs, and eggs.

2. In a large skillet over medium heat, melt butter with oil. For each pancake, place 2 heaping tablespoons sweet potato mixture in pan and flatten to a pancake about 4 inches in diameter. Cook until each side is browned and appears dry (10 minutes on the first side, 8 minutes on the second side). Serve immediately.

Serves 6.

RABAT RICE PILAF

Toasted nuts, dried currants, diced dried apricots, shredded carrots, or minced fresh herbs will add variety to this basic pilaf. If served with beef or lamb, substitute beef stock for the chicken stock.

    2 tablespoons butter
    1 onion, minced
    1 carrot, finely diced
    2 ½ cups long-grain white rice
    4 ½ cups chicken stock
    ½ tablespoon salt
    ¼ teaspoon freshly ground pepper

In a medium saucepan over medium heat, melt butter. Sauté onion and carrot until softened but not browned (about 6 minutes). Add rice, stock, salt, and pepper. Stir to combine. Cover and cook over low to medium heat until liquid is absorbed (about 25 minutes). Serve warm.

Serves 8.

Multigrain Pilaf   Use 1 cup long-grain white rice; 1 cup wheat berries, rye berries, triticale berries, or barley; and ½ cup wild rice. Increase chicken stock to 5 cups. Cook pilaf for 40 minutes.

ARROZ VERDE

Tone down the heat in this rice dish by omitting the diced green chiles.

    1 onion, diced
    2 cloves garlic, minced
    2 tablespoons vegetable oil
    ½ cup minced parsley
    2 cups long-grain white rice
    4 ½ cups chicken stock
    2 teaspoons salt
    8 green onions, minced
    ½ cup minced cilantro
    1 small can (3 ½ oz) diced green
        chiles

1. In a medium saucepan over medium heat, sauté onion and garlic in oil until softened and translucent (3 to 4 minutes). Stir in parsley, rice, chicken stock, and salt.

2. Cover and simmer over low heat until all liquid is absorbed (18 to 20 minutes). Remove from heat and stir in green onions, cilantro, and diced green chiles. Serve warm.

Serves 8.

TOMATO-RICE CASSEROLE

Make this easy accompaniment to barbecued steak in stages: Cook the rice and combine with the other ingredients, then hold in a casserole and bake shortly before serving.

    3 tablespoons vegetable oil
    1 ½ cups long-grain white rice
    1 large onion, finely chopped
    1 clove garlic, minced
    1 can (15 oz) tomato sauce
    1 ½ cups chicken stock
    ¾ teaspoon each salt and ground
        cumin
    ⅛ teaspoon cayenne pepper
    ¾ cup ripe olive wedges
    2 cups grated Monterey jack cheese

1. Preheat oven to 325° F. Grease a 1 ½ to 2-quart casserole. In a large deep saucepan, heat oil over medium heat; stir in rice and coat with oil. Add onion and garlic and sauté until onion browns lightly. Mix in tomato sauce, stock, salt, cumin, and cayenne. Bring to a boil over medium-high heat, reduce heat to low, and cover. Cook until rice is almost tender (about 20 minutes).

2. Mix in olive wedges and 1 cup of the cheese. Turn into prepared casserole. Sprinkle with remaining cheese. Bake, uncovered, until cheese is melted and lightly browned (about 15 minutes).

Serves 6 to 8.

FONTINA POLENTA

Polenta can be prepared at the last minute or hours ahead. Top it with Fresh Tomato Sauce (see page 115) and sprinkle with basil. Some grilled Italian sausage would round out a wonderful Sunday supper menu.

    2 ½ cups chicken stock
    1 cup polenta (coarse cornmeal)
    1 tablespoon butter
    1 ¼ teaspoons salt
    2 tablespoons whipping cream
        (optional)
    ½ cup grated fontina cheese

1. In a large saucepan over medium-high heat, bring stock to a boil. Reduce heat to medium. Add polenta by the tablespoon, stirring constantly to prevent lumps from forming. Continue stirring as mixture cooks (about 20 minutes). Polenta will pull away from sides of pan.

2. Stir in butter, salt, and cream (if used). Top with grated fontina and serve immediately.

Serves 6.

Baked Fontina Polenta   Prepare Fontina Polenta as directed, reserving grated fontina. Pour polenta into a buttered 8- by 8-inch baking pan. Cover with plastic wrap if not serving immediately. At serving time, preheat oven to 375° F. Sprinkle polenta with grated fontina and bake until cheese melts (15 to 20 minutes).

Creamy Gorgonzola Polenta   Omit fontina cheese. Stir 4 ounces crumbled Gorgonzola cheese into warm polenta with butter and salt.

BORRACHO BEANS

Drunken (*borracho*) beans accompany myriad entrées from south of the border. They can be garnished with salsa and sour cream for extra flavor. To prepare beans, soak 2½ cups dried beans 8 to 10 hours, drain liquid, add fresh water to cover, and simmer 2 hours until tender. Borracho Beans can be made as much as one week ahead and kept in the refrigerator until needed.

½ pound bacon, diced
2 onions, diced
2 cloves garlic, diced
6 cups cooked black beans
2 teaspoons salt
1 teaspoon each pepper and toasted cumin seed
1 can (12 oz) beer

1. In a 6-quart bean pot or deep stockpot over medium heat, cook bacon until some of the fat is rendered (4 minutes). Stir in onions and garlic and sauté until onion is translucent (4 to 5 minutes).

2. Add beans, salt, pepper, cumin seed, and beer. Simmer 25 minutes. Serve warm or refrigerate up to 1 week; reheat to serve.

Serves 8 to 10.

COUSCOUS WITH MUSHROOMS

Shaped like tiny pellets, couscous is a Moroccan pasta that is as versatile as rice. If you use the instant type, as this recipe does, it is ready in minutes. Couscous can be found with the rice and pasta at well-stocked supermarkets.

(continued)

From Venice comes Fontina Polenta, shown here with grilled Italian sausages.

(continued from page 113)

   3 cups chicken stock
   2 cups quick-cooking couscous
   3 green onions, thinly sliced
   3 to 4 tablespoons toasted pine nuts
     or sliced almonds
   ½ cup thinly sliced mushrooms
    Minced parsley, for garnish

1. In a large saucepan over medium-high heat, bring stock to a boil. Stir in couscous, onions, nuts, and mushrooms.

2. Immediately remove from heat, cover, and let stand until liquid is absorbed (5 minutes). Serve garnished with parsley.

Serves 4.

PASTA WITH BROCCOLI AND SNOW PEAS

Use this one-pot technique for any pasta tossed with vegetables; blanching the vegetables in the same pot used later for the pasta will save cleanup time.

   3 shallots, minced
   3 tablespoons butter
   1 bunch broccoli, cut into florets
   ½ pound snow peas
   1 pound dried fusilli pasta
   1 cup (5 oz) grated Asiago cheese
   ½ teaspoon hot-pepper flakes
    Freshly ground black pepper, to
    taste

1. In a large saucepan over medium heat, sauté shallots in butter until softened (about 3 minutes); remove from pan and reserve.

2. In same pan, bring water to a boil. Boil broccoli until tender (3 to 4 minutes). Remove with a slotted spoon and reserve. Blanch snow peas in boiling water until bright green (about 30 seconds); remove with a slotted spoon and reserve. Return water to a boil and stir in pasta. Boil until pasta is just tender (about 12 minutes). Drain in colander.

3. In a large bowl, combine pasta, broccoli, snow peas, and reserved shallots. Toss with ½ cup of the Asiago cheese and hot pepper flakes. Transfer to a serving bowl. Sprinkle with remaining cheese and season with pepper.

Serves 6 to 8.

FEATURE

PANTRY SAUCES AND RELISHES

If you have a few hours to spend in the kitchen above and beyond the time expended for meal preparation, set aside an afternoon or evening to put up a shelf-full of homemade specialty foods. These fancy items are costly to buy when ready-made. By preparing them yourself, you will be able to stock a pantry with premium products at a more affordable price. A selection of relishes and sauces will embellish your cooking and add sparkle to meals. Packaged in pretty containers, they also make welcome gifts.

MARINATED ONIONS

Store these piquant onion slices in the refrigerator, ready to toss in a salad, place on a pizza, or garnish a hamburger.

   1 large red onion, thinly sliced
   ⅓ cup red wine vinegar
   ½ cup water
   1 tablespoon sugar
   ½ teaspoon salt
   5 or 6 peppercorns
   1 teaspoon dried oregano
   1 teaspoon dried basil

1. In a large saucepan, bring onion, vinegar, the water, sugar, salt, peppercorns, oregano, and basil to a boil. Reduce heat to low and simmer, uncovered, until onion is tender (about 8 minutes).

2. Chill onion in the cooking liquid 2 to 12 hours. Store, covered, in refrigerator up to 1 week.

Makes about 2 cups.

PINEAPPLE SALSA

Fresh fruit salsas satisfy the taste for salad and fruit in one dish. Peaches, nectarines, or plums can also be used. Serve as a condiment with pork, chicken, or duck.

   ½ pineapple, diced in ¼-inch pieces
   2 medium tomatoes, diced
   1 small cucumber, seeded and
    diced
   2 shallots, minced
   ½ jalapeño chile, minced
   ¼ cup minced cilantro
   2 tablespoons lime juice
   1 tablespoon each white wine
    vinegar and vegetable oil
   ½ teaspoon salt

In a medium bowl stir together all ingredients. Cover and refrigerate at least 1 hour.

Makes 4 cups.

SOUTH-OF-THE-BORDER SALSA

This versatile sauce can serve as a dip for crisp tortilla chips or as a spicy marinade for poultry or fish. Stir the salsa into a soup to spice up a light lunch with the avocado variation. Avocado Salsa is a delicious condiment that can be used in the same way as guacamole. Since avocados are perishable, prepare the variation no more than one day ahead.

   3 large tomatoes, coarsely chopped
   1 small onion, finely diced
   2 cloves garlic, minced
    Juice of 2 limes
   1 jalapeño chile, minced
   1 teaspoon salt
   1 bunch cilantro, minced

In a medium bowl, stir together tomatoes, onion, garlic, lime juice, chile, salt, and cilantro. Let rest for at least 30 minutes before serving.

Makes 3 ½ cups.

Avocado Salsa Follow South-of-the-Border Salsa recipe, but substitute 3 large, ripe (but not soft), coarsely chopped avocados and 3 fresh tomatillos (paper husks removed, fruit washed, dried, and diced) for the tomatoes.

Makes 4 cups.

PESTO SAUCE

Use this vibrantly green sauce to brush on Italian flat bread, to toss with buttered fresh pasta, to rub on chicken breasts before broiling, or to add in a thin layer to Potato Gratin (see page 111). For variety, try Pesto With Sun-Dried Tomatoes, below.

  2 *cups fresh basil leaves*
  4 *cloves garlic*
1 ¼ *cups olive oil*
  ½ *teaspoon salt*
  1 *cup grated Parmesan cheese*
  ¼ *cup pine nuts or walnuts*

In a blender or food processor, purée basil and garlic with olive oil. Blend in salt, cheese, and nuts. Seal tightly in one or two airtight containers. Store in the refrigerator up to 3 weeks or in the freezer up to 6 months.

Makes 2 cups.

Pesto With Sun-Dried Tomatoes

Follow Pesto Sauce recipe, but substitute 1 ounce sun-dried tomatoes for 1 cup of the basil leaves. To reconstitute tomatoes, cover with boiling water and let rest for 30 minutes. Drain, pat dry, and purée as directed.

FRESH TOMATO SAUCE

Fresh herbs enhance the flavor of this sauce but, in a pinch, dried herbs can be substituted. Canned tomatoes are often superior in flavor to tomatoes out of season. They are also convenient, allowing last-minute preparation.

  2 *pounds fresh tomatoes, peeled*
     and seeded (see page 56) or
     1 can (28 oz) whole plum
     tomatoes
  2 *tablespoons olive oil*
  1 *medium onion, diced*
  3 *cloves garlic, minced*
  ¼ *cup chopped fresh parsley or*
     2 teaspoons dried parsley
  2 *tablespoons chopped fresh basil or*
     1 teaspoon dried basil
  1 *tablespoon chopped fresh oregano*
     or 1 teaspoon dried oregano
  ½ *teaspoon sugar*
  1 *teaspoon salt*
  ½ *teaspoon freshly ground pepper*

1. Chop peeled and seeded fresh tomatoes into medium dice. If using canned tomatoes, drain, discard juice, and dice.

2. In a medium saucepan over medium heat, heat oil and sauté onion 5 minutes. Add garlic and sauté 5 minutes more. Stir in tomatoes, parsley, basil, oregano, sugar, salt, and pepper. Simmer 20 minutes. Use immediately or store, tightly covered, in the refrigerator for 1 week or in an airtight container in the freezer for 1 month.

Makes about 2 cups.

Spicy Tomato Sauce   Add ½ teaspoon ground dried chiles to sauce.

TOMATO-PEARL ONION CHUTNEY

The easiest way to peel a pearl onion is to dip it in boiling water for 3 minutes, cut off the end, and then squeeze the onion out of the skin.

 10 *ounces pearl onions*
  1 *large yellow onion, minced*
  2 *cloves garlic, minced*
  1 *tablespoon olive oil*
  5 *tomatoes, diced*
  1 *tablespoon minced fresh ginger*
  2 *tablespoons tomato paste*
  1 *teaspoon dry mustard*
  2 *tablespoons apple cider vinegar*
  ½ *teaspoon salt*
  1 *tablespoon honey*
  ¼ *teaspoon ground dried red chiles*
  ¼ *cup raisins*
  2 *tablespoons parsley, minced*
  1 *teaspoon fresh oregano, minced*
 10 *ounces pearl onions, peeled*

In a medium saucepan over medium heat, sauté yellow onion and garlic in oil for 5 minutes; add tomatoes, ginger, tomato paste, dry mustard, vinegar, salt, honey, dried chiles, raisins, parsley, and oregano. Cook for 20 minutes. Add pearl onions and cook for 25 minutes more. Cool slightly before serving.

Makes 3 ¼ cups.

Luxurious flavor and delicate texture are combined in this Mediterranean fruit-filled dessert known as Cassata.

DESSERTS

Desserts are an opportunity for the cook to make a grand statement with relatively little effort. Most desserts can be prepared ahead of serving time and held without problem until needed. There's a recipe for every sweet tooth in this final chapter: fruits served in simple wine sauces (see page 120) or baked in a custardy batter (see page 118); a gooey brownie sundae (see page 125) or a rum-and-coffee-flavored sponge cake (see page 128); a frozen confection of ice cream and candied fruit (see page 130) or a chocolate waffle (see page 128); plus a stellar collection of fabulous ice cream sauces.

DESSERTS WITH FRUIT

Fruit is a welcome conclusion to any meal, whether served alone, baked in a delicate batter, marinated in spirits, or crushed and streaked through luscious whipped cream. Some of the recipes in this section are best made with fresh fruit at their seasonal peak; others work just as well with fruit that is frozen or canned. All are tempting and easy. Zinfandel Pears and Peaches (see page 120) is a delicious sauce made of wine-poached fruit intriguingly flavored with herbs. Fruit Fool (see page 121) is an English favorite that tosses together mashed sugared strawberries with whipped cream. Warm Figs With Gorgonzola (see page 120) contrasts the sweetness of ripe figs with the savory creaminess of a cheese accompaniment.

TART RED CHERRY CLAFOUTIS

Clafoutis is a French pudding made with fresh, canned, or frozen fruit. Blueberries, blackberries, peaches, or raspberries can be used instead of cherries. Vanilla ice cream is a dramatic accent for this simple dessert. The batter can be prepared ahead through step 3 early in the day and left out at cool room temperature until needed. Forty minutes before serving, proceed with step 4.

3 tablespoons butter
1 pound tart red cherries, pitted if fresh, drained if canned
1 cup sugar
½ cup flour
6 eggs, separated
1 ⅓ cups milk
⅛ teaspoon salt
1 teaspoon vanilla extract
⅛ teaspoon cream of tartar
Confectioners' sugar, for garnish
Vanilla ice cream, for accompaniment (optional)

1. Using 1 tablespoon of the butter, grease a shallow, 10-inch diameter baking or gratin dish. Preheat oven to 350° F.

2. Toss cherries with ¼ cup sugar and place in buttered baking dish. Dot cherries with remaining butter.

3. In a large bowl, whisk remaining sugar, flour, egg yolks, milk, salt, and vanilla.

4. Beat egg whites with cream of tartar to form soft peaks. Fold into flour mixture and pour over cherries in prepared dish. Bake until light golden brown (about 35 minutes). Dust with confectioners' sugar, and serve warm with vanilla ice cream (if desired).

Serves 6.

Tart Red Cherry Clafoutis, a French fruit pudding, is most delicious when served warm.

FEATURE

FRESH FRUIT SHELLS

On special occasions you can dress up sorbets by serving them frozen in the fruits from which they were made or in fruits with a complementary flavor. Hollowed-out lemons, limes, Granny Smith apples, kiwifruits, mangoes, guavas, plums, peaches, oranges, apricots, and giant strawberries make perfect serving containers. Simply scoop out the centers of the fruits, freeze the shells, then fill with the appropriate sorbets. Wrap tightly and return to the freezer until time for serving. For an especially festive presentation, line a large grapevine basket with moss or leaves and decorate it with such flowers as sweet peas, roses, nasturtiums, and honeysuckle. Arrange the sorbet-filled frozen fruits in the basket and let your guests pick out their favorites. Most supermarkets have a selection of sorbets in the frozen food section. Look for sorbets at take-out ice cream stores as well.

FRESH FRUIT MARINATED IN WINE

An assortment of seasonal fruits marinated in sweet Muscat wine makes a light, refreshing dessert. Of course, a glass of the same wine would taste fine along with it. Try to combine some tart fruits like oranges and pineapple with low-acid types like pears or bananas, but don't use too much tart fruit or the acidity will overpower the wine.

Choose three or four of the following, depending on what is in season: strawberries, hulled, split if large; cantaloupe, honeydew, or other firm melon, in cubes or balls; orange or tangerine sections, all white pith removed; peaches or nectarines, unpeeled, sliced; blueberries or huckleberries; red, green, or purple grapes, especially Muscat types; mango, peeled and cut into wedges; papaya, peeled and diced; pears, peeled, cored, and diced; fully ripe pineapple, in chunks; bananas, peeled and sliced.

4 cups assorted fresh fruit (see above)
1 cup sweet Muscat Blanc, Muscat Canelli, or Malvasia Bianca
Lemon juice to taste (omit if using citrus fruits)
Mint leaves, for garnish

1. Combine the cut-up fruit in a large bowl, pour in the wine, and toss to moisten the fruit thoroughly with wine. Marinate in the refrigerator 1 to 4 hours.

2. Taste a piece of the sweetest fruit and a piece of the most tart. Add lemon juice if necessary. Serve with a garnish of fresh mint.

Serves 4.

BAKED CRANBERRY APPLES

Baking apples is an old-fashioned preparation that works equally well with pears and quince. Cranberries and pecans add a festive touch. Granny Smiths or pippins are the apples of choice in this recipe, but any tart apple will do.

8 large tart apples
1 orange
½ cup pecans, toasted
4 tablespoons butter, melted
1 cup cranberries
⅓ cup maple syrup or honey
1 teaspoon ground cinnamon

1. Preheat oven to 350° F. Slice tops from apples. Carefully remove cores, taking care not to cut through to bottoms.

2. Peel skin from orange, leaving the bitter white membrane. Dice orange peel. Juice orange. Discard membrane. Coarsely chop pecans. Drizzle 2 tablespoons of the melted butter in the bottom of a 9- by 12-inch baking dish. In a small mixing bowl combine cranberries, orange peel, orange juice, pecans, remaining butter, maple syrup, and cinnamon.

3. Place ⅛ of the mixture into each cored apple. Put apples into baking dish. Cover pan with aluminum foil. Bake for 20 minutes. Remove foil and bake until a knife inserted in the side of apples meets no resistance (5 minutes). Apples will be tender but should still hold their shape.

Serves 8.

ZINFANDEL PEARS

Pears, peaches, apples, and quince are among the many fruits that taste sensational when poached in red wine. Serve warm with a scoop of vanilla ice cream melting over the fruit; chilled in a wineglass; as the filling of a fruit tart; or warm with Chocolate Fudge Sauce (see page 131). Mint is in the same herb family as basil and may be substituted for the basil in the recipe.

6 pears
1 small bunch fresh basil, plus basil leaves for garnish
2 cups zinfandel wine
½ cup sugar

1. Peel pears. Core pears by cutting a cone-shaped wedge from the bottom of each. Leave stems intact. Discard seeds and cores. Wash and julienne a bunch of basil.

2. Place wine and sugar in a medium nonaluminum saucepan. Add julienned basil and bring mixture to a boil over medium-high heat. Place pears upright in poaching liquid, reduce heat, and simmer until pears are tender and do not offer resistance when pierced with a sharp knife (about 20 minutes).

3. Remove fruit with a slotted spoon to a serving dish. Return syrup to a boil and reduce by half to about 1 cup (about 10 minutes). Pour syrup over pears and cool for 3 hours in refrigerator.

4. To serve, place pears in stemmed glasses, spooning some of the cooking juices over each fruit. Garnish with basil leaves.

Serves 6.

Zinfandel Peaches   Follow recipe for Zinfandel Pears; substitute 6 peaches for pears. Peel peaches with a sharp knife, or dip in a pan of boiling water for about 1 minute to loosen skin and peel by hand. Halve and remove pit. Place in poaching liquid and cook until tender (15 to 20 minutes). Proceed with recipe.

WARM FIGS WITH GORGONZOLA

The appeal of sweet figs with salty cheese is delightful. A nonsweet walnut or dense whole wheat bread would be a delicious companion.

2 tablespoons honey
1 tablespoon lemon juice
8 large ripe figs
¾ pound Gorgonzola cheese
¼ pound cream cheese (optional)

1. Preheat oven to 350° F. In a small saucepan, combine honey and lemon juice and cook over low heat, stirring, until honey melts. Lightly brush outside of figs with honey mixture. Cut figs in half and place cut side up on a baking sheet. Lightly brush cut surfaces with honey mixture. Bake until warmed through and slightly softened (7 to 10 minutes). Remove from oven and let stand 10 minutes.

2. To serve, place warm figs on a platter accompanied by Gorgonzola in one piece. Or, serve each guest a small plate with 2 fig halves and a small wedge of Gorgonzola. If desired, Gorgonzola can be blended with cream cheese for a milder flavor and packed into a crock.

Serves 8.

FRUIT FOOL

Crushed raspberries, peaches, apricots, blackberries, or blueberries work equally well for this old-fashioned English dessert, although crushed gooseberries are the traditional choice. The juice released from the berries stains the whipped cream a lovely color.

> 2 *pints strawberries*
> 2 *cups confectioners' sugar*
> 2 *cups whipping cream*
>   *Cream Cheese Cookies (see page 129), for accompaniment*

1. Wash strawberries and remove stems; pat berries dry. In a large bowl, mash berries with a potato masher or fork. Sift confectioners' sugar over berries and stir to combine well. Macerate 1 hour.

2. Whip cream to soft peaks. Stir strawberries to mix berries and juices, and gently fold whipped cream into them. Some white streaks of cream may remain. Serve in glass dessert bowls accompanied by Cream Cheese Cookies.

Serves 8.

PEACH AND PECAN BREAD PUDDING

Assemble this dessert early in the day and relax. The bread will absorb the custard while the dish rests in the refrigerator.

> 12 *slices (about about ¾ in. thick) French bread*
> ½ *cup butter, melted*
> 4 *cups half-and-half*
> 1¼ *cups sugar*
> 10 *egg yolks*
> 1 *teaspoon vanilla extract Pinch salt*
> 4 *large peaches, peeled, pitted, and thinly sliced*
> 1 *cup toasted pecan halves Vanilla ice cream or whipped cream, for accompaniment*

1. Preheat oven to 425° F. Brush bread with some of the melted butter. Put bread slices on a baking sheet and bake until golden brown (about 10 minutes).

2. In a medium saucepan over medium-low heat, bring half-and-half to a simmer (bubbles will appear at edge of pan). In a 3-quart bowl, beat sugar with egg yolks; whisk hot half-and-half into egg-sugar mixture. Stir in vanilla and salt; set aside.

3. Pour remaining butter into a 9- by 12-inch baking dish. Place 6 bread slices in dish; strain half of egg-custard mixture through a wire mesh strainer over bread. Distribute sliced peaches over bread-custard mixture; top with pecans. Arrange remaining bread over fruit and strain remaining egg-custard mixture over bread. Let stand 1 hour, covered with plastic wrap, or refrigerate up to 6 hours.

4. If refrigerated, remove from refrigerator about 2 hours before serving. Preheat oven to 325° F. Bake, uncovered, until golden brown and slightly crusty (about 1¾ hours). Serve warm, cut into squares and topped with vanilla ice cream or whipped cream.

Serves 8 to 10.

As easy on the cook as it is sublime to eat, this Peach and Pecan Bread Pudding can be assembled ahead of time.

Reminiscent of chocolate truffles, Chocolate-Filled Chocolate Nests feature raspberry preserves beneath a layer of chocolate filling.

COOKIES AND CAKES

Diets or no, a meal seems incomplete without a "little something" sweet to finish it off. Just the right cookie might satisfy the craving. Try Layered Orange Bars (see page 124) or Chinese Almond Cookies (see page 124), or any or all of the Quick Cookies on pages 128 and 129. For some of us, though, only a piece of cake will do. In that case, offer a big slice of Ginger-Nectarine Upside-Down Cake (see page 126), or Mom's Double Dutch Chocolate Cake (see page 127), or, if you're in a Continental mood, Coffee Semifreddo (see page 128). The beauty of all these baked delights is that they must be made ahead. There's no fussing in the kitchen after dinner to get dessert organized.

CHOCOLATE-FILLED CHOCOLATE NESTS

A creamy chocolate filling conceals a raspberry layer atop the crisp cocoa press-in pastry.

> ¼ cup raspberry jam or preserves
> 4 ounces semisweet chocolate, coarsely chopped
> 2 tablespoons granulated sugar
> 2 tablespoons butter
> ¼ cup whipping cream

Cocoa Pastry

> 1 cup flour
> 1 tablespoon unsweetened cocoa
> 3 tablespoons confectioners' sugar
> ⅓ cup firm butter
> 1 egg yolk
> 2 teaspoons water

1. Preheat oven to 350° F. Pinch off 1-inch balls of Cocoa Pastry and press into ungreased 1 ¾-inch muffin pans. Bake until lightly browned and firm when touched gently (10 to 15 minutes).

2. Let tart shells cool in pans on wire racks. Carefully remove shells from muffin pans. Spoon a scant ½ teaspoon raspberry jam into each.

3. In a heavy pan over low heat, combine chocolate, sugar, and butter. Heat, stirring occasionally, until chocolate and butter melt and sugar is dissolved. Add whipping cream; stir over medium heat until mixture is hot to the touch (2 to 3 minutes). Remove from heat and let stand until cooled to room temperature (about 20 minutes).

4. Spoon about ½ tablespoon of the chocolate filling into each tart shell. Let stand at room temperature until filling is set (about 1 hour).

Makes 2 dozen cookies.

Cocoa Pastry In a bowl stir together flour, cocoa, and sugar to combine thoroughly. Using a pastry blender or 2 knives, cut in butter until mixture resembles coarse crumbs. In a small bowl, combine egg yolk and the water; beat until blended. Add egg mixture to flour mixture, stirring with a fork until dough clings together. Use your hands to press dough into a smooth ball.

FEATURE

FRENCH BRANDIED FRUITS

Brandied fruits are a wonderful way to use the fruits of the season, adding new ones to the crock as they ripen. Enjoy brandied fruits as the French do, spooned over vanilla ice cream. Fill a jar from the crock for a special gift any time; everyone loves receiving summer fruits in the dead of winter.

> 9 cups diced mixed fruit, such as strawberries, blackberries, Bing cherries, pineapple, apricots, peaches, nectarines, seedless grapes, or other seasonal fruits
> 5 cups sugar
> 5 cups firmly packed light brown sugar
> 1 quart brandy

1. Prepare fruit. Peaches, nectarines, and apricots should be peeled, stoned, and chopped. Pineapple should be peeled, cored, and cubed. Cherries should be pitted. All fruit should be chopped to roughly the same size as the cherries.

2. In a very large bowl combine sugars. Add fruit and toss to coat. Cover the bowl and let stand 1 hour, tossing every 15 minutes.

3. Transfer fruit to a 1 ½-gallon crock and pour in brandy. Place a plate on top to weight down fruit. Store in a cool place. Fruit will be ready to eat in a month, but definitely improves with age.

Makes about 4 quarts.

Note More fruit can be added at any time. Toss each 2 cups fruit in ⅔ cup each white and firmly packed brown sugar and add enough brandy to cover.

LAYERED ORANGE BARS

This standard bar-cookie recipe has several irresistible variations. In addition to the basic orange-accented version, you will want to try eye-catching Chocolate-Drizzled Pecan Bars.

  ¼ cup flour
  ½ teaspoon baking powder
  2 eggs
  1 cup firmly packed dark brown
      sugar
  1 teaspoon vanilla extract
  1 tablespoon grated orange peel
  1 cup chopped walnuts
  1½ cups flaked coconut

Orange Pastry

  ½ cup butter, softened
  ½ cup granulated sugar
  1 teaspoon grated orange peel
  1 cup flour

Orange Glaze

  1 cup confectioners' sugar
  1 teapoon grated orange peel
  1½ tablespoons orange juice

1. Preheat oven to 375º F. Prepare Orange Pastry; press firmly and evenly over bottom of a greased 9- by 13-inch baking pan. Bake for 10 minutes, then remove pastry from oven. Reduce temperature to 350º F.

2. In a small bowl combine flour and baking powder; stir to combine thoroughly. In mixer bowl combine eggs and brown sugar; beat until well mixed. Blend in vanilla and orange peel. Gradually beat in flour mixture until well combined. Stir in walnuts and coconut. Spread mixture over partially baked pastry.

These buttery but crisp Chinese Almond Cookies are a delicious finale to stir-fry dinners.

3. Bake until well browned and set in center (20 to 25 minutes). Remove pan to a rack; drizzle with glaze while warm. Let stand until glaze is set, then cut into bars. Remove from pan when cool.

Makes 3 dozen bars.

Orange Pastry   In mixer bowl combine butter, sugar, and orange peel; beat until fluffy. Gradually stir in flour until mixture is well combined (dough will be crumbly).

Orange Glaze   Combine confectioners' sugar and orange peel in a small bowl; stir in orange juice until icing is smooth.

Chocolate-Drizzled Pecan Bars

Omit orange peel from filling; substitute chopped pecans for walnuts. Increase vanilla to 1½ teaspoons. Omit orange peel from pastry; substitute ½ teaspoon vanilla. Omit glaze. While cookies are cooling, melt 1 square (1 oz) semisweet baking chocolate with ½ teaspoon vegetable oil in a small, heavy pan over low heat. Drizzle melted chocolate over baked cookies from the tip of a teaspoon. Cut into bars after chocolate sets.

CHINESE ALMOND COOKIES

When selecting from the varied attractions of certain Chinese take-out restaurants, many people find rich almond cookies, packaged to go in a waxed-paper bag, virtually irresistible. They are just as compelling when baked at home and served as the conclusion to a Chinese stir-fried dinner. Making the cookies with a combination of butter and lard brings together the best quality of each ingredient—the flavor of butter and the tender crispness that lard imparts to pastry.

  2 cups flour
  ½ teaspoon baking powder
  ½ cup each butter or margarine
      and lard, softened
  1 cup sugar
  1 teaspoon almond extract
  ½ teaspoon vanilla extract
  2 egg yolks
  ⅓ cup (approximately) blanched
      almonds
  2 teaspoons water

1. In a medium bowl, stir together flour and baking powder to combine thoroughly; set aside. Preheat oven to 350º F.

2. In mixer bowl combine butter and lard; beat until fluffy. Add sugar and beat until well combined. Blend in almond and vanilla extracts, then 1 egg yolk. Gradually add flour mixture, beating until well combined.

3. Shape dough into 1-inch balls. Place about 1½ inches apart on lightly greased baking sheets. Slightly flatten each cookie

with your fingertips; press an almond into center.

4. In a small bowl, beat remaining egg yolk with the 2 teaspoons water until blended. Lightly brush top of each cookie with egg-yolk mixture.

5. Bake until cookies are golden brown and feel firm when touched lightly (15 to 18 minutes). Let stand on baking sheets for 1 to 2 minutes, then transfer to wire racks to cool.

Makes about forty-two 2-inch cookies.

BROWNIE À LA MODE

When eaten alone, this rich, gooey brownie is a terrific snack, but layered in a shallow bowl with vanilla ice cream and fudge sauce, it is transformed into a chocolate lover's fantasy.

    4 ounces unsweetened chocolate,
        coarsely chopped
    ½ cup unsalted butter
    1½ cups sugar
    3 eggs
    1½ teaspoons vanilla extract
    ¾ cup flour

    ¼ teaspoon salt
    1 cup toasted pecans (optional)
    1 pint vanilla ice cream
        Chocolate Fudge Sauce (see
            page 131)

1. Preheat oven to 350° F. Line an 8- by 8-inch baking pan with parchment paper, or generously butter and flour.

2. In a medium metal bowl, combine chocolate and butter. Place bowl in a shallow pan of water over low heat. Stir, while chocolate and butter are melting, for about 5 minutes.

3. Stir sugar into chocolate mixture while still warm. Add eggs and vanilla, mixing to combine. Sift together flour and salt; fold into chocolate mixture along with pecans (if used). Place in prepared pan and bake until a wooden skewer inserted 2 inches from edge comes out with small moist crumbs clinging to it (about 30 minutes; brownies should be slightly underdone). Cool 20 minutes in pan on wire rack before serving.

4. Cut brownie into 16 squares. Place one square in a stemmed serving dish, top with one scoop vanilla ice cream, place a second brownie on the vanilla ice cream, top with another small scoop of vanilla ice cream, and drizzle with Chocolate Fudge Sauce. Repeat with remaining brownies, ice cream, and sauce.

Serves 8.

A brownie makes a luscious snack all by itself; layered with ice cream and fudge sauce, it becomes pure fantasy.

Versatile Vanilla-Nutmeg Pound Cake is the basis for a variety of upscale yet simple desserts.

VANILLA-NUTMEG POUND CAKE

This versatile vanilla pound cake can be dressed up with Chocolate Fudge Sauce (see page 131) or Zinfandel Peaches (see page 120).

> 4 cups cake flour
> 2 teaspoons baking soda
> 1 teaspoon each salt and ground nutmeg
> 1 cup unsalted butter, softened
> 2 cups granulated sugar
> 2 eggs
> 1 tablespoon vanilla extract
> 2 cups buttermilk or sour cream
> Confectioners' sugar, for dusting

1. Butter and flour a 12-cup tube pan. Preheat oven to 350° F. Sift flour, baking soda, salt, and nutmeg together.

2. Cream butter and sugar until light and fluffy. Add eggs, one at a time, beating well after each egg is added. Stir in vanilla.

3. Stir half of the sifted flour mixture into the butter-sugar mixture. Add 1 cup of the buttermilk. Add the other half of the flour mixture, then the remaining buttermilk.

4. Pour batter into prepared tube pan and bake until a wooden skewer inserted 2 inches from edge comes out clean (about 1 hour and 5 minutes). Cool cake in pan 10 to 15 minutes; invert onto a cooling rack, remove pan, and cool completely before serving. Transfer to a serving plate. Dust with confectioners' sugar.

Serves 12.

GINGER-NECTARINE UPSIDE-DOWN CAKE

Gingerbread is even better when baked on a layer of nectarine, peach, or pear slices. When turned upside down after baking, the fruit slices glow under a buttery brown-sugar glaze that drips delicately down the sides of the cake.

> 1 cup firmly packed light brown sugar
> 6 tablespoons unsalted butter, melted
> 3 nectarines
> 2 ½ cups flour

2 teaspoons baking soda
½ teaspoon ground cinnamon
2 teaspoons ground ginger
⅛ teaspoon ground nutmeg
⅛ teaspoon ground cardamom
  (optional)
½ teaspoon salt
½ cup dark molasses
1 cup boiling water
1 scant cup unsalted butter,
  melted, or safflower oil
1 cup granulated sugar
2 eggs, lightly beaten
2 teaspoons finely grated orange
  peel (optional)
  Whipped cream, for accompaniment

1. Preheat oven to 350º F. Butter sides of a 10- by 3-inch springform pan. Stir the brown sugar into the 6 tablespoons melted butter; spread evenly in the bottom of pan. Halve nectarines, pit, and cut fruit into ½-inch slices. Arrange slices (packed closely together) in concentric circles on sugar in bottom of pan.

2. Sift together the flour, baking soda, cinnamon, ginger, nutmeg, cardamom (if used), and salt; set aside. Combine molasses and water in a bowl; set aside.

3. In a large bowl, beat the 1 cup melted butter and granulated sugar until light. Beat in the eggs and orange peel (if used). Add the molasses mixture. Stir in dry ingredients; beat until well blended. Pour batter into the fruit-lined pan. Bake until a wooden skewer comes out clean and cake springs back when lightly touched in center (about 1 hour). Cover top of cake with parchment paper if it begins to burn at the edges.

4. Allow cake to cool in pan for 30 minutes. Invert cake on serving platter, remove cake pan, and allow glaze to drip down sides of cake. Serve while still warm or at room temperature with whipped cream.

Serves 10 to 12.

RHUBARB COFFEE CAKE

Discard the dark green leaves of the rhubarb, which are toxic. Although botanically a vegetable, rhubarb is considered a fruit by most cooks and diners.

Filling

4 cups rhubarb (about 8 stalks)
½ cup sugar
¼ cup flour
2 tablespoons butter
2 teaspoons ground cinnamon

Batter

¾ cup butter
1 cup sugar
2 eggs
1 teaspoon vanilla extract
1½ cups all-purpose flour
½ cup whole wheat flour
1 teaspoon baking powder
¼ teaspoon baking soda
  Pinch salt
  Grated peel of 1 lemon
1 cup plain yogurt

Topping

¼ cup butter
½ cup firmly packed brown sugar
1 teaspoon ground cinnamon
½ cup flour

1. Preheat oven to 400º F. Butter and flour a 9-inch springform pan.

2. *To make filling:* Wash and dry rhubarb stalks. Slice into 1-inch pieces and place in a medium bowl. Toss with sugar, flour, butter, and cinnamon. Set aside.

3. *To make batter:* In a large mixing bowl, beat butter and sugar together until light and fluffy. Beat in eggs and vanilla. Sift flours, baking powder, baking soda, and salt. Stir lemon peel into yogurt. Fold half of sifted flour mixture into butter-sugar-egg mixture. Fold in yogurt-lemon peel. Fold in remaining flour. Mix well.

4. *To make topping:* In a small bowl, mix butter, brown sugar, and cinnamon. Mix in flour until crumbly.

5. Place half the batter in prepared pan. Cover batter with filling. Top with remaining batter. Sprinkle on topping. Bake for 1 hour and 10 minutes. Cool in pan 10 minutes; carefully remove pan sides; cool completely on wire rack.

Serves 8.

MOM'S DOUBLE DUTCH CHOCOLATE CAKE

This cake is easier to make than a packaged mix and just as foolproof. The chocolate frosting is a snap as well if you follow the simple steps for melting chocolate described in the recipe. This technique works especially well for white chocolate, which tends to scorch very easily.

2¼ cups flour
1¼ cups baking soda
1 teaspoon salt
2¼ cups firmly packed dark brown
  sugar
1 cup butter, melted
½ cup unsweetened cocoa
1 cup water
2 eggs
1 tablespoon vanilla extract
⅔ cup sour cream

Chocolate Frosting

14 ounces semisweet chocolate
1⅓ cups sour cream, at room
  temperature
½ teaspoon vanilla extract
½ cup unsalted butter

1. Preheat oven to 350º F. Line bottom of two 8-inch-diameter cake pans with parchment paper, or butter and flour bottoms and sides.

2. Sift together flour, baking soda, and salt; set aside. In a small saucepan over low heat, melt brown sugar, butter, and cocoa in the water; cool slightly. In a large bowl, stir together eggs, vanilla, and sour cream. Add cocoa mixture to egg mixture, then stir in sifted flour mixture. Divide evenly between prepared cake pans.

3. Bake until cake is dry on top and a wooden skewer inserted 2 inches from edge comes out clean (30 to 35 minutes). Cool 10 minutes. Slip a knife around edge of each cake pan, invert cakes onto a cooling rack, and cool completely.

4. Place one cake layer on an 8-inch cardboard cake round or serving dish. Spread layer with ¾ cup frosting. Top with second layer and frost top and sides of cake.

Serves 8 to 10.

Chocolate Frosting Fill a large skillet with water to a depth of 1 ½ inches and bring to a boil. Chop semisweet chocolate into pea-sized pieces and place in a metal mixing bowl. Turn off heat under skillet, place mixing bowl of chocolate in hot water, and stir until chocolate is melted. Stir in sour cream, vanilla, and butter until smooth. Let rest at room temperature until spreading consistency (15 to 30 minutes), stirring occasionally.

Makes about 2 ½ cups.

COFFEE SEMIFREDDO

Semifreddo means *half-chilled* in Italian. This lovely dessert multiplies readily and stores well in the freezer. It is customarily served just slightly melting.

> *4 eggs*
> *1 cup confectioners' sugar*
> *2 tablespoons milk*
> *4 tablespoons butter*
> *1 teaspoon vanilla extract*
> *½ cup flour*
> *1 teaspoon baking powder*
> *½ teaspoon salt*
> *Confectioners' sugar, for dusting*
> *3 tablespoons rum*
> *¼ cup unsweetened cocoa*
> *1 pint coffee ice cream, softened*
> *Chocolate Fudge Sauce (see page 131), for accompaniment*

1. Preheat oven to 350° F. Line an 11- by 17- by 1-inch baking pan with parchment paper (or butter and flour pan). In a small saucepan over medium-low heat, place milk and butter and heat until butter is melted. Remove from heat and cool until tepid.

2. In a large bowl, beat eggs and confectioners' sugar together with a wire whisk until mixture is pale yellow and thickened to consistency of mayonnaise.

3. Sift together flour, baking powder, and salt. Using a rubber spatula, gently fold flour mixture into eggs.

4. Scoop 1 cup batter into a small mixing bowl and whisk together with milk-butter mixture. Fold mixture into batter. This will enable the heavy milk-butter mixture to be easily and completely folded into the light, airy batter without deflating it. Pour batter into prepared pan and bake until cake is pale golden brown and dry on top, and springs back when gently pressed with finger (20 to 22 minutes).

5. Cool 2 to 3 minutes in pan. Loosen edges of cake from pan with a small knife. Dust a tea towel with confectioners' sugar. Invert cake onto sugar-dusted towel; carefully peel away parchment paper from cake roll. Cool completely.

6. *To assemble semifreddo:* Cut sponge cake roll into 3 equal rectangles, each 5 ¼ inches by 11 inches. Sprinkle cake layers with rum; dust with some of the cocoa.

7. Place one cake layer on a serving tray. Cover with about 1 cup softened ice cream. Top with a second layer and cover with 1 cup more ice cream; cover with third layer and freeze.

8. Twenty minutes before serving, remove cake from freezer and let rest at room temperature. Dust with remaining cocoa. Slice about 1 inch thick and place each slice on a chilled dessert plate. Drizzle with Chocolate Fudge Sauce. Serve immediately.

Serves 8 to 10.

FROZEN FINALES

A big reason for the popularity of frozen desserts is that they make life so much easier for the host. Made ahead, they remove some of the hustle and bustle that surround entertaining. From a quick and easy Mile-High Strawberry Pie (see page 130) to a sophisticated Sicilian Cassata (see page 130) to surprising Chocolate Waffles With Ice Cream (see page 130), frozen desserts fit the diversity of today's tastes and the demands of our fast-paced life-style.

BASICS

QUICK COOKIES

Cookies are a wonderful dessert. They can make an attractive centerpiece, glamorize a plate of fruit, or garnish a bowl of ice cream. Taking only minutes to stir together and baking in 10 to 15 minutes, cookies are one of the easiest and quickest desserts to prepare. Whether baked and waiting in the freezer or sitting, ready to bake, in the refrigerator, cookies are also the perfect do-ahead dessert. Offering a selection of personal favorites can become your trademark. Even a selection of small cookies can look like a substantial dessert.

Refrigerator cookies such as Cream Cheese Cookies (see opposite page) and Susan's Triple-Chocolate Cookies (see opposite page) are best served the same day they are baked. If necessary, the dough can be prepared up to one week in advance and stored in the refrigerator, wrapped in foil, ready to slice and bake. These doughs also freeze well if you are planning a large party or anticipating several houseguests. Cream Cheese Cookies (see opposite page) can be dressed up with confectioners' sugar, garnished with raspberry jam or chocolate sprinkles, or filled with peanut butter and dipped in chocolate.

RUTHEE'S IRISH LACE COOKIES

Inexpensive rolled oats take the place of chopped pecans in this crisp, elegant cookie. If making these cookies ahead, store airtight after baking. Recrisp by warming on a baking sheet in a 350° F oven 5 minutes. Cool completely before serving.

> *½ cup unsalted butter, plus butter for greasing*
> *4 tablespoons flour, plus flour for dusting*
> *1 cup firmly packed brown sugar*
> *1 tablespoon vanilla extract*

2 tablespoons milk
1 cup old-fashioned rolled oats

1. Preheat oven to 350° F. Grease and flour 2 baking sheets.

2. Cream butter and sugar. Add vanilla; stir in flour, milk, and rolled oats. Drop batter by the tablespoon onto prepared baking sheets; allow room for cookies to spread to about 3 inches in diameter. Each baking sheet will hold about 6 cookies.

3. Bake until cookies flatten and look dry (10 minutes). Let cookies cool for 4 to 5 minutes on baking sheets. Lift from baking sheet with a metal spatula and cool completely.

Makes 2 dozen cookies.

CREAM CHEESE COOKIES

These make wonderful refrigerator cookies—simply roll the dough into a cylinder, wrap tightly to seal, and chill. The dough can be frozen for up to three months, an asset for the busy cook. Decorate with chocolate sprinkles, a dot of cherry jam, or a whole toasted pecan. Thinner cookies (which bake in less time) can be cut and filled with a layer of cool Chocolate Fudge Sauce (see page 131) or raspberry jam. Dust the tops with confectioners' sugar. The dough can also be pressed into miniature tart tins and filled with lemon curd. For yet another variation, cut rounds, bake, then dip one half of each cookie in melted chocolate.

½ cup unsalted butter, at room
   temperature
3 ounces cream cheese, at room
   temperature
2 cups granulated sugar
2 eggs
1 teaspoon vanilla extract
   Grated peel of 1 lemon
4 cups flour
1 teaspoon baking powder
½ teaspoon salt
½ cup raspberry jam
   Confectioners' sugar, for dusting

1. Cream butter, cream cheese, and granulated sugar until light and fluffy. Add eggs, one at a time, beating well after each addition. Stir in vanilla and lemon peel.

2. Sift together flour, baking powder, and salt. Stir into butter–cream cheese mixture.

3. Roll dough into a log about 18 inches long. Place on a 20-inch-long sheet of aluminum foil, roll up, and seal ends. Chill 2 hours or freeze for up to 3 months.

4. To bake, preheat oven to 350° F. Slice dough into ⅜-inch-thick rounds and place on parchment-lined baking sheets. Spoon ½ teaspoon jam in center of each cookie. Bake until firm on top and golden brown on underside (8 to 10 minutes). Remove from baking sheet to a cooling rack. Dust with confectioners' sugar before serving.

Makes about 4 dozen cookies.

SUSAN'S TRIPLE-CHOCOLATE COOKIES

Chocoholics never feel cheated when these triple-rich cookies are the only dessert served. Use a stainless steel mixing bowl and make this a one-bowl recipe.

4 ounces unsweetened chocolate,
   chopped roughly
12 ounces semisweet chocolate,
   chopped roughly
4 tablespoons unsalted butter
½ cup flour
½ teaspoon baking powder
½ teaspoon baking soda
⅛ teaspoon salt
4 eggs
2 cups sugar
1 tablespoon dark rum
1 teaspoon vanilla extract
2 cups chocolate chips
2 cups chopped walnuts

1. Fill a shallow pan with 1 ½ inches water; bring to a boil over medium heat. Place chocolates and butter in a 2-quart metal mixing bowl. Place bowl in the shallow pan of boiling water and turn off heat. Stir to mix chocolates and butter while they melt.

2. Sift together flour, baking powder, baking soda, and salt onto a piece of aluminum foil or parchment paper.

3. Beat eggs, sugar, rum, and vanilla into melted chocolate mixture until mixture thickens. Stir in sifted flour mixture and combine thoroughly. Stir in chocolate chips and walnuts. Let mixture sit until easy to shape (5 to 10 minutes); it will be sticky.

4. Place dough on a sheet of aluminum foil about 18 inches long and roll into a log 2 inches in diameter. (For a more elegant cookie, roll 2 cylinders each about 1 inch in diameter.) Wrap carefully and chill overnight.

5. Preheat oven to 350° F. Line baking sheets with aluminum foil. Slice cookie dough with a hot knife. Place slices on foil. Bake until cracks form on top of cookies and surfaces appear dry; interiors of cookies as seen through cracks will be moist (10 to 12 minutes). Let cool 5 minutes on baking sheets before removing to a wire rack to finish cooling.

Makes 2 dozen large cookies or 4 dozen small cookies.

Easy-to-make Mile-High Strawberry Pie can be prepared and decorated ahead of time, then frozen until needed.

Chocolate Waffles With Ice Cream are evidence enough that waffles needn't be limited to breakfast menus.

SICILIAN CASSATA

Cassata can be either fruit-filled ice cream, as it is here, or a rich layer cake with ricotta cheese, fruit, chocolate, and cream.

> 3 tablespoons dark rum or
> amaretto
> 1 tablespoon orange-flavored
> liqueur
> ¾ cup mixed candied fruit, chopped
> ¾ cup whipping cream
> 1 quart French vanilla ice cream,
> slightly softened
> ½ cup pistachio nuts, chopped
> ½ cup coarsely chopped semisweet
> chocolate
> Whipped cream, candied cherries,
> and cocoa powder, for
> garnish (optional)

1. Combine rum, liqueur, and candied fruit in a small bowl; set aside for at least half an hour.

2. Meanwhile, line a 2-quart loaf pan or mold with a large piece of plastic wrap, pressing it well into the corners. In a medium bowl, whip the cream to soft peaks.

3. Spoon softened ice cream into a large bowl; fold in rum-fruit mixture, pistachio nuts, and chocolate. Gently fold in whipped cream.

4. Pour into plastic-lined pan. Tap the pan against a cutting board several times to fill the corners. Cover with plastic wrap and freeze overnight.

5. To serve, invert the pan on a chilled platter. Lift off the pan and remove the plastic wrap. Garnish cassata with whipped cream rosettes, candied cherries, or a light dusting of cocoa (if desired). Cut into slices.

Serves 8 to 10.

MILE-HIGH STRAWBERRY PIE

Any berry can be substituted in this quick dessert.

> 1 package (10 oz) frozen strawber-
> ries or raspberries in syrup,
> thawed
> About ½ cup sugar, or to taste
> 1 tablespoon lemon juice
> 2 large egg whites

> ¾ cup whipping cream
> 1 baked pie shell or graham
> cracker crust (9 in.)

In a large bowl, combine berries, sugar, lemon juice, and egg whites. Beat with an electric mixer until soft peaks form and mixture is very thick (15 to 20 minutes). In a separate bowl, whip the cream to soft peaks and fold into berry mixture. Gently pile filling high in pie crust and freeze until firm. About 30 minutes before serving, transfer pie from freezer to refrigerator.

Serves 8 to 10.

CHOCOLATE WAFFLES WITH ICE CREAM

With or without nuts, these chocolaty waffles make a wonderful base for ice cream and sauces.

> 1 ½ cups flour
> ¼ cup cocoa powder
> 1 teaspoon baking powder
> 1 teaspoon baking soda
> ⅓ cup sugar
> 2 cups buttermilk
> ½ cup vegetable oil or melted butter
> 2 large eggs, separated
> 1 teaspoon vanilla extract
> Pinch cream of tartar
> 1 cup chopped pecans (optional)
> Ice cream, for accompaniment

1. Sift together flour, cocoa, baking powder, baking soda, and sugar. Make a well in center of sifted dry ingredients.

2. In a separate bowl mix buttermilk, oil, egg yolks, and vanilla. Pour into the well and mix with dry ingredients.

3. Beat egg whites with cream of tartar until soft peaks form. Gradually fold into batter, one third at a time. Fold in pecans (if used).

4. Cook in waffle iron according to manufacturer's instructions. Top with ice cream.

Makes 4 large waffles.

TOPPINGS FOR ICE CREAM

An ice cream dessert can be dressed up or down by the sauce that covers it. Sundaes are perfect last-minute finales to impromptu meals. Sauces and toppings for ice cream run the gamut from elegant Brandied Fruit (see page 123) to such fabulous, rich creations as Almond-Raisin-Fudge Sauce. The following toppings can be made ahead of time, making it easy to concoct everyone's ice cream dream.

ALMOND-RAISIN-FUDGE SAUCE

Toasting the nuts helps bring out their flavor.

¼ cup unsalted butter
2 ounces unsweetened chocolate
¼ cup unsweetened cocoa powder
¾ cup sugar
⅔ cup whipping cream
   Pinch of salt
1 teaspoon vanilla extract
½ cup raisins, coarsely chopped
¼ cup chopped or slivered almonds, toasted

In a heavy small saucepan, melt butter and chocolate over low heat. Stir in cocoa, sugar, cream, and salt. Bring slowly to a boil. Remove from heat and add vanilla, raisins, and almonds. Serve warm or at room temperature.

Makes about 1½ cups.

CHOCOLATE FUDGE SAUCE

Every cook should have a recipe for a fabulous chocolate sauce. This is it. Spoon into tiny tart shells and top with a rosette of whipped cream and a sprinkling of toasted pistachio nuts.

1 cup whipping cream
8 ounces semisweet chocolate, chopped
4 tablespoons unsalted butter
¼ cup firmly packed brown sugar
2 tablespoons light corn syrup

In a small saucepan, heat cream over medium heat. Stir in chocolate, butter, brown sugar, and corn syrup. Cool slightly before serving.

Makes about 2 cups.

CHOCOLATE-RASPBERRY SAUCE

This is one instance in which frozen berries are better than fresh.

1 package (10 oz) raspberries frozen in syrup
¼ cup sugar
5 ounces semisweet chocolate, chopped into ½-inch pieces
2 tablespoons unsalted butter, softened

1. Thaw raspberries in their syrup. Mash berries to a mushlike consistency.

2. In a heavy small saucepan, bring sugar and berries to a boil. Add chocolate and butter and cook, stirring constantly, until melted.

3. Serve hot, or cool to room temperature and refrigerate. Sauce will keep for several weeks. To use, reheat over hot water.

Makes about 1¼ cups.

CINNAMON-BLUEBERRY SAUCE

Frozen blueberries may be substituted for fresh.

2 cups blueberries
1 tablespoon ground cinnamon
½ cup sugar
8 tablespoons unsalted butter
2 tablespoons lemon juice

In a heavy small saucepan combine all ingredients. Cook over medium heat until berries break and sauce thickens (about 5 minutes). Serve warm. Sauce can be refrigerated and reheated.

Makes about 1½ cups.

PINEAPPLE SAUCE

This sweet, aromatic sauce will quickly become a favorite.

1 large pineapple (about 4 lb)
½ cup sugar

1. Peel, core, and chop pineapple. Reserve about 2 cups. In a food processor fitted with a steel blade or in a blender in batches, purée remaining pineapple.

2. In a medium saucepan, bring the puréed pineapple and sugar to a boil over medium heat. Simmer, stirring occasionally, about 5 minutes.

3. Strain through a sieve, pressing hard to extract all the liquid. Skim off the froth and add the reserved pineapple. Cover and chill.

Makes about 3 cups.

Dress your favorite ice cream up or down by adding just the right topping for the occasion.

INDEX

*Note: Page numbers in italics refer
to illustrations.*

C A L I F O R N I A
CULINARY ACADEMY

The California Culinary Academy was founded in San Francisco in 1977 as a professional school for chef training. Unique among chef training schools, the Academy is situated near the heart of downtown San Francisco, a city internationally acclaimed for its world-class dining establishments. One of the first such schools in the western United States, the Academy is now recognized as a leader and innovator in the Culinary Arts. The Academy's proximity to several wine-producing regions is unparalleled among American culinary schools. Courses, special tastings, field trips, and food- and wine-pairing contests for students focus on this unique opportunity.

The Academy has nine professional kitchens for practical training including a pastry shop, bakery, candy kitchen, garde manger, butchery, three production kitchens, and a fully-equipped demonstration kitchen, as well as three classrooms. Additional learning facilities include three student-staffed restaurants open to the general public for lunch and dinner five days per week and a retail shop for the sale of products made by students. The Academy has an instructional staff of 17 chef instructors, four maitre d'hotel instructors, and six restaurant and kitchen management instructors. The Academy's Educational Advisory Committee includes Julia Child, Robert Mondavi, Jeremiah Tower, Martin Yan, Richard Swig, Bert Cutino, Hubert Keller, and André Fournier.

Curriculum

The Academy offers a curriculum focusing on the fundamentals of modern classical cooking and baking. The professional curriculum covers every aspect of food preparation, beginning with knife skills and advancing through stocks, soups, sauces, mousses, salads, vegetables, seafood, poultry, meats, breads, and desserts, providing students with a complete understanding of the intricacies of professional cooking. Special weekend and evening cooking and restaurant management classes are offered by the Academy. Students, professionals in the foodservice industry, and the general public are invited to attend these classes. Special courses for large groups can be custom-designed.

Whether your goal is to work in a traditional American or European restaurant, open your own restaurant or catering business, broaden your culinary knowledge, or perfect your cooking technique, the California Culinary Academy can help you. For most aspiring chefs in America, the dream of studying in the classrooms and kitchens of Europe and Asia is out of reach. At the California Culinary Academy we are dedicated to making that educational experience available to you.

Restaurant Patrons: Visitors to the California Culinary Academy may dine in one of the Academy's three restaurants: The Academy Grill, The Carême Room, and Cyril's. The Academy Grill, The Carême Room and Cyril's are all training facilities for our students. We hope you enjoy visiting our center for culinary education and we appreciate your interest in the California Culinary Academy.

For more information: For more information or to visit the Academy, call 1-800-BAY-CHEF (1-800-229-2433) or, if you live within the San Francisco Bay Area, 415-771-3536.

U.S. MEASURE AND METRIC CONVERSION CHART

Formulas for Exact Measures	Symbol	When you know:	Multiply by	To find:	Rounded Measures for Quick Reference		
Mass (weight)	oz	ounces	28.35	grams	1 oz		= 30g
	lb	pounds	0.45	kilograms	4 oz		= 115 g
	g	grams	0.035	ounces	8 oz		= 225 g
	kg	kilograms	2.2	pounds	16 oz	= 1lb	= 450 g
					32 oz	= 2lb	= 900 g
					36 oz	= 2¼ lb	= 1,000 g (1 kg)
Volume	tsp	teaspoons	5.0	milliliters	¼ tsp.	= 1/24 oz	= 1 ml
	tbsp	tablespoons	15.0	milliliters	½ tsp	= 1/12 oz	= 2 ml
	fl oz	fluid ounces	29.57	milliliters	1 tsp	= ⅙ oz	= 5 ml
	c	cups	0.24	liters	1 tbsp	= ½ oz	= 15 ml
	pt	pints	0.47	liters	1c	= 8 oz	= 250 ml
	qt	quarts	0.95	liters	2c (1 pt)	= 16 oz	= 500 ml
	gal	gallons	3.785	liters	4c (1 qt)	= 32 oz	= 1 l
	ml	milliliters	0.034	fluid ounces	4 qt (1 gal)	= 128 oz	= 3¾ l
Length	in.	inches	2.54	centimeters	⅜ in.	= 1 cm	
	ft	feet	30.48	centimeters	1 in.	= 2.5 cm	
	yd	yards	0.9144	meters	2 in	= 5 cm	
	mi	miles	1.609	kilometers	2 ½ in.	= 6.5 cm	
	km	kilometers	0.621	miles	12 in. (1 ft)	= 30 cm	
	m	meters	1.094	yards	1 yd	= 90 cm	
	cm	centimeters	0.39	inches	100 ft	= 30 m	
					1 mi	= 1.6 km	
Temperature	°F	Fahrenheit	5/9 (after subtracting 32)	Celsius	32°F	= 0°C	
					68°F	= 20°C	
	°C	Celsius	9/5 (then add 32)	Fahrenheit	212°F	= 100°C	
Area	in^2	square inches	6.452	square centimeters	1 $in.^2$	= 6.5cm^2	
	ft^2	square feet	929.0	square centimeters	1 ft^2	= 930 cm^2	
	yd^2	square yards	8,361.0	square centimeters	1 yd^2	= 8,360 cm^2	
	a	acres	0.4047	hectares	1 a	= 4,050 m^2	